PATRONAGE or
PARTNERSHIP

PATRONAGE or PARTNERSHIP

Local Capacity Building in Humanitarian Crises

Edited by
IAN SMILLIE

for the Humanitarianism and War Project

KUMARIAN
PRESS

Patronage or Partnership: Local Capacity Building in Humanitarian Crises
Published 2001 in the United States of America by Kumarian Press, Inc.
1294 Blue Hills Avenue, Bloomfield, CT 06002 USA.

Index by Back Words Indexing
Proofread by Lloyd C. John, II

Production and design by ediType
The text of this book is in 10/12 Adobe Sabon.

Printed in USA on acid-free paper by Thomson-Shore, Inc.

Text printed with vegetable oil–based ink.

∞ The paper used in this publication meets the minimum requirements of the American National Standard for Information Sciences—Permanence of Paper for Printed Library Materials, ANSI Z39.48—1984.

Library of Congress Cataloging-in-Publication Data

Smillie, Ian
    Patronage or partnership : local capacity building in humanitarian crises / Ian Smillie.
      p. cm.
    "For the Humanitarianism and War Project."
    Includes bibliographical references and index.
    ISBN 1-56549-130-0 (cloth : alk. paper) – ISBN 1-56549-129-7 (pbk. : alk. paper)
    1. Disaster relief – Developing countries – Citizen participation. 2. Humanitarian assistance – Developing countries – Citizen participation. 3. Community development – Developing countries. I. Humanitarianism and War Project. II. Title.

HV555.D44 S56 2001
363.34'8'091724 – dc21

2001023031

National Library of Canada cataloguing in publication data

Main entry under title:

Patronage or partnership : local capacity building in humanitarian crises

Co-published by Kumarian Press.
Includes bibliographical references.
ISBN 0-88936-944-5

1. Emergency management – Developing countries.
2. Humanitarian assistance – Developing countries.
3. International relief – Developing countries.
4. Crisis management – Developing countries.
I. Smillie, Ian.
II. International Development Research Centre (Canada)

HV553.P37 2001   363.3'988'09712'4   C2001-980027-4

---

10 09 08 07 06 05 04 03 02 01   10 9 8 7 6 5 4 3 2 1   First Printing 2001

Contents

Foreword

One of the core commitments of most international humanitarian organizations is to strengthen the capacity of local agencies to respond to crises and to participate more fully in their respective civil societies. To do anything less, the agencies argue persuasively, would be to leave those societies vulnerable to recurring emergencies. The track record of humanitarian organizations, however, is better in delivering life-saving assistance than in strengthening local capacity.

The externality of major international relief undertakings raises serious questions about the scale and appropriateness of the assistance provided. The essentially foreign character of such interventions also works against the expressed preference of the agencies for greater local participation and mutuality. In the heat of each new crisis, the scramble to save lives often eclipses the goal of partnership with local institutions. Moreover, patterns of relationships established during the relief phases of conflicts, many of them distressingly long-lived, are difficult to alter as reconstruction and development possibilities open up.

More than three years in the gestation process, this book reviews recent experiences in strengthening local institutions, governmental and nongovernmental alike, in six countries on five continents. It examines various aspects of the tensions between international initiatives to save lives, or, in the case of postconflict settings, to reconstruct the fabric of societies, and the parallel and sometimes competing international commitment to "capacitation." The story is a variegated and uneven one, with many successes and failures in the particular crises examined in this study. The candid review of experience that follows, however, provides a necessary step in the process of revisiting a perennial issue and charting a more effective course.

That, in fact, is the purpose of the Humanitarianism and War Project, under whose auspices the book has been written. The Project, an independent policy-research initiative based at Tufts University (see the brief explanation about the Project at the back of this volume), seeks to assist practitioner organizations to reflect on their experience and to adapt their policies and programs accordingly. Drawing on frontline insights from selected settings, the volume proceeds inductively from field data to broader conclusions. The spirit of the writing, too, is in keeping with the approach that animates the project. "In an era of slash-and-burn exposés of bungled aid efforts," writes Smillie in his introduction, "the book balances candor with constructiveness."

There are, it goes without saying, no easy solutions to the dilemmas inherent in building institutional capacity, and this book, to its credit, does not attempt to provide any. If all-purpose solutions were available, they would have been identified and implemented well before now. What Smillie and his collaborators do provide, however, is a demonstration of the importance of struggling—country by country, conflict by conflict— with the vexing dilemmas of capacity building in all of their complexity. The varied experience marshaled and examined under a common rubric offers the reader and the institutional actors some clear pointers for the future.

Experiences of individual countries flesh out Smillie's initial presentation of history, definitions, and a typology of capacity building. There is no doubt among the writers about the need for strengthening local institutions, although the difficulties of succeeding in today's conflicts emerge in stark terms. Readers will be struck by how different capacity building looks when viewed from the ground up rather than from agency headquarters. Providing further context and realism, Smillie frames capacity building in terms of such larger issues as competing understandings of "civil society," trends and tensions in North-South cooperation, and the ever more insistent need for fundamental reforms in international humanitarian- and development-assistance methodologies and institutions.

Strengthening local institutions is a major objective of Canada's International Development Research Centre in Ottawa (IDRC), which has provided significant funding for the research and writing of this volume. Dr. Neclâ Tschirgi, IDRC's team leader in its Peacebuilding and Reconstruction Program, has underscored from the start of the undertaking the need to tackle the difficult issue of capacitation and the need to do so in collaboration with colleagues and institutions from the countries in conflict, incorporating local perspectives throughout. We are grateful for IDRC's support and encouragement.

Other funds have been provided by supporters of the Humanitarianism and War Project, listed by name on the Project's web site (see back of the volume). We wish to thank all of our contributors for making this work possible. Special thanks go as well to CARE Canada, which in the spring of 2001 hosted a discussion with government officials, NGOs, and others in Ottawa on the issues discussed in the book. We also extend appreciation to our editor Mary Lhowe, who has worked with the individual contributors to refine their contributions and to harmonize their prose. Other Project staff, including its former coordinator, Laura

Sadovnikoff, assisted at earlier points in the process when the project was located at Brown University's Watson Institute.

The Project welcomes comments from readers. We are committed to refining our understanding of these issues as we continue to engage the international community.

LARRY MINEAR, Director
Humanitarianism and War Project

Introduction

IAN SMILLIE

It is early 1998, on the outskirts of Bujumbura, the capital of Burundi. "People are dying like flies," says an understandably emotional American missionary running a refugee camp for four thousand Hutus. Asked by a reporter about a series of nearby conflict resolution workshops being run by a British nongovernmental organization, the missionary watches four more corpses as they are carried out of the makeshift shelter he has constructed. The missionary says, "I do not like to criticize other groups ... but I wish someone was giving me that sort of money."

Stories like this one, which appeared in the *Sunday Times* under the headline "Burundi 'peace-shops' squander British aid,"[1] encapsulate the dilemma that this book seeks to address. The dilemma is the tradeoff between outsiders doing things themselves—meeting human needs in the midst of a humanitarian emergency—and working to build longer-term capacities among local organizations so that people will be better able to deal with their own problems.

Much has been written in recent years about the need to build local capacities in emergency and postemergency situations. Good intentions notwithstanding, outsiders appear to have great difficulty working effectively with local organizations—civil society, nongovernmental organizations (NGOs), community organizations, local government authorities—during humanitarian emergencies. When they do, the relationship is more often one of patronage than partnership. For a local organization, the task is more often about following the instructions of others than about meeting its own objectives. Five years—even ten years—after the emergencies in Sri Lanka, Sierra Leone, and Mozambique began, local organizations do not seem better able to cope with humanitarian assistance than when they started. Is this true? If so, why? Is it because local organizations are congenitally deficient? Is it because outsiders know best, or because they do not know enough? Is it because the urgency of saving lives preempts all other considerations? Or is there another reason?

This book goes beyond rhetoric and prescriptive nostrums and examines the dynamics of what actually happens on the ground during and after emergencies. Case studies written by international aid practitioners and journalists have been enhanced by commentary from the point of view of the people and organizations most affected by wars. Kathy Mangones writes from her vantage point as the executive director of a Haitian NGO umbrella organization attempting to function under military rule after the overthrow of President Jean-Bertrand Aristide. Goran Todorović survived the Bosnian war while working for an international relief agency in Sarajevo, but the greater challenge was his attempt to establish a postwar organization that could help build local civil society. Thomas Turay accepted the assignment to write a chapter on Sierra Leone following a series of peacebuilding workshops in 1998, only to become trapped during the January 1999 Revolutionary United Front (RUF) incursion into Freetown, barely escaping with his three daughters and his life. To these chapters are added firsthand accounts of the problems and opportunities created by the would-be kindness of strangers in Sri Lanka, Guatemala, and Mozambique.

The chapters present a cross section of emergencies in Africa, Asia, Latin America, and the Caribbean. The cases were selected to bring out different aspects of the challenge at different moments in time. The chapter on Bosnia looks at the immediate reconstruction following the Dayton Peace Accords. The chapter on Mozambique takes a longer postwar view, while the chapter on Sri Lanka deals with an ongoing conflict. The Sierra Leone case deals with the immediacy, panic, and confusion of war.

Each chapter presents a different perspective on the relationship between international humanitarian actors and local civil society. Stephen Lubkemann's chapter on Mozambique highlights reasons for success in the rural health efforts of a European aid agency. Mike Leffert applies a journalist's eye to problems encountered by women returning to Guatemala after years of gender training provided by well-meaning international agencies in Mexican refugee camps.

In Bosnia, the story is one of external agencies looking for fast and efficient service delivery and dressing it in the language of civil society. The Haitian case demonstrates that much-maligned food aid can actually play a key role in building local capacities and local self-esteem, even during the worst of times. Thomas Turay describes a personal descent into aid-agency hell in Sierra Leone, and the return, at least, of hope. Although the book is about a form of aid delivery, it is not written primarily from the perspective of the people who deliver it. Rather, most of the chapters are written from the perspective of the people who receive it.

The primary purpose of the book is to identify and examine innovative practices that have contributed to building short- and long-term local capacities, which are then brought to bear on the challenges of emergency assistance, peacebuilding, reconstruction, and development. The book also distills real-life experience and aims to encourage reflection among practitioners, thereby setting it apart from most traditional analyses. In an era of slash-and-burn exposés of bungled aid efforts, the book balances candor with constructiveness.

Chapter 1 reviews the international development literature on capacity building and finds that, while the language has been successfully transferred to humanitarian organizations and complex emergencies, there are very real problems in making the reality fit the words. The chapter expands the definition of the term *capacity building* and discusses the very real constraints faced by practitioners: knowledge, time, the sources of and expectations behind available funding. It is worth keeping in mind from the outset, however, that—theory and definitions aside—the purpose of capacity building is straightforward. In chapter 7, Thomas Turay says it well:

> I understand capacity building as a process through which people of a given society are motivated to transform their physical, socioeconomic, cultural, political, and spiritual environments for their own well-being and the advancement of their society. Capacity building is about empowering people to take control of their lives. It enables people to rediscover their strengths and limitations, and the opportunities to develop their fullest potential. The process enables people to build self-confidence and self-respect, and to improve the quality of their lives, utilizing their own resources, both human and nonhuman. Capacity building provides opportunities for local organizations to establish networks at both local and international levels. Capacity building is also a process of creating opportunities for people to be creative and imaginative, to dream, and to be able to live their dreams.

Chapter 2 examines the relationship between external humanitarian actors and Bosnian civil society at three moments in time. The first section examines the situation at the end of 1996, two years after the Dayton Peace Accords. This was a period of early transition from relief and rehabilitation to efforts dealing with longer-term social and economic issues. The second section describes a specific effort by one international NGO to work with civil society; it charts this NGO's progress from confident proposal-writing to the complex reality of helping traumatized people form organizations where none existed before. The final section is a sobering reflection on the progress made by Bosnian civil society and external agencies' progress in understanding that society at the start of the twenty-first century.

Chapter 3 deals with Haiti. It examines the provision of alternative types of food aid following the 1991 military coup d'état. The focus is not the prevalent critique of traditional food aid; rather, it is on attempts by Haitians to create alternative food aid programs to strengthen local food production and to promote the institutional development of local organizations during a highly volatile political moment in a country with endemic structural problems. The perspective is unabashedly that of Haitian civil society—a diverse collection of organizations and groups reflecting the vibrancy of Haitian organizational expression and Haitian commitment to social change.

The fourth chapter considers the challenges and possibilities in building local capacity in the health sector in Mozambique over the last two years of a long civil war, and the transition to reconstruction and longer-term development. The chapter examines the building of local capacity in two distinct yet critically interrelated senses. Narrowly, it examines the interaction among international actors (donors and operational agencies) and national actors (in particular the ministry of health) in rebuilding the modern health sector's local-service capacity in a postwar situation. It also examines how foreign aid in the health sector has contributed to a broader sense of local capacity and to the potential for a genuine civil society. These changes follow a long history of heavy-handed state intervention and a political culture in which disengagement became the primary strategy for dealing with it.

Chapter 5 deals with Sri Lanka. Once a beacon of hope and an exemplar of good development, Sri Lanka has suffered almost two decades of debilitating civil war. A country with a well-developed civil society, Sri Lanka has nevertheless suffered from serious human rights abuse perpetrated by both sides in the conflict, and it has seen its long-standing commitment to democratic process repeatedly challenged by assassination and constitutional manipulation. This chapter explores the relationship over time among outsiders, local organizations of civil society, government, and the Liberation Tigers of Tamil Eelam. It asks whether humanitarian assistance in Sri Lanka—intended to end suffering by addressing the effects of war—is failing because of its inability or unwillingness to address the causes of war.

Chapter 6 considers relationships and capacities generated during the fourteen-year period in which forty-five thousand Guatemalans took refuge in camps in Mexico. It focuses particularly on international support for women's organizations in refugee camps and the acquisition of greater gender awareness among both Guatemalan men and women in the camps. Conditions in the camps bore little resemblance to everyday life, and for many women this was not altogether bad. Many took advantage of the time to organize, meet, discuss, and learn. What they learned, however, could not necessarily have been predicted from what was taught. The chapter follows returnees to Guatemala in the mid- and late 1990s, finding a notable dispersion of women's organizations, along with a decline in international efforts at organizing returnees and a regression to traditional gender roles. The chapter argues that emergencies, by definition, mark a break with a population's history, often accompanied by shifts in environment, production, community ties, and relations with outside actors. The exceptional nature of these shifts places severe limitations on external efforts at long-lasting change. In fact, the social relations created by new dependencies during a prolonged emergency may disguise underlying realities, giving false indications of both change and the sustainability of new ideas.

In chapter 7, Thomas Turay describes going back to Sierra Leone at the end of 1998. The Revolutionary United Front attack on Freetown in January 1999 unexpectedly cut him off from his family—and from the assignment. He spent the next twelve months working with local and international agencies, observing their interaction and their isolation firsthand, while at the same time trying to rescue his three daughters from behind rebel lines. This is an unanticipated and highly personal firsthand account of what happens when hell breaks loose, when theories fall victim to panic, and when aid agencies confront their worst fears. It is also a story of possibilities, with important lessons for outsiders from those on the inside.

The eighth and final chapter draws together the lessons, potential lessons, and anomalies in the case-study chapters, with crosscutting themes and policy considerations for practitioners, international humanitarian organizations, and organizations in countries attempting to cope with emergencies and with international help.

Information about each of the contributors appears at the back of the volume. Many other individuals assisted in the development of this book. Matt Creelman, Isabel Soares, and Bob Maguire provided valuable assistance on Guatemala, Mozambique, and Haiti, respectively. Larry Minear, director of the Humanitarianism and War Project, accepted the book's ambitious premise without demur, and he supported it throughout a gestation period that included endless electronic transfers and disappearing files, not to mention the occasional disappearing author. Without the support of Neclâ Tschirgi at the International Development Research Centre, the book would not have been written. And without the assistance of Mary Lhowe it would not be as polished as it is. The contributors, however, take full responsibility for their own work as well as any errors or omissions.

Note

1. Andrew Malone, "Burundi 'peace-shops' squander British aid," *Sunday Times*, March 29, 1998, 20.

Chapter 1

Capacity Building and the Humanitarian Enterprise

IAN SMILLIE

What is "capacity building"? That is the problem.
—MICK MOORE

In recent years there has been a perceptible upturn in commentary on building local capacities in emergency and postemergency situations. Despite this trend, many relief programs remain characterized by their preponderant externality—as demonstrated by their sources of input and their accountabilities in their approach to management and in their dependence on expatriate staff. Agencies often fail to recognize local resources and skills, and they miss real opportunities to include civil society—NGOs, community organizations, trade unions, religious organizations, professional bodies, foundations, local government—in the management of relief and peacebuilding. Channeling bilateral and multilateral resources through international NGOs can shift accountability and responsibility away from national and local leaders, undermining local capacity and creating further dependence. Emergency assistance can create tensions among local organizations and between refugee and host populations over access to external resources. In short, relief assistance can undermine rather than strengthen indigenous capacity.

The reality of what often happens in emergency assistance programs flies in the face of stated donor policy and oft-expressed good intentions. Virtually every serious major external actor in emergency situations is committed to strengthening local capacity. But clearly, this is easier said than done. Knowing *whom* to work with (for example, women, traditional leaders, or indigenous NGOs) is as important as knowing *how* to work with them. Sometimes the wrong capacities may be enhanced, or the capacities of the wrong people may be strengthened, as in the case of freelance militia in Somalia or Hutu militia in the Goma camps. Gender is an especially important area of concern. Women may have been protected from violence in some emergencies, but in many they have been targeted, and in most the burden for children and for the care and feeding of their families has increased.

Capacity Building: Some History

Capacity building, often used synonymously with *institution building, institutional development,* and *organizational development,* is in some ways as old as development assistance itself. Slogans such as "helping people to help themselves" point directly at capacity building. The proverb "teach a man to fish" is about building capacity for self-sufficiency. In the 1950s and 1960s, community development focused on building self-help capacities within rural communities. A major purpose of technical assistance has always been to enhance the capacities of individuals and institutions through training, research, and counterpart relationships. Schools, vocational training, and universities all aim to build human capacities for self-development.

The 1969 Pearson Commission Report on international development—the first of many such commissions—spoke extensively of the need to build administrative capacity in developing countries, especially capacity to absorb political and economic change.[1] In 1974, the United Nations Research Institute for Social Development (UNRISD) coined the term *capacitation,* suggesting that

> A "capacitating" operation does not try so much to define or control the future as to establish present conditions or capacities that will permit a given society to meet its problems in the future. The emphasis in such an approach is not on setting future appropriate output targets but on diagnosing current weaknesses and potentials, finding appropriate policies and constantly monitoring the course of development.[2]

Peter Morgan has tracked the concept of capacity building from its origins in the 1950s and 1960s, when it was based to a large extent on the idea of equipping developing countries with a basic inventory of public sector institutions and, later, strengthening them to improve their performance. By the 1980s, the idea of institutional development had gained several new features. In addition to government, the private sector and NGOs had been added to the mix. The time frame had also changed, with institutional development seen as a longer-term process of restructuring and institutional change. It had become "more concerned about the adaptability and responsiveness of development institutions...[and it had] moved beyond the framework of individual organizations. For the first time institutional analysis began to look at sectoral perspectives and at groups of institutions. . . . Finally, institutional development began to address itself to the sustainability issue—not just the 'what works?' question, but the 'what lasts?' question."[3]

Despite its long history, growing sophistication, and a renewed emphasis in the 1990s, capacity building, or the way it has been managed, has in many cases resulted in the opposite of what was intended. Capacities have not been built, institutions have failed, organizations have not met expectations. In a damning critique of international assistance to Rwanda prior to the genocide, Peter Uvin discusses the capacity building efforts of Belgium, Switzerland, and the United Nations Development Program (UNDP):

> As Rwanda's farmers were facing crises without precedent, as inequality and corruption reached endemic proportions, as hope for the future was extinguished, and as violence, hatred and human rights abuses became government policy, the international community was congratulating Rwanda for its improved capacity to overcome its "limited absorptive capacity," and to "improve its capacity to design and implement development projects."[4]

The realization of failure is not new. Writing less dramatically in 1978—a time so long past in the development experience that age almost disqualifies it from relevance—John Oxenham and Robert Chambers described the weakness of capacity building as it was then conceived: an effort basically designed and implemented by outsiders. Usually styled as "technical assistance" or "technical cooperation," capacity building judged what people did not know and what they required. "Providing specialist people-services necessarily implies that [outsiders] have the expertise which the people lack and must transmit it to the people. So the people 'to be developed' start out on an unequal footing. . . . the fairly strong human bias towards authoritarianism is legitimized and reinforced through the explicit authority of professional expertise."[5]

Writing in 1984, Majid Rahnema, a former aid official and once a minister in the government of Iran, criticized the idea of community development by outsiders "as if [villagers] could not develop themselves. This infantilization of the deprived population . . . is the primary reason why development activities do not take root in the life of communities."[6] A decade later, he observed that instead of enhancing the development process or reducing poverty, capacity building had too often enhanced the abilities of predatory governments, building "their capacity to 'milk' their own people, and . . . the assistance they receive from their richer foreign patrons."[7] These early critics foreshadowed the call for and the widespread acceptance by the early 1990s of *participatory development* and *empowerment*—terms that are also fraught with definitional problems. But the story is getting ahead of itself, and a more systematic consideration of capacity building typologies is in order before determining their relevance to the emergencies and postconflict situations of the twenty-first century.

A Typology of Capacity Building

What is "capacity building"? That is the problem. It includes everything that was covered by the different definitions of "institution building" and much more besides.... Aid agencies would be wise to have no truck with the new jargon of "capacity building" and to insist on using language and terms that have identifiable and precise meanings.[8]

Moore's imprecation notwithstanding, it is impossible to avoid a term that is in such widespread use. Part of its definitional problem has to do with target and purpose. In some cases individuals, a community, or an organization are to be strengthened. In others, the target is a sector, such as agricultural or health, while in others the target may be an entire societal subset. Alan Fowler has helped to sort this out by separating organizational development from sectoral development and institutional development, the latter representing a broad cross section of organizations, such as informal sector entrepreneurs, or "civil society."

A second area of necessary clarification has to do with the purpose of a capacity building effort. In some cases, capacity building may be seen as the means to an end—for example, enhancing the capacity of a local NGO to deliver emergency assistance. In others, the end may be more important than the means—the development of an organization capable of developing and managing its own programs and strategies independently of outsiders. In some cases, the process of capacity building may be more important than either the means or the ends—such as the stimulation of greater coherence around an issue or within a community. Figure 1.1, adapted from a typology created by Fowler, is an attempt to distinguish both target and purpose in capacity building.

This sort of typology suggests that capacity building is considerably more complex than originally conceived in the training programs and technical assistance of the early development decades. It also suggests that capacity building requires serious attention to target and purpose, as well as to considerations of process. And it helps to explain why capacity building seems to have had little success over four or five decades of experimentation. The reason is that it was usually and unambitiously lodged in the upper-left sector (under "Means") of figure 1.1, strengthening the capacity of organizations to carry out specific functions, often designed by outsiders.

Figure 1.1: Concepts of Capacity Building

	Means	*Process*	*Ends*
Building the capacity of an organization: organizational development	Strengthens the organization's ability to perform specific functions, such as refugee-camp management	Builds coherence within internal operations; develops the possibility of continued learning and adaptation	Improves the organization's viability, sustainability, and impact in relation to its mission
Building the capacity of an institutional subsector (e.g., health, credit, emergency assistance): sectoral development	Strengthens the ability of the sector or subsector to improve its overall impact	Develops mutually supporting relations and understanding within the sector or subsector	Achieves confident and meaningful interaction with other sectors and social actors based on shared strategies and learning
Building the capacity of civil society: institutional development	Improves the ability of primary stakeholders to identify and carry out activities to solve problems	Enables and stimulates better interaction, communication, conflict resolution in society, enhancing social capital	Increases the ability of primary stakeholders to engage with and influence the political arena and the socioeconomic system in accordance with their interests

Source: Adapted from Alan Fowler, *Striking a Balance: A Guide to Enhancing the Effectiveness of NGOs in International Development* (London: Earthscan, 1997), 188.

Where emergencies are concerned, an early and prominent effort to move the discussion out of this first sector and into the area of ends was the Capacities and Vulnerability Analysis (CVA), developed by Mary Anderson and Peter Woodrow in 1989.[9] The CVA is based on the idea that in emergencies, individuals and groups have capacities in addition to the obvious vulnerabilities. In the past, the tendency was for outsiders to focus mainly on vulnerabilities, often becoming preoccupied with symptoms rather than causes. Using the CVA approach, those wishing to assist are urged to identify both capacities and vulnerabilities, building the former and reducing the latter. Essentially, the Capabilities and Vulnerability Analysis uses the idea that outsiders cannot develop others, but that they can help to create an environment and processes that help people on the path to their own development. This is especially true in emergencies, in which investments in longer-term capacities may have considerable impact on people's ability to reconstruct their lives after outsiders are gone.

The CVA is not far removed from Participatory Rural Appraisal (PRA) techniques developed in the early 1990s. These emerged from a greater awareness among development professionals that there was a considerable gap between the objectives and the results of many rural development efforts. The problem often grew from outsiders' profound lack of understanding of people and context and on the weak involvement in or absence of intended beneficiaries from the planning and implementation of projects. PRA has developed rapidly since its inception, becoming "a family of approaches and methods to enable local people to share, enhance and analyze their knowledge of life and conditions, and to plan, act, monitor and evaluate."[10] PRA provides a systematic approach to learning about people and context, recognizing and building on the capacities of individuals and communities. In PRA, the emphasis is as much on process as on ends.

Much has been written in recent years about the coping strategies that people employ in times of trouble—efforts to reduce their vulnerability and to recover as quickly as possible. Considerably less thought has been given to the coping strategies of local organizations in an emergency. They, too, have capacities and vulnerabilities that may be exploited or become exploitative as an emergency deepens. For example, outsiders frequently view the activities of local NGOs as opportunistic and donor-driven.

In some cases these organizations may "take sides" or become "corrupt." In Afghanistan, many local NGOs channeled aid funds into the war chests of local military commanders and were therefore disparaged and written off by donors. But it is worth considering the issue from another angle. Just as international NGOs are obliged to do things in accordance with donor demands, in Afghanistan some may have had little choice but to appease commanders in order to create space for themselves in their work with local communities.[11]

The War-Torn Societies Project (WSP), which operated between 1994 and 1998 as a joint effort of UNRISD and the Geneva Graduate Institute of International Studies, sought to move capacity building into the lower-right-hand sector of Figure 1.1. It tried to influence the political arena and the socioeconomic system in accordance with their own interests and perceptions. Using a participatory-action research process, the project operated in four countries: Somalia, Guatemala, Eritrea, and Mozambique. Its premise was that "postconflict rehabilitation typically involves a whole range of actors—internal and external—but... it is often hampered by these actors' lack of understanding of how some of the basic issues and priorities involved in rehabilitation relate to each other."[12] The project aimed to identify priorities for the country's policy agenda, recognizing explicitly a number of key issues typically ignored in a postwar situation:

- that power struggles may not have been resolved, and that an election does not necessarily resolve underlying problems (elections may not lead to sustainable power-sharing arrangements);
- that war may have destroyed or discredited traditional social structures, and that their replacements may be weak and may lack legitimacy;
- that postwar governments, cognizant of the urgency and the challenges facing them, may be tempted into authoritarian solutions that work against inclusion, dialogue, and credibility;
- that people's high expectations may be contrasted with low delivery capacities in government;
- that there may be little space for neutral or impartial dialogue;
- that external actors may continue to play divisive roles.

The Importance of a Healthy Civil Society

In recent years, much discussion about capacity building has moved from nuts-and-bolts questions about self-help and teaching a man to fish, to a higher plane in which civil society looms large. Men (or women) may well know how to fish, but may be prevented from deriving a living from their labors by vested interests, an authoritarian regime, environmental problems, or by a conflict that has forced them from the site of their livelihood. Solutions to such problems go beyond standard human resource development efforts, often falling into a broader societal domain. Like capacity building, *civil society* is a much-used and much-abused term, one that in the space of only a handful of years has found its way onto the covers of dozens of books. Writers on civil society draw inspiration from Hegel, de Tocqueville, and Gramsci, and most owe at least a nod to Robert Putnam's 1993 study of democracy in Italy.[13] Putnam was the first to put some empirical clothing on the concept of civil society, demonstrating that long traditions of associational life in northern Italy—unlike in the south—have created the "social capital" responsible there for good governance and a vibrant economy.

The weakness or absence of civil society in much of the developing world has come to be seen as a reason for bad governance, human rights abuse, weak democracy, state collapse, and war. It follows that one way to reduce conflict or to regain stability in a postconflict situation is to strengthen civil society. Strengthening civil society or, more particularly, strengthening the capacity of civil society, has therefore become an important preoccupation of the aid establishment in recent years. The various arguments that comprise this emerging objective have been summarized by Paul Harvey:

A strong civil society is crucial to development. In complex political emergencies, civil society and social capital are badly eroded.
Given that there is no government to work with, governance capacity needs to be rebuilt from the bottom up, together with civil
society and social capital. It is hoped that this will marginalize existing predatory authorities. Strengthening non-military interests will
create a platform for peace by allowing space and a voice for civil
society to express its desire for peace.[14]

There are some suggestions, however, that the civil society discourse
has a strong Western European bias, and that it needs refinement. Even
where civil society in the south has been strong, it has not been able to
prevent disaster. Sri Lanka has a relatively large and mature civil society,
but Paikiasothy Saravanamuttu argues that because, historically, much
of it had a role in welfare, it was both co-opted and ill-equipped to
deal with the creeping authoritarianism of government in the 1970s and
1980s. Two violent uprisings in the south and a civil war in the north
led to increasing state-managed violence and political ruthlessness, with
a concomitant attack on an already weakened and politically impotent
civil society.[15]

Peter Uvin makes the same point about Rwanda, a country with "an
extremely high civil society density."[16] Rwandan civil society, however,
was unable to prevent or mitigate one of the worst societal crimes of
the modern era, Uvin finds, mainly because it had little interest in doing
so. As reasons, he cites government and ethnic co-optation, a dangerous political climate for dissidents, and donor funding with an explicitly
"apolitical" agenda. In short, courageous proponents of human rights
and democracy notwithstanding, neither Sri Lanka nor Rwanda had
civil societies of the size and type described by Putnam and the broader
literature on connections among democracy, human rights, and civil
society.

Harvey suggests that during an emergency, civil society is, in fact,
simultaneously emerging, as well as being undermined and contested. He
suggests five linked processes that affect civil society during a complex
political emergency:

- an extreme process of disengagement of civil society from the state;

- a fallback on primary groupings within civil society. Kinship, tribal,
  religious, and traditional political structures serve as coping strategies for people in response to state collapse;

- military strategies, extreme scarcity, and displacement that undermine civil society;

- predatory local authorities contesting the space of civil society, moving into the parallel economy, and attempting to create support by drawing on neo-patrimonial ties based on ethnicity;

- the continued strength of civil society at a local level, both in the parallel economy and in traditional institutions.[17]

These challenges should not suggest, however, that the promotion of civil society as a cornerstone of democracy, human rights, and a culture of inclusion is misplaced. Putnam found that the process had taken five hundred years or more in Italy; thus, a decade of small, uncertain aid infusions cannot be expected to have achieved much so far. What is becoming clear, however, is that support for civil society writ large—clubs, trade unions, NGOs, welfare societies, and self-help groups—may not do much for democracy unless these organizations are explicitly committed to their own independence from government, and more broadly to principles of pluralism, democracy, and human rights.

Why Build Local Capacities?

A second and more traditional reason for building local capacities relates to changes in the relative roles of the state and civil society in the provision of basic services. In some cases there is a specific and practical intent to capacity building. Where government has collapsed, or where it is a combatant in a two-sided conflict, there are good reasons to promote nongovernmental delivery mechanisms for emergency assistance. Building local capacities in such situations can make assistance more effective and more efficient in the short run, as well as in longer-term, postconflict peacebuilding and reconstruction. In this area, some see a neoliberal conspiracy to push back the state—an integral part of draconian structural adjustment policies. In this scenario, civil society—essentially client NGOs—is expected to do the best it can to fill the widest gaps in social services.

Whether this is true or not, some believe that the rise of NGOs *has* been at the expense of the state. Mozambique is a frequently cited example, as in the following observation from Antonio Donini:

> Relief agencies—and NGOs in particular, some of which have programmes larger than those of the largest bilateral donor—have become the chief provider of public welfare and important sources of employment. They also further weaken government structures by siphoning off the remaining trained and competent local professionals...who are attracted by the higher and regular salaries paid by the outsiders.[18]

This is complex and contested territory, as the chapter on Mozambique will demonstrate. And the statement is not universally true. NGOs are a small part of the social service scene in most countries, and, in some, governments actually welcome and generously subsidize the work of the voluntary sector: health services in Zimbabwe, Tanzania, Kenya, and Uganda are good examples.

Toward a Definition of Capacity Building

After almost half a century of conceptual refinement and considerable shortcomings in practice, capacity development has moved beyond simple ideas of organizations and human resource development. Peter Morgan argues that

> Capacity development is therefore a more normative and less technique-oriented concept than institutional strengthening or institutional development.... It is the ability of individuals, groups, institutions, organizations and societies to identify and meet development challenges over time.... It implies reshaping the relationship between donors and developing countries with the objective of making endogenous capacities the central focus of attention.... It sets the strengthening or development of individual organizations in a much broader framework of sectoral or national efforts to improve development capabilities.[19]

Deborah Eade, writing about the Oxfam experience of capacity building, adds that capacity building does not begin and end with NGOs or with donors.

> Nor is "civil society" independent of, much less an alternative to, the state. Rather, capacity building involves the whole network of relationships in society: within, between and among households, neighborhoods, grassroots or community-based organizations, unions, religious confessions, training institutions, research bodies, government ministries, the private sector, NGOs and donor agencies—whether official or nongovernmental, Northern or Southern. Capacity building is also concerned with creating new relationships of mutuality and reciprocity within a given society and beyond.[20]

These definitions, and others like them, draw on the (mostly inconclusive) capacity building experience of several decades. The definitions are long and vague, and invoke all manner of good things—something for which their authors often apologize.[21] The problem is not so much the definitions as the context into which they must fit. Because contexts differ so widely and because the intent of a capacity building effort may differ from one agency or one situation to another, writers offer general, all-inclusive, and high-sounding definitions. These no doubt bewilder the average field-based project officer who must decide whether to give a training course or to "build civil society"—or, more pointedly, whether to forget about the long term and to take immediate action in aid of people who are "dying like flies" in the here and now.

Practitioners may take some solace from an apocryphal story about Christopher Wren, surveying construction on St. Paul's Cathedral. Coming across a stonemason, he asked what the man was doing. "Cutting stone," came the answer. Later, he met another stonemason and asked the same question. "I am building a cathedral," the man replied. Thus, context, purpose, and target will ensure that an appropriate approach in one situation is inappropriate in another. A simpler definition of capacity building in emergency situations has been developed by Sue Lautze and John Hammock, who observed that "capacity building is any intervention designed to reinforce or create strengths upon which communities can draw to offset disaster-related vulnerability."[22]

The problem, of course, is not so much the intention to reinforce or create strengths, but whether in fact strengths actually result from the effort. The chapter on Guatemala demonstrates that what is intended is not always what happens. Knowing what to do and what not to do becomes, therefore, the critical issue.

What to Do? Issues in Capacity Building

The following sections deal with key issues that arise in capacity building efforts: training, timing, and the capacity of those who would build capacity in others.

When in Doubt, Train

Despite improved understanding among development agencies about the complexities of capacity building, in practice such work boils down too often to giving the intended beneficiary a training program. In Bosnia, two years after the Dayton Peace Accords, the fledgling Bosnian NGO community was attempting to handle enormous psychosocial upheaval, feeding programs for refugees, reconstruction of homes, microcredit, and a hundred other challenges that few were equipped to deal with. There were at the time at least six capacity building programs being offered by international NGOs and United Nations agencies, all of them generic training courses on basic issues of NGO management. At a 1997 meeting that discussed the NGO sector as a whole, several Bosnian NGO managers agreed that while they might need such training, none ever wanted to attend another program on how to write a mission statement or how to write a project proposal.[23]

The long-term vision of many of the Bosnian organizations may have been unclear, but the problem was not so much one of mission statements as one of survival in a climate in which donors themselves had no long-term perspective, doling out small grants in three- and six-month tranches. How to write a project proposal was a generic issue, to be sure, not least because every donor required a different format, and because few would accept proposals written in the Bosnian language. In fact, the courses had all the hallmarks of the capacity building style criticized by Oxenham and Chambers in 1978: telling people what they need, essentially so they could conform with the management standards and programming requirements of outsiders.

Bosnia is discussed at greater length in chapter 2. Criticism of the Bosnian situation notwithstanding, training may be precisely what a community-based organization (CBO) or an NGO needs. But determining genuine needs is no easy task. Much has been written on capacity assessment, the best of it describing a range of responses that become more complex and time-consuming, depending on the depth of change required. The intent in building the capacity of a particular NGO, for example, may be to enable it to undertake specific functions or to help the organization manage itself better. Or it may aim to build longer-term viability, strength, and sustainability.

Depending on the existing capacities of the organization, all that may be required at the function end of the spectrum is information, for example, on how to manage a feeding program. Managing a feeding program in an unstable and dangerous situation, however, requires deeper knowledge and experience. Managing for greater efficiency and effectiveness may require significant organizational change. Helping to build an NGO's longer-term financial viability or helping it to become an effective advocate for humanitarian issues will require time and may require changes in attitudes and individual behavior. In each case, training may or may not be indicated, but short-term boilerplate courses are rarely likely to suffice. Figure 1.2 suggests that the difficulty and the time required will depend on the depth of change required.

Time and Timing

In much of the current literature, there is clear recognition that the most effective kinds of capacity building take time, and that short-term efforts applied on a piecemeal basis have limited impact. Writing about development rather than emergency situations, Peter Morgan says that the normal three- to five-year donor time frame is inadequate. "Capacity issues are seen as long-term problems that can take—as in the case of public sector reform—fifteen to twenty years to address in a serious way.

Figure 1.2: Time and Complexity in Organizational Change

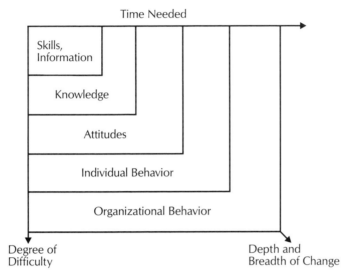

Source: Adapted from Fowler, *Striking a Balance*, 193 (see Fig. 1.1), and Piers Campbell, "Relations between Northern and Southern NGOs: Effective Partnerships for Sustainable Development" (Geneva: International Council of Voluntary Agencies, 1989).

The development of effective, viable organizations is seen as a long-term evolutionary process that requires patience and consistency."[24]

What does this imply for those working in emergency situations, where there are real pressures to act urgently? Obviously, many emergencies, especially in the early stages, do not lend themselves to long-term planning or capacity building. International relief agencies must act to alleviate suffering as best they can and as quickly as possible. But there is a problem of mind-set where timing is concerned, exacerbated by institutional donors whose funding is limited to very short time horizons. This issue is raised with poignancy in chapter 3 on Haiti. The mind-set means there is often no time to identify, much less to strengthen, local capacities; no time to study local coping mechanisms; no time to work with local NGOs; and not much time to think about the longer-term requirements that will come with reconstruction and postconflict attempts to rebuild normalcy.

Although this sort of situation is undesirable, it is also understandable, up to a point. But many of today's complex emergencies have been going on for five, ten, and more years. During such an extended time frame, it *is* possible to learn more about local communities and cultures, and to build longer-term relationships with local organizations. By 1997, the war in Sierra Leone was in its sixth year. But with the exception of the Sierra Leone Red Cross and some church-related organizations, very few Sierra Leonean NGOs had been able to attract funding or any other form of institutional support from their northern counterparts. For international NGOs with an interest, the reason given for so little interaction were problems of probity. Sierra Leonean NGOs believed, however, that their honesty was subject to monitoring, contracts, and the creation of adequate checks and balances. They were particularly unhappy that internationals gave this "excuse" for what could only be seen as avoidance of serious capacity building efforts. As a result, most Sierra Leonean NGOs believed that they were no more capable of effective efforts in 1997 than they had been in 1991.[25] More recent events in Sierra Leone will be considered in the chapter by Thomas Turay.

The Capacity to Build Capacity

One of the reasons that outsiders have focused so resolutely on generic training and the transfer of information to improve basic functions has to do with time. Another has to do with emergency field-workers themselves. Often young, overworked, operating in high-stress situations, and subject to sudden reassignment, few are equipped or mandated to gain a deep understanding of communities in conflict, whether local civil society organizations or NGOs. In short, their capacity to build capacity is limited. As Lautze and Hammock put it, "This lack of capacity to use or build capacity is also due to limited institutional knowledge, a lack of previous experience with capacity building and a dearth of case studies focusing on how to work with populations in crisis. It is not surprising, then, that truly effective means of working with local populations are neither taught formally in training seminars nor exchanged informally among more and lesser experienced staff."[26]

A further issue has to do with money: can a funding agency also provide effective support for capacity building? Many do, but the pitfalls are enormous. Whatever form the capacity building takes, beneficiaries may participate only because they think they see a gleam of silver at the end of the tunnel. If their purpose in participating is largely financial, effective change may be compromised from the outset. A second issue, even if the first is not a problem, is that the capacity building agency may attempt to instill ideas and priorities that are in line with its own funding and programming mandates, instead of working to build independent ways of thinking and working in the intended beneficiary. The Karachi-based NGO Resource Centre aims to build short- and long-term strategic and management capacities in Pakistani NGOs. When established in 1987, the center made a deliberate decision to avoid involvement in the funding of its partner organizations, because it believed that this would lead, sooner or later, to damaging compromises on the part of both giver and receiver. In a book on the experience of African NGOs, Rick James says that the question of "whose purpose organizational development is serving—the Northern NGO or the Southern NGO" must be rigorously addressed.[27]

Interim Conclusions

It is possible that the capacity building discourse (this chapter included) sets the bar too high. If, after fifty years of effort, capacity building still proves to be difficult in development settings where it is a priority, how much more difficult will it likely be in emergency settings, where the primary and most immediate goal is to save lives? Where capacity builders lack the mandate, capacity building skills, understanding of the local context, and staying power, mistakes inevitably will be made.

Several interim conclusions can be drawn from the literature on capacity building and emergencies. The most prominent is that in order to be effective, a capacity building approach must be clear in its purpose: does it intend to create a specific capacity within a single organization, or does it aim to build the institution and its capacity to undertake independent thought and action? Second, the target must be clear—whether a single organization, a sectoral activity such as health delivery, or an institutional subset such as civil society. The time required and the complexity of the exercise will increase depending on the depth of change envisaged. The simple transfer of information may not require great effort, but building knowledge, changing behavior, and altering attitudes require investments with significantly different orders of magnitude.

In approaching the question of civil society, outsiders need to build their own understanding while exercising caution. Attempts to build civil society are important, but civil society may be contested space during a volatile and politicized emergency, simultaneously emerging and contracting, part solution and perhaps part problem. Training is not a panacea; while it has a role to play, it is not in any way synonymous with capacity building. A major issue has to do with the capacity of potential capacity builders: in emergencies such capacities may be limited. And a general lesson about capacity building, one now decades old, is that builders must have good knowledge of "buildees," their society, and the context in which the effort is expected to take place. There is no substitute for a clear understanding and analysis of the local situation, something that cannot be achieved without the intimate participation of those affected.

These tidy prescriptions—uncontentious and fairly commonsensical—flow from the literature. The chapters that follow will demonstrate how difficult it is to convert what looks, on the printed page, like common sense into concrete action in the midst of a complex emergency and its aftermath.

Notes

1. Lester B. Pearson, *Partners in Development* (New York: Praeger, 1969), 232.

2. Marshall Wolfe, *Elusive Development* (London and Atlantic Highlands, N.J.: Zed Books; Geneva: United Nations Research Institute for Social Development, 1996), quoted in Deborah Eade, *Capacity Building: An Approach to People-Centred Development* (Oxford: Oxfam, 1997), 16.

3. Peter Morgan, "Capacity Development—An Introduction," in *Emerging Issues in Capacity Development* (Ottawa: Institute on Governance, 1994), 9.

4. Peter Uvin, *Aiding Violence: The Development Enterprise in Rwanda* (West Hartford, Conn.: Kumarian Press, 1998), 89. Quotations are from a World Bank report.

5. John Oxenham and Robert Chambers, "Organising Education and Training for Rural Development: Problems and Challenges," quoted in Bernard Lecomte, *Project Aid: Limitations and Alternatives* (Paris: Organization for Economic Cooperation and Development, 1986), 45.

6. Majid Rahnema, "The Grassroots of the Future," quoted in Lecomte, *Project Aid*, 43.

7. Majid Rahnema, "Poverty," in *The Development Dictionary*, ed. Wolfgang Sachs (London: Zed Books, 1992), 166.

8. Mick Moore, "Promoting Good Government by Supporting Institutional Development," *Institute of Development Studies Bulletin* 26, no. 2 (1995), quoted in Eade, *Capacity Building*, 1.

9. Mary B. Anderson and Peter J. Woodrow, *Rising from the Ashes: Development Strategies in Times of Disaster* (Boulder, Colo.: Westview Press, 1989).

10. Robert Chambers, *Whose Reality Counts? Putting the Last First* (London: Intermediate Technology Publications, 1997), 102.

11. This theme is discussed by Jonathan Goodhand and Peter Chamberlain in "Dancing with the Prince: NGOs' Survival Strategies in the Afghan Conflict," *Development in States of War* (Oxford: Oxfam, 1996), 38–50.

12. Matthias Stiefel, *Rebuilding after War: A Summary Report of the War-Torn Societies Project* (Geneva: War-Torn Societies Project and Nations Research Institute for Social Development, 1998), 5.

13. Robert D. Putnam, *Making Democracy Work: Civic Traditions in Modern Italy* (Princeton: Princeton University Press, 1993).

14. Paul Harvey, "Rehabilitation in Complex Political Emergencies: Is Rebuilding Civil Society the Answer?" *Disasters* 22, no. 3 (1998): 203.

15. Paikiasothy Saravanamuttu, "Sri Lanka: Civil Society, the Nation, and the State-Building Challenge," in *Civil Society and the Aid Industry*, ed. Alison Van Rooy (London: Earthscan, 1998), 104–33.

16. Uvin, *Aiding Violence*, 166.

17. Harvey, "Rehabilitation in Complex Political Emergencies," 208.

18. Antonio Donini, "The Bureaucracy and the Free Spirits: Stagnation and Innovation in the Relationship between the UN and NGOs," *Third World Quarterly* 16, no. 3 (1995): 436.

19. Morgan, "Capacity Development," 10–11.

20. Eade, *Capacity Building*, 21–22.

21. In fairness, Morgan has written much more extensively about capacity building than the selection of one paragraph might imply. Eade has written a thoughtful and thought-provoking book on the subject.

22. Sue Lautze and John Hammock, *Coping with Crisis, Coping with Aid: Capacity Building, Coping Mechanisms, and Dependency, Linking Relief and Development* (New York: United Nations Department of Humanitarian Affairs, 1996), 2.

23. Author's personal discussions at the meeting.

24. Morgan, "Capacity Development," 12.

25. Ian Smillie, "Sierra Leone," *NGOs in Complex Emergencies Project* (Ottawa: CARE Canada, 1997), 12.

26. Lautze and Hammock, *Coping with Crisis*, 10–11.

27. Rick James, *Demystifying Organization Development: Practical Capacity-Building Experiences of African NGOs* (Oxford: International Training and NGO Research Centre, 1998), 169.

Chapter 2

Reconstructing Bosnia, Constructing Civil Society

Disjuncture and Convergence

IAN SMILLIE and GORAN TODOROVIĆ

They came here, not for us, but for them.
—COMMENTS AT AN NGO MEETING IN SARAJEVO

This chapter covers four years following the 1995 Dayton Peace Accords, which gave birth to an independent Bosnia. The chapter studies the relationship between external humanitarian actors and Bosnian civil society at three moments after the Dayton accords. The first section examines the situation at the end of 1996, about two years after Dayton, a period of early transition from relief and rehabilitation to efforts dealing with longer-term social and economic issues. The second section describes a specific effort by one international nongovernmental organization to build civil society. It charts the organization's progress from the confident proposal-writing stage to the complex reality of working with traumatized people to form organizations where none had existed before. This part of the chapter is set in January 1998, three years after Dayton—when support for the building of civil society had risen to prominence on the donor agenda. The final section is a sobering reflection on the progress that had been made by Bosnian civil society, and the understanding of that progress by external agencies at the start of the twenty-first century.

A brief word on terminology and recent events may be useful for those unfamiliar with the outcome of the 1995 Dayton Peace Accords. The accords led to the creation of the Republic of Bosnia and Herzegovina (hereafter called "Bosnia"), a federal arrangement with two "entities"—the Bosnia Serb Republic, with a largely Serbian population, and the Federation of Bosnia and Herzegovina, comprised of a majority of Muslims and Croats.

The Dayton accords were backed by 52,000 North Atlantic Treaty

25

SUM Incorporated

Organization peacekeepers. At the end of 1996, more than a million
Bosnian refugees and displaced persons remained in other parts of former
Yugoslavia or elsewhere in Europe. (Five years earlier, the 1991 census
had placed the total population at 4.4 million.) Also at the end of 1996,
35 percent of the country's roads and 40 percent of the bridges were
damaged, and much of the health and education systems were still not
functioning. Electricity, water, and sewage systems were in varying states

of disrepair. Unemployment in Bosnia was estimated at 45 to 85 percent, and the cost of priority reconstruction was estimated by the World Bank at three billion dollars over a three-year period.[1]

December 1996 — Civil Society in Bosnia and Herzegovina

Although expressions such as *civil society* and *NGO community* are frequently used to describe the totality of NGOs in Bosnia, by the end of 1996 it was still far from being a community with coherence or sense of common purpose. The only partial exception would have been organizations involved with women and those concerned about human rights. The number of organizations is somewhat unclear and is made more confusing by varied definitions of what civil society or even an NGO actually was. There were probably several hundred associations—football clubs, youth associations and the like, many dating from pre-war days.

In September 1996, the International Council of Voluntary Agencies (ICVA) estimated that there were ninety-eight local NGOs working on reconstruction, infrastructure development, human rights, and women's issues. Most of these had been established since 1993, but some were less than a year old. Many worked within a restricted geographic area, while a handful worked on a wider basis. Few, if any, had any identity throughout the entities of Bosnia, the Serb Republic, and the federation. There was a large imbalance in the geographic location and work of NGOs. Many were clustered in Sarajevo and Tuzla—the two largest cities in Bosnia—and there had been very slow NGO growth in the Serb Republic.

The estimates of international NGOs ranged from 156 (by the ICVA) to 240 (by the federation government). Most of the major international NGOs were present—International Rescue Committee (IRC), Médecins sans Frontières (MSF), CARE, World Vision, Oxfam, Adventist Development and Relief Agency (ADRA), Catholic Relief Services (CRS). Many of the others were either very small ad hoc organizations formed in response to this crisis or NGOs that were relatively unknown in other parts of the world.

Many local NGOs were formed as conversions of projects established by international NGOs wanting to "leave something behind" or by the local staff of these organizations wanting to strike out on their own. Plavi Most in Bihac, established by the local staff of CARE, assumed responsibility for some of the CARE activities in the area, and then went on to develop new projects with support from the United Nations High Commissioner for Refugees (UNHCR), the World Bank, and the European Community. Viva Zena in Tuzla was originally a project funded by a group of individual German donors to support women and orphans.

It then registered itself as an independent Bosnian NGO. Three different organizations named Amica established themselves as the inheritors of projects established by a small German organization, Amica. Bospo and Bosfam in Tuzla inherited project and program activity initiated by the Danish Refugee Council and Oxfam, respectively.

Other organizations had formed spontaneously to deal with local problems and to take advantage of special funding made available by donors. Few had developed out of community spirit, however, and many operated without boards of directors or anything resembling the sort of "constituency" that Western NGOs take for granted. Apart, perhaps, from the human rights organizations, many had little understanding of their place in civil society or their potential for advocacy and for work beyond simple service delivery. Like the international NGOs they emulated, many were quick to fall into competition with each other, vying for donor attention and funding.

UNHCR has been criticized elsewhere for ignoring local organizations and favoring international NGOs. In Bosnia, however, UNHCR made a special point after 1994 to channel as much of its funding as possible through local organizations, creating many opportunities in the process for the establishment of new NGOs. With additional funding through the European Community Humanitarian Office (ECHO), the Bosnian Women's Initiative (managed by UNHCR), the World Bank, and others, a wide range of new possibilities for broadening an organization's funding base and for consolidating early programming efforts had become available by the end of 1996. Many embassies, including those of Canada, France, and the Netherlands, also initiated small grants programs for Bosnian organizations.

In recognition of the newness of the NGO sector and its fragility, several international organizations also organized capacity building programs. The United States Agency for International Development (USAID), for example, supported an umbrella grant managed by the International Rescue Committee. The umbrella grant aimed to strengthen local, community-oriented NGOs with training and technical assistance as well as project assistance. Delphi International's Star Project was similar, supporting non-nationalistic women's organizations throughout former Yugoslavia with both project and sustainability support. The Independent Bureau for Humanitarian Affairs (IBHA), funded by UNHCR, provided training courses and direct consultancy services to Bosnian NGOs, and the Organization for Security and Cooperation in Europe (OSCE) facilitated and hosted meetings, training, and logistical support, with emphasis on human rights, cross-ethnic activities, and women's organizations.

ICVA, a Geneva-based NGO umbrella organization, had established a rare external operation, setting up offices in three countries of the former Yugoslavia and in both entities of Bosnia. ICVA's main purpose was to foster communication and cooperation among the NGOs and to facilitate a coherent NGO interface on issues common to NATO's Implementation Force (IFOR), the Office of the High Representative,[2] UNHCR, OSCE, the World Bank and other multinational institutions, the governments of the entities, and, in Bosnia, the cantonal and municipal governments. ICVA provided information and networking services to international and local NGOs, and it promoted appropriate NGO legislation within Bosnia. It helped to establish an informal NGO Council aimed at coordinating the efforts of international and some local NGOs.

This description does not cover all the capacity building efforts available at the end of 1996. The Soros Foundation, the New Bosnia Fund, the Independent Bureau for Humanitarian Affairs, and others created special initiatives to finance and strengthen local NGO capacity, either generally or in specific sectors.

Given the amount and variety of funding available, given the support from international NGOs for the creation of new offspring, and given the capacity building programs available, it might have been assumed that the Bosnian NGO community had a bright future. This would have been a serious error.

Problems Facing Civil Society

Like many countries emerging from communism and command economies, Bosnia faced a major challenge in reorienting government attitudes toward both the private and nonprofit sectors. Government officials readily admitted that, as recently as 1993 or 1994, they had no idea what an NGO was, or what the establishment of a nonprofit sector might mean. Some were cautiously positive about its emergence, while others were openly hostile. At the cantonal level, officials could be very supportive because they saw what NGOs could accomplish, but there was concern about the lack of coordination and the emphasis on some sectors and geographic areas to the exclusion of others. Some officials, however, were suspicious and regarded much NGO activity as an incursion into areas of government responsibility. Some viewed income-generation efforts as little more than black marketeering.

Given the historical and political legacy of pre-war Bosnia, a degree of government hostility was perhaps not surprising. The personal ambivalence toward NGOs was also understandable: many government departments and social service centers had received very little donor attention over the previous four years, while NGOs, in many cases, were viewed as having been overfunded.

Also at the end of 1996 there was no legal framework as such for the nonprofit sector. Most NGOs were rightly confused by the array of laws under which they had to register and work. Some registered under an old law governing associations in general, but many expected soon to have to re-register under the Ministry of Social Welfare. A new law governing humanitarian organizations was anticipated, but it would have left important issues such as taxation to other departments.

The heavy burden of salary taxes for businesses in Bosnia applied also to NGOs. Payroll taxes and social security increased basic salaries by 100 percent or more, and the tax exemptions common in other countries were not always available for local organizations. Income generation and NGO microenterprise efforts were similarly susceptible to heavy rates of taxation. In fact, there were different tax regimes in both the Bosnian and Croat areas of the federation, as well as in the Serb Republic, and regulations differed in both letter and interpretation from canton to canton. Adding to the burden, many donors refused to allow their contributions to pay taxes, placing their beneficiary organization in an impossible situation. At least one Bosnian NGO had established a bank account in the neighboring country of Croatia to avoid such taxes (and to accede to donor concerns), a risky, semilegal, and ultimately unsustainable practice.

Another problem had to do with the excessive and opportunistic growth of NGOs. Some NGOs had been funded far beyond their capacity for good management. Organizations less than a year old were charged with managing a project portfolio in excess of a million dollars, something that would be unheard of in other parts of Europe and North America. This supply-driven situation represented little more than opportunism on the part of both donor and recipient. On the part of the donor, it resulted from a search for executing agencies, no matter how new, how fragile, how competent. On the part of some NGOs, it represented little more than a search for security and employment. In many cases it was simply the inability to say no in the face of need, opportunity, and optimism.

Changes in donor priorities was another of the most serious problems for Bosnian organizations two years after Dayton. A high proportion of organizations had been formed to deal with the psychosocial problems of those with whom they lived—widows, orphans, the elderly, the handicapped, and those traumatized by war, violence, and the loss of their homes. Through 1994, 1995, and much of 1996, this was the overwhelming priority in the country, and the locus around which many NGOs had formed. These needs were also reflected clearly as donor funding priorities.

By the end of 1996, however, new priorities had come to the fore. The reconstruction of houses and public infrastructure such as schools and clinics was a new and obvious area of need, attracting increased donor attention. Some, notably the World Bank, were placing increasing emphasis on the economy, and they began to create NGO-related funding mechanisms for microenterprise development. As funding for psycho social work declined, however, a serious problem began to emerge. Many, if not most, local NGOs were formed to deal with psychosocial problems. They felt that changing donor priorities ignored the continuing problems facing the tens of thousands of people with whom they worked. Need remained extremely high, and in many cases the possibility of real psychosocial healing was just beginning.

Because of rapidly declining funds, however, many NGOs despaired for the people with whom they worked. Much NGO psychosocial activity was expensive, isolated, and unconnected to potential government allies, services, and policies. The need had not diminished, but neither NGOs nor their supporters had a coherent medium-term view of what to do. Also, because many of the Bosnian NGOs and their workers had a social welfare orientation, they were unequipped (and in some cases uninterested) in working on reconstruction and microenterprise development. Because funding was drying up in one programming area, however, NGOs, in order to survive, were being drawn to new areas in which they had no special expertise and little interest.

Time frames also became troublesome. Most Bosnian NGOs were being forced by donor funding techniques to live with extremely short time horizons. Many could not predict—for themselves, their staff, or their beneficiaries—where funding would come from in three months. Virtually all donor grant mechanisms had a time frame of one year or less. Some were for six months or even three, and yet an organization could wait months from the date of application for a decision, and months for the receipt of funds.

European Union (EU) support for a local initiative in Banja Luka, for example, was based on a project proposal submitted in April 1995; it was not approved until seventeen months later, in October 1996. The actual agreement with the NGO was not signed until May 1997, but, by then, the proposal was barely relevant to the changed situation.[3] This sort of tardiness—more common than not—created great insecurity within organizations. It made long-term planning (not to mention strategic planning) impossible, and it encouraged NGOs to chase whatever new donor fund or priority emerged rather than to focus on their own aims and objectives. Short time frames required a permanent proposal-writing capacity and added to the reporting burden and the likelihood of shoddy implementation.

Capacity Building and Sustainability

Although there was, by the end of 1996, a wide range of capacity building efforts for NGOs, such efforts formed a very small proportion of the funding going to NGOs. Capacity building was too often equated simply with training. There was little coordination among the providers of this training; identification of needs tended to favor the interests and perceptions of donors rather than those of NGOs. "What Is an NGO?" "Strategic Planning," "How to Develop a Mission Statement," and "Project Design and Reporting" were common topics in the courses being provided. While these were no doubt useful for some NGOs, many NGOs complained that they had been through the same courses many times, and that much of it was very general and had little relevance to existing realities. For many, the problem was not how to write a report, but how to write six reports, in English, in six different formats every quarter, or even every month.

When donors first began funding and establishing local organizations, there was little talk of sustainability. By late 1996, however, like the weather, everybody was talking about the sustainability of Bosnian NGOs. And, like the weather, few were doing anything about it.

Then and now there was little likelihood of financial support to NGOs from government. And local philanthropy—unheard of in the past—in a war-damaged economy with massive unemployment was not a realistic possibility in the short or the medium term. Even in the longer term, funding from sources such as the Bosnian diaspora was likely to be ethnically based, and could actually work against a pluralistic, multiethnic society.

Some donors and international NGOs addressed the problem in a forthright manner, recognizing that NGOs cannot survive and plan for their own futures unless they have a secure financial base. In Tuzla, for example, the European Community Humanitarian Office (ECHO) was providing a management adviser and some of the running costs for a local NGO that showed promise. Terre des Hommes was providing all the core costs of the organization that emerged from its efforts in 1996, and it would continue to provide core costs on a declining scale over a five-year period. In its Local Initiatives Project, the World Bank provided running costs and allowed NGOs to retain the interest earned on microenterprise loans. In time, NGOs would also perhaps be permitted to retain ownership of the revolving loan fund.

These examples, however, were not just rare; they were virtually unique. Some of the NGOs created by international agencies had been "dumped." They had been given basic project funds for a year, a little training perhaps, and then set adrift in a sea of jargon about sustainability. Most NGOs, including several regarded by donors as the best and the strongest, faced extremely severe financial difficulties because of core funding shortfalls.

Despite its good intentions in channeling funding through local NGOs, UNHCR was perhaps one of the most prominent culprits in setting organizations up for a fall. Its rigid adherence to implementation costs and its avoidance of organizational costs, combined with the fact that it was the biggest source of local NGO funding for three years, created a community of organizations that lived an almost completely unsustainable hand-to-mouth existence. Many other donors were no better, telling NGOs that they would not fund salaries, overheads, and other core costs, for fear that some sort of "dependency" might develop.

Some of this reflected donor naïveté about the NGO reality in Bosnia. Some of it was simply opportunism, using local organizations as cheap delivery mechanisms, regardless of the longer-term societal cost. International NGOs could not be exempted from such criticism, especially those that transformed their projects into a local organization before hitchhiking home. Having done this, one prominent international organization reviewed the progress of its progeny in August 1996, and found an organization that was—not surprisingly—fighting for its financial life, despite its good programming reputation. "Having invested in the creation of local NGOs," the evaluation states (a year too late), "we now have a responsibility to support them through their transition to a sustainable independent sector. Given the crucial role played by a strong NGO sector in democratic society, we should all consider this a serious issue that constitutes a threat to the future of a multiparty, democratic Bosnia and continue to invest energy and resources into supporting local NGOs."[4]

Civil Society and/or Service Delivery

It is perhaps worth pausing to consider the second issue raised in the preceding quotation. Donors (and many international NGOs) characterize their interest in supporting local NGOs as an investment in a strong, pluralist, socially integrated civil society. And yet what was happening in Bosnia at this time was entirely different: in funding NGOs, donors essentially sought—and found—cheap service delivery. Given the problems and constraints mentioned above, given the manner in which the international players worked with local organizations, it is possible to view this trend as a weakening rather than a strengthening of civil society. NGO observer Paul Stubbs suggests that the development of NGOs and civil society is characterized "as *either* the key social development force constraining the potential extremes of state and market, *or* as an essentially residualist model of social welfare."[5] The latter model would view NGOs as a cheap substitute for social welfare activities that once were within the purview of the state. Despite the ringing declarations of donor support for civil society, this model, in practice, was the fact of life for NGOs in Bosnia Herzegovina at the end of 1996. By treating NGOs as cheap executing agencies and by ignoring what it would take to strengthen the sector properly, donors not only threatened the emergence of a genuine civil society, but they stood to lose their executing agencies as well.

Project Phoenix

Blame for the disintegration of Yugoslavia and the ensuing war has been laid at many doors. For some, the downfall was a direct outcome of the economic collapse that accompanied massive borrowing and a muddled effort to convert a communist command structure into something resembling a market economy. For others, the cause was the rise of ethnic and regional nationalisms, released from a forty-year deep freeze after the death of Marshal Tito. For still others the cause was simply political opportunism and corruption amid confusion caused by economic disarray and a power vacuum. All were contributing factors.

What made the contributing factors more menacing, however, was the lack of institutional and public resistance to trends that in other European countries would have been halted before they reached dangerous proportions. The absence of a free press, weak or nonexistent concepts of political democracy, and a stunted civil society made Yugoslavia and its component parts highly vulnerable to political opportunists and predators.

With hindsight, and in the aftermath of war, these weaknesses were more visible, and by 1997 and 1998 some international actors had begun to see the contradiction in their efforts to find cheap local service delivery and their stated desire to build civil society. This section describes the efforts of one international NGO to strengthen civil society and what it began to learn in the process.

The Proposal

In February 1997, CARE International in Bosnia submitted a proposal to the Norwegian Agency for Development Cooperation (NORAD) through CARE Norway for a two-year Project Phoenix.[6] Project Phoenix would "facilitate the growth of Bosnian Civil Society by providing technical and material support to sixteen grassroots organizations that are now reconstituting themselves or are being created for the first time to meet social and community needs caused by the recent war." The project spoke of "assisting groups to assess their own training and organizational needs, [to] facilitate technical support and training where required, and [to] assist in the rebuilding of communications and information links where appropriate." Organizations would be selected on the basis of "mutually shared values and principles" that would include a commitment to tolerance and diversity; to community life and public good; and to widening the space for social and political activity at the grassroots level.

There would be a period of "intensive collaboration" focusing on "self-defined needs assessment . . . consultative meetings and the development of linkages and forums with other associations and formal bodies, both locally and internationally." CARE aimed to "break down barriers that currently isolate communities and groups, building up opportunities and ways to create links and networks." Work with the sixteen associations would be phased, with each organization receiving ten months of intensive interaction before being "rotated off the project."

The proposal listed a series of anticipated outputs (sixteen local associations assisted through twenty technical-assistance seminars, six networking conferences, and so on) as well as broader qualitative outcomes such as enhanced community identity, self-reliance, and self-determination through the participation of ordinary citizens. The proposal also stated:

> As well, the project will be developed with the goal of strengthening a pluralistic and diversified civic foundation that will enhance the social welfare of the entire community, especially the most disadvantaged populations. One of the biggest strengths of this project is its ripple effect.... Beneficiaries will have acquired new professional techniques, a repertoire of skills and modalities. This informed sense of knowledge and acquisition of new professional tools will not only increase their sense of professionalism, it will also help them to perform their jobs and to deliver their services to their clients more effectively. CARE's collaboration could also lead to the formation of other new associations that will build on the lessons learned and develop new and innovative strategies to meet the changing needs of a postwar population.

The confident tone of the proposal minimized any doubts about CARE's ability to tackle the problems described. The organization had begun working in the former Yugoslavia at the height of the war, providing medical care, psychosocial assistance, food, shelter, medicine, and clothing. One project had provided assistance since 1994 to extremely vulnerable individuals (EVIs) in thirty-two communities. CARE worked on stress and trauma training for teachers, house reconstruction for returning refugees, and, at the height of the siege of Sarajevo, it provided solar-powered emergency water purifiers, spring development, and water-containment tanks.

CARE, therefore, had a track record in Bosnia. It had worked extensively with the three ethnic communities, had supported local self-help efforts, and had thought through some of the larger implications of what it proposed in Project Phoenix. Confident that NORAD would support the project (it was approved in July 1997), CARE began operations a few months earlier, in May. Little in CARE's background or in the confident project proposal would have led anyone to believe that, within six months, the project and CARE's understanding of civil society would be profoundly altered.

Getting Started

CARE's first problem was to identify civil society organizations. These fell broadly into three categories that sometimes overlapped. First, there were organizations formed to help others—often called nongovernmental organizations and commonly referred to now in Bosnia as NGOs. Understandably, many of these in the Bosnia of mid-1997 had a distinct welfare approach. Second, there were organizations formed to advocate change, such as human rights groups or those working for a free press. Third, there were those formed out of self-interest: membership groups, cooperatives, trade unions.

A high proportion remained unregistered, few had developed formal structures, and even fewer had anything that even vaguely resembled an income and budget. The government view of such organizations continued to vary, not least because there were still, structurally speaking, three governments. Each held different and fluctuating views of civil society, and each had different and largely inadequate laws governing the functioning of such organizations. Attitudes ranged from tolerance to indifference to open hostility. Given the political situation and the economic state of affairs, financial support from government for any kind of civil society organization or NGO remained, in 1997 and 1998, out of the question.

CARE soon discovered that a lot of its original ideas were not going to work. The idea of finding up-and-coming organizations that needed intensive management or financial training was not realistic. As noted in the first part of this chapter, several international agencies had already established capacity building projects, and most local organizations had attended one or even several of the training sessions. They complained that their real needs—mostly financial and political—were being ignored in favor of lengthy sessions on how to prepare mission statements, project proposals, and reports. Some had already learned these basic tricks of the trade and did not need, or at least did not want, this sort of capacity building. And some organizations, in CARE's estimation, had become little more than contractors for donors, a poor reflection of the sort of civil society that CARE hoped to foster.

Starting its selection process, CARE cast its conceptual net wider than originally planned and soon discovered that it would have trouble narrowing the number of organizations to the project target of sixteen. Hundreds had mushroomed since the war ended. Some were more interested in themselves than anybody else, and this too started CARE thinking. Self-help was perhaps as sustainable in the long run—if not more so—than social welfare activities on behalf of others.

Meeting with fledgling groups, CARE staff also discovered that once they had shed ideas about training in management and finance, there was no road map on how to deal with civil society. Intensive regular meetings no longer seemed appropriate; the idea of rotating organizations out after ten months no longer made sense. The most basic ideas about where to start, what to do, how to do it, and even how to justify it had to be rethought. Groups, for example, were suspicious, fearing that CARE had a political agenda. For many, traumatized by war and "ethnic cleansing," textbook ideas about reconciliation were unwelcome, and they feared a plot to force them into unwanted activities or travel "to the other side."

Banja Luka

CARE planned to work with groups in Eastern Slavonija (part of Croatia), in the Federation of Bosnia-Herzegovina and in the western Serb Republic, with an emphasis there on Banja Luka. The second-largest city in Bosnia, Banja Luka has a population of about 200,000 and, in 1998, refugees and displaced persons added perhaps 70,000. Before the war, it had equal numbers of Serbs and Muslims, with a smaller Croat population. Early in the war, however, Banja Luka was taken by Serb forces and, thereafter, became a Serb stronghold. Ethnic cleansing took a serious toll on the non-Serb population, many of whom left after their jobs disappeared, when they were evicted from their homes, or when they became victims of humiliation and violence. For much of the war, the city was under a military blockade, with only occasional relief convoys getting though. Until the war turned against the Bosnian Serb army in the summer of 1995, Banja Luka was spared the worst of the war. Then, however, it suffered a massive influx of tens of thousands of Serbian refugees moving in advance of a disintegrating front.

Following Dayton, recovery began almost immediately in federation territory, but international sanctions on the Serb Republic were not lifted until April 1996, and aid was further restricted or withheld because of the government's noncompliance with key aspects of the peace accord. By the end of 1996, production was only 10 percent of its pre-war figure in the Serb Republic, and unemployment in the nonagricultural sector—officially recognized at 61 percent and largely unchanged the following summer[7]—was probably much higher. At the end of 1997, the overall gross domestic product of the Serb Republic was less than a quarter of its pre-war level or, as one report put it, "equivalent to that of a small city in the European Union."[8]

Three Civil Society Organizations

VIDRA Women's Action. The group formed in Banja Luka in the summer of 1997, when sixteen women began talking about how to create jobs for themselves. Many were unemployed professionals; some had lost their husbands during the war; some had worked with relief agencies and saw an opportunity in foreign assistance. Some were Serbs, some were

Muslims, and some were Croats. The one thing they had in common apart from their mutual acquaintance was the need for employment. With help from a Danish NGO, they got enough money and the additional membership required for legal registration.

But meeting in their homes or in borrowed offices, they looked and felt unprofessional. In order to convince project donors that they were serious, they felt that an office, a phone, and a fax machine, along with basic meeting facilities, were essential. In the end, after considerable discussion, that is what CARE provided: six months rent for an office, some tables and chairs, a computer, a phone, and fax. Within weeks, the organization had developed proposals for several funding agencies. One project aimed to train women in bookkeeping and office financial management. A second was a training and information program on the legal rights of women. The third focused on psychosocial assistance for trauma victims of the war. A fourth, Open Eyes, aimed to work with children and youth on cultural problems that would emphasize tolerance, problem solving, and kindness. At the end of 1997, members wrote to CARE: "VIDRA knows that the project we gave you will not provide a long-term solution, but with it we can perhaps find a way to create self-sustainability for our organization."[9] Perhaps. They had a long way to go, however, with only one of their four projects funded by the beginning of 1998.

Asked why such organizations did not exist before the war, the VIDRA executive committee agreed unanimously that there simply had been no need. Government took care of everything; it was a different society; "everything was good." Regarding the future, however, they said they were very optimistic. There was a new government, and that could make their work easier, with new legislation for nonprofit organizations and other forms of support. They wanted to get out of the humanitarian dependence they found themselves in, and they hoped to develop joint projects with other organizations—internationally, throughout the Republic of Bosnia-Herzegovina, and within the Serb Republic.

Student Union, Faculty of Economics, University of Banja Luka. The student union started in 1995 with 150 members. By 1998 it was involved in a range of student activities—organizing guest lecturers, artists, writers, sports and cultural events, and activity for students' rights. It had a student radio program; it published a regular magazine; and it was trying to reestablish international relationships that had broken down during the war. The union was, members said, nonpolitical. But they were functioning in a highly political environment, and they wanted to reconnect with the world. The university, strapped for cash, could not do it for them, and the union decided to do it themselves.

CARE assisted them with office furniture and a photocopier that members could use on a cost-recovery basis. CARE also provided a small grant for seed capital to purchase hard-to-get textbooks and supplies at wholesale prices, for resale through their own shop. They hoped that this would generate enough money to sustain the union financially over the next few years.

The executive was full of ideas: to bring in business professors from other countries; to start a company that would assist students with jobs when they graduated; to create student-exchange programs with other countries. "CARE gave us an opportunity to grow up," said the union president. But not enough, it seems, to consider relations with other parts of Bosnia-Herzegovina. Many students were killed during the war, the president said, adding, "It will take time."

The Elderly Club 15–100. Before the war, the elderly in the former Yugoslavia were loosely organized through local associations of pensioners. With the upheavals of war, much of this changed. In January 1998, pensioners—reduced to a notional income of about seventeen American dollars per month—were waiting, as they had for years, for government support to arrive. Families had been torn apart by the war and many young people had left, becoming immigrants or refugees in Europe and North America. Many of those left behind were obliged to seek assistance from one of the relief centers established by the Adventist Development and Relief Agency or the Austrian Red Cross. By January 1998, two years after Dayton, little had changed.

During the war, CARE had provided a home help service for those most in need, and many Banja Lukans knew the organization. When the idea of resuscitating some form of joint action arose, the pensioners who had attended the first meetings were confused. The biggest need was for jobs, they said. There was much debate, however, about what they could do to help rebuild their damaged society. Nine of them, representing nine different communities, kept coming to the meetings, and they began to discuss things they could do, rather than what they needed for themselves. In the group were Serbs, Croats, and Muslims, but, as with VIDRA, this was accidental and not a CARE requirement. They talked about the past, about the 30,000 mixed marriages in Banja Luka, about how ethnic hatred had never been a feature of life until the war. They feared that the lack of jobs, family breakup, and the influx of 70,000 refugees from other parts of the country were leading to violence, robbery, and continuing social disintegration.

Maybe they could create a drop-in center to facilitate activities, discussion groups, and training programs for young people. They asked CARE to provide computers as a draw for the training programs, and they asked for help to find a building. In the end, they persuaded the civic authorities to provide a building themselves, and CARE assisted with repairs and with establishing a canteen that could help cover running costs. They named their group "15–100" because they wanted the center to be a place where people of all ages could meet, and where they could discuss the future together.

In some ways, there was nothing very profound about the Elderly Club 15–100: a drop-in center, training programs, and possibly inter-generational and interethnic peacebuilding. As with VIDRA and the student union, the total start-up cost for CARE was less than six thousand U.S. dollars, although the group was expected to request more assistance as time passed. The developmental indicators of output and outcome would be vague and ephemeral. The project might work; in five years there could be a vibrant center from which peace and harmony would radiate throughout the community. Or it might simply disappear. For a relatively small investment, however, CARE had created an opportunity for a group of citizens to build new meaning in their lives and, instead of dwelling on the past, to work for the future.

Lessons

CARE staff spent several months meeting and brainstorming with the groups, developing relationships and group self-confidence. Stated baldly, however, the tangible support provided by CARE to these three groups in Banja Luka was as follows:

- a newly formed women's group without a penny to its name was given money to rent a downtown office for six months;
- the student union in the university's faculty of economics received a photocopier and a little seed capital;
- a group of elderly pensioners, many of them living off meager international relief supplies, was given computers.

How might these expenditures be justified by an organization working to build civil society in a war-torn part of Bosnia? How would CARE justify itself to the donor? It would undoubtedly provide quantitative indicators of accomplishment: so many groups supported, so many members benefiting. Qualitative indicators would be more difficult: some of the groups might become financially or in other ways more independent. Some might be more democratic (whatever that means) after their CARE experience; there may have been more interethnic contact, and, as a result, some reconciliation. Greater pluralism may have been fostered, peace built, and civil society strengthened. Most of the report, however, would have to be anecdotal, as is this description.

The most useful result of the project might have been what CARE did not have in great quantity when it began: knowledge about Bosnian civil society, and how outsiders can and cannot interface with it. One of the greatest shortcomings of the several bilateral, multilateral, and NGO-supported capacity building projects in Bosnian civil society at the start of 1998, in fact, was the lack of public information about what was being learned. Like others before it, CARE started with some platitudes and a boilerplate project design that proved inadequate. CARE then learned that:

- working with civil society organizations in a postcommunist, postwar situation is not easy. The platitudes that catch a donor's eye provide few real guidelines in the cold light of morning;

- despite decades of communism and a bloody civil war, Bosnian civil society was much more vibrant than assumed;

- many civil society organizations were unregistered and loosely constituted, but that made them no less real and no less important;

- working with fledgling organizations takes time. They cannot be rushed or quickly rotated out. The one-year project funded by NORAD probably needed two, three, or even more years to run to its logical conclusion;

- partnership has to mean something. In CARE's case it meant working through Bosnian staff in getting to know the organization's members and making a decision in reasonable time.[10] It meant letting the association determine its own needs and its own time frame as much as possible, within a budget allocation in most cases of less than ten thousand American dollars. It meant keeping the paper requirements to a minimum. It meant scrapping the idea that capacity building is synonymous with training, and it meant understanding that organizational life is more than mission statements and project proposals;

- self-help groups are no less legitimate than groups that want to help others. They may, in fact, constitute an important first line in civil society.

A final lesson may emerge more slowly and it may be far from universal. Well-intentioned outsiders may want to build peace and foster reconciliation in places where terrible ethnic-related atrocities have taken place. However, as the student-union official said, "It will take time." In areas where wounds are raw, forcing the pace may make things worse. Peace is a natural human desire, and if the right conditions can be created, it may develop of its own accord. Writing about Rwanda, Peter Uvin takes a more proactive position, cautioning against excessive optimism about the democratizing and stabilizing impact of NGOs. "NGOs do not promote pluralism and tolerance in society if they do not seek to do so. In other words, civil society organizations' positive effects do not follow automatically from their existence, but must be targeted."[11]

The View at the Start of a New Century

When speaking of Bosnian NGOs, the so-called third sector, or civil society as a whole, we refer in reality only to the years after 1992 and more especially to the period after the signing of the Dayton Peace Accords in 1995. There was little in the way of an observable civil society as such in Yugoslavia's socialist state. Very few nongovernmental organizations represented the interest of specific categories of people, and social programs were mainly directed by the government. Bosnian NGOs arose during the war as a side effect of the great influx of international NGOs and donors. In that respect, Bosnia is unique: as the first European humanitarian emergency in this generation, it attracted almost every known international NGO and donor agency, creating an environment that was and remains highly complex.

At the start of the twenty-first century, civil society in Bosnia remained well behind other Eastern and Central European countries in transition. The irony is that after World War II, Yugoslavia was, in many respects, well ahead of other Eastern and Central European countries. In 2000, estimates ranged from 1,000 to 1,500 Bosnian organizations, compared with 30,000 civil associations in the Czech Republic or 5,000 registered associations and 10,000 Russian organizations in Moscow alone. If there is any validity in the numbers, however, the increase in Bosnia between 1996 and 2000 represented a tenfold rate of growth.

While other Eastern European countries struggle mainly with economic and political reforms, Bosnia has, in addition, been scarred by a long war, during which thousands of people were killed and more than one million became refugees or internally displaced. Parts of the country were totally devastated. The war brought about economic collapse, and the political environment remains one of the most complex in the world. Bosnia still lacks the basic preconditions for a strong NGO sector. There is no tradition of charitable and voluntary action; the public has little understanding of NGOs; and local authorities still see NGOs more as competition than allies. They retain a simplistic view of NGOs as foes of the government, as competitors for international funds. Bosnian and international organizations certainly made efforts, however, to create coordinating and support mechanisms. Three examples follow.

Bosnia and Herzegovina NGO Council

This Bosnian consultative and lobbying body was founded in Banja Luka in November 1997. It was a significant step for NGOs from both entities, who wanted to create better understanding and coordination among themselves. As a non-ethnic coalition—consisting of eighteen regional NGO forums—it was something of a first in Bosnia. From the outset, however, there were problems: lack of trust; long debates about who could speak on behalf of the third sector; whether the council should have a permanent president, formal statutes, and so on. At the beginning of 1999, however, they finally reached agreement on an organizational structure and secretariat. By the end of the year, the council had sought financial assistance from the World Bank (refused), the Charles Mott Foundation (refused), USAID (no interest in its work), and the British Embassy (no response). Its only support after eighteen months was a small grant from the EU for "local initiatives."

The Bosnian NGO Foundation

In 1998, five international NGOs (World Vision, CARE, ICVA, IRC, and CRS) sponsored an initiative to create a Bosnian NGO Foundation. The purpose of the foundation was to accumulate funds that would be invested, and whose proceeds would help pay for training and advocacy as well as grant support. The invested funds would also supplement international funding after the major donors had left the country. By the end of 1999, the foundation was officially organized, with a Bosnian board of directors, an international advisory committee, and a small secretariat.

As a first effort, the foundation conducted a survey of Bosnian civil society organizations, covering a wide range of issues. Initial core funding was provided by the five sponsoring agencies, and an additional Can. $500,000 was committed by the Canadian International Development Agency (CIDA) for a sustaining endowment. In November 2000, however, CIDA's promise of support was canceled in favor of a project fund, not unlike the nonsustaining "support" of all the other donors in Bosnia.

UNHCR made a tentative offer of support (U.S.$400,000), but the official who was involved left Bosnia and interest faded. Requests to USAID, the British Department for International Development (DFID), Sida, other bilateral agencies, the EU, the World Bank, and foundations with a stated interest in building civil society fell on deaf ears, and by the beginning of 2000, the initiative was still in question, surviving mainly on tiny project-based contributions.

The Civil Society Development Program

In 1997, a Danish organization, Dialogue Development, was engaged by the European Community (EC) to develop a European Union approach to civil society. Questionnaires, consultations, and voluminous background papers were produced, and, by the end of 1997, a plan had begun to take shape. This effort was characterized alternatively as a civil society development program and as the creation of a civil society and democratization institute.[12] It was proposed that the initiative be managed by a Bosnian advisory board, with donor participation. The initiative overlapped with some of what the Bosnian NGO Foundation was attempting, but it was projected as a programming partner for the EC. Reflecting the model developed for other EC-supported initiatives in Eastern Europe, the proposal contained references to Bulgaria that its authors had forgotten to replace with the word "Bosnia." Although much talked about among Bosnian civil society organizations in 1997 and 1998, the proposal disappeared with the transfer from Sarajevo of its main EC supporter.

Additional Problems

While the international community has made some positive and many ill-advised efforts to assist local organizations, the biggest proportion of civil society funding was, four years after Dayton, still directed through international NGOs. Along with their governments and other donors, the international NGOs became the main decision makers in the country, providing funding, support, ideas, and priorities, often with little regard for the historical, economic, and social circumstances that shape Bosnian civil society. Donor agencies have supported local NGOs, acting as mentors, catalysts, and funders, but often they have induced or even forced the creation of local NGOs without any long-term strategy. From the Bosnian NGO point of view, the situation was made worse by international mentors who made three- and five-year plans for themselves, but who refused to consider such time frames for locals.

Responsibility for the underdevelopment of Bosnia's third sector must be shared jointly by international and local organizations. The international community failed in a number of important ways:

1. International organizations did not use the political instruments at their disposal to encourage a more productive dialogue between the Bosnian government and local civil society organizations. A 1999 survey conducted by the NGO Foundation for Bosnia and Herzegovina found that government authorities knew little or nothing of the NGOs' role and work. NGOs said that the government believed them to be unnecessary and harmful or simply saw them as competition. Decisions of great importance continued to be made for (or were imposed upon) the people of Bosnia and Herzegovina by the international community through the Office of the High Representative which, in fact, ruled the country as a form of protectorate.

The international community never seemed to grasp the importance of a more aggressive strategy in support of the civic movement. Instead, it equated democracy with elections, thinking that by imposing a democratic electoral process—organized and overseen by the OSCE—it could create a democratic society. Unfortunately, elections or not, a majority of the same politicians who had led Bosnia into war remained at the policy helm. Lasting changes that may eventually remove chauvinistic leaders are more likely to be initiated at the grassroots level. Such changes are more likely with an informed public and if citizens understand how to influence policy. In that regard, civil society is an ideal vehicle to bring about meaningful change in Bosnia, but its visibility and influence need to be strengthened. Bosnian NGOs need financial sustainability, voice, and a legitimate role in working with their government and with the international community. Four years after Dayton, the international community still failed to provide substantive support and guidance.

2. International assistance to Bosnia during and after the war was the costliest in recent humanitarian history. How much reached people in need, and how much was spent on the personnel and infrastructure of international agencies, may never be known, but Bosnians are very sensitive on this question and on the cost of supporting the NATO effort. According to some reports, the cost of maintaining NATO troops for one day at the peak of the effort was five million dollars, enough to support most existing social programs for a year.

3. Since 1995, the country's legal system has been well within the purview of the international community. Unfortunately, little effort was invested in lobbying for better and more favorable laws to regulate the work of NGOs and civic organizations. Most NGOs regarded the legal framework as a major handicap. There are two sets of laws (Serb Republic and federation), but no central law to regulate NGO work throughout the country. In practice, this means that an NGO needs to have two separate registrations in order to operate legally in both entities.

4. Key international donors and NGOs have serious coordination problems at the policy level and in their work; many prefer "bricks and mortar" projects to the more difficult social programming.

5. Despite much talk of participation and consultation, donors essentially ignore Bosnian NGOs when preparing their projects and programs, focusing on their own priorities and agendas. In the NGO Foundation survey, 54 percent of respondents said that their relationship with donors was inadequate, and that domestic NGOs were seen only as a source of cheap labor. Donors rarely met with NGOs as a group, and were usually guarded about what they said and what conclusions they reached in discussions. While most donors say their doors are open to anyone, in reality it is not easy for Bosnian NGOs to get through them.

6. Little attention is given to authentic Bosnian initiatives and to mechanisms that will ultimately take over the work being done by foreigners. Initiatives conceived by and for Bosnians are rare, and those that have been initiated have largely been ignored.

7. It is widely believed by Bosnian NGOs that as long as there is money for international NGOs in Bosnia, they will not leave. Further, international NGOs will rarely advise donors to work through Bosnian organizations as long as there are financial possibilities for themselves.

Bosnian civil society itself bears some of the responsibility for these ongoing problems. One of the biggest problems is leadership. Most NGOs were established by individuals with personal courage, vision, and commitment. However, most Bosnian NGOs are not based on membership, and few have much support in the communities where they work. This means that leaders take on great personal responsibility. When the leader moves, the organization often finds itself in trouble because of poor teamwork and because finding a replacement is a major problem. Many leaders have spent more time with donors and at international conferences than they have with their peers, so they lose contact with the community of which they are a part.

There is an additional problem: the international community sees only a small, unrepresentative group of Bosnian NGO leaders, and these few are becoming opinion makers for the donor community. For example, in Bijeljina in the Serb Republic, there is an office of the local Helsinki Committee for Human Rights. It took some time before NGOs started blooming in that region, but because the local Helsinki Committee was among the first (and because their leaders showed great courage in criticizing local Serb authorities), it gained the sympathy and interest of key international players, to the exclusion of many others. Whenever foreigners visited Bijeljina, they went mainly to the leaders of the Helsinki Committee, bewildering and offending other local NGOs.

The lack of NGO street smarts—basic management expertise and donor savvy—is a further problem. In particular, local NGOs have difficulties in communication with foreigners, and they are unfamiliar with general NGO management and developmental norms as understood in other countries. Bosnian NGOs seem more willing to learn from their own mistakes than to use lessons that have been learned by others or to build on experience from other countries in transition. To be fair, communication difficulties are part of the reason for this problem. And NGOs in Bosnia are so preoccupied with their own survival that there is hardly time for reading or networking with others.

Lack of vision should be added to the list of weaknesses. At both the local and state level, NGOs have difficulties in developing a vision for their growth, their course of action, and their medium- and long-term plans. In the exceptional case when vision *is* more developed, the NGO usually lacks the wherewithal to implement it, and everything stays at the level of nicely presented ideas.

The NGO public image is weak. NGOs are poorly represented in the media, so the public has little opportunity to find out what they are doing. Journalists have little idea how to present or deal with the third sector, seeing it mainly in humanitarian terms and underestimating its strength. NGOs themselves have underestimated the importance of the media and have not developed an understanding of how or why to engage it.

Transparency and credibility are urgent problems for Bosnian civil society. Few organizations are willing to share information in public about their work. As a result, they cannot count on significant growth in public support. The lack of transparency in government is thus reciprocated among NGOs, reinforcing old patterns of secrecy and mistrust. In recent years, the Bosnian branch of the Soros Foundation was one of the few organizations that produced an annual report with financial statements. Despite their rarity, such examples are important for the Bosnian third sector.

People working within NGOs are uncomfortable admitting that their work is, in fact, political. Almost every NGO intervention can be seen in some way as a political activity. For example, if an NGO is dealing with human rights, it is realistic to expect that most of its beneficiaries will be victims of human rights abuse. In the Bosnian context, this means members of a minority. By helping the minority, NGOs may confront local authorities that may not be doing everything they should or could on behalf of the victims. Other NGOs helping refugees return home may confront authorities that prefer the new status quo. By refusing to acknowledge the political nature of their work, organizations make strategic errors and miss important opportunities for influencing both government and donor agencies.

Because the third sector is still a relatively new phenomenon, local authorities still have great problems in accepting that groups and individuals outside the traditional government structure can contribute something to society. In a few cases, donors have attempted to induce cooperation between NGOs and unwilling government structures. On the other hand, many NGOs still do not understand that in some cases they can benefit from closer relationships with government. Instead, many isolate themselves, submerging themselves in program activities. The resulting vacuum represents a loss for all.

Conclusions

During the war (until end of 1995) and in the transition period immediately after the war (most of 1996), the international community was right in giving priority to international NGOs for the implementation of programs. Because of the political complexity of the region, because the wounds of war were fresh, because there was restricted freedom of movement and great need for specific emergency skills, international agencies were the major vehicle for meaningful and timely humanitarian assistance. During that period, international organizations were able to educate their local staff and to prepare them for the postwar period. However, once the war was over, many donors still wanted to work with foreign NGOs rather than local organizations.

Most agree that international NGOs should depart as soon as possible, but in an organized manner, leaving sustainable mechanisms in place for the support of civil society after they have left. However, Bosnian NGOs believe that most will not leave as long as there is money available for them. The problem at the turn of the century was how to address this late transition phase issue, and how to design policy interventions that would encourage greater meaningful investment in local organizations and local capacities before the money started to dry up.

It is clear that the success of the international agencies—even during the war years—was due in large part to the knowledge, hard work, and risk-taking of local staff. It is fair and reasonable now to expect a payback. During the crisis, foreigners were needed for their knowledge, their money, and their neutrality. The crisis is ending, and local people need to cope with problems by themselves. Solutions from outside may help, but they will never resolve problems.

Post-Dayton Bosnia is, in essence, an ethnic microcosm of the old Yugoslavia. It is engaged in an attempt to rebuild the tolerance that disappeared so quickly in the early 1990s. Much of the current emphasis is on economic recovery. Understandably, people need jobs, and there are massive reconstruction requirements. As stated in a World Bank discussion paper (September 1996), "The Government of the Republic of Bosnia and Herzegovina has expressed its firm determination to rebuild the country as fast as it can. There is equal determination to achieve this goal, not through a system of command and control, but as far as possible through the initiative of private individuals, organized in a modern market economy. It is hoped that in this process of reconstruction and reform, the critical elements of a pluralistic, multiethnic society will be re-established and strengthened."

Like many other donors and investors, the World Bank places a great deal of faith in the idea that a revived and prosperous market economy will lead to peace and security. Historian Michael Ignatieff is more than a little dismissive of this as the key to change. "Speaking as a liberal," he writes, "I would say that it is time to jettison the traditional liberal fiction—enunciated since the days of Adam Smith—that global commerce will pacify the world, that everyone's objective interest in prosperity gives everyone an interest in social peace. Yugoslavia demonstrates that when ethnic groups feel their identity, culture and survival at stake, they are willing to lay waste to what was one of Eastern Europe's most prosperous economies."[13]

Rebuilding tolerance and pluralism in Bosnia and Herzegovina is perhaps more important than anywhere else in the former Yugoslavia. It is important because, without it, the Dayton Peace Accords, hundreds of thousands of lives, hundreds of millions of dollars spent trying to reach a settlement, and the hope of a united Bosnia and Herzegovina will be lost. Democracy is more than the economy. It is more than political parties and elections. A free press is an essential part, but it is only one part. Accountability, legitimacy, and competence in public life are the key, and these can only be achieved through the active participation of the electorate, buoyed by a strong, plural, associational base, by a web of social, cultural, and functional relationships which can act as a "societal glue" and as a counterbalance to the market and the state. The alternative for Bosnia and Herzegovina, well-known to citizens of the former Yugoslavia, is paternalism, exploitation, corruption, and war.

Notes

1. For an earlier study by the Humanitarianism and War Project that examines the crisis and international response through 1993, see Larry Minear et al., *Humanitarian Action in the Former Yugoslavia: The U.N.'s Role 1991–1993* (Providence, R.I.: Watson Institute, 1994).

2. The High Representative was appointed by the Organization for Security and Cooperation in Europe, which assumed the responsibilities that NATO conferred on it after the Dayton accords.

3. European Union, *Project Fiche No. 15-0 Democracy (B7-7001),* May 10, 1999.

4. Confidential Oxfam Great Britain evaluation of a Bosnian NGO, 1996.

5. Paul Stubbs, *Social Reconstruction and Social Development in Croatia and Slovenia: The Role of the NGO Sector,* Research Report R6274 (Zagreb: Overseas Development Authority, 1996).

6. CARE International is a group of several CARE organizations in Europe, North America, and Australia. When Project Phoenix was initiated, CARE Canada was the "lead agency" for the former Yugoslavia, with headquarters in Zagreb and several offices throughout the republics; these offices were formed in the early 1990s.

7. World Bank, *Bosnia and Herzegovina: From Recovery to Sustainable Growth* (Washington, D.C.: World Bank, 1997), 8; European Commission and World Bank, *Bosnia and Herzegovina: Implementation of the Priority Reconstruction Program—Status Report to the Donor Community,* November 1997, 6.

8. Office of the High Representative, *Outlook for 1998,* Sarajevo, December 1997.

9. VIDRA letter to CARE in Banja Luka, November 14, 1997 (translation).

10. Making commitments relatively quickly was done for two reasons, according to project manager Nevin Orange. CARE did not want to discourage groups by making too many demands on them at first. The second reason was more practical. Funding arrived late, "allowing us very little time to do the job responsibly, which also led us to other lessons like only committing small amounts of money to a larger number of groups which—practically speaking—lessened the risk while allowing us to reach more groups. Nevertheless, the bottom line is that this approach fostered trust, allowed us to meet and work informally and

as partners with the groups, and put us in the positive position of learning the other lessons..." (correspondence with the author, February 25, 1998).

11. Peter Uvin, *Aiding Violence: The Development Enterprise in Rwanda* (West Hartford, Conn.: Kumarian Press, 1998), 168.

12. Dialogue Development, *European Union Civil Society Development Project in Bosnia and Herzegovina,* Copenhagen, November 1997.

13. Michael Ignatieff, "Nationalism and the Narcissism of Minor Differences," *Queen's Quarterly* 102, no. 1 (spring 1995).

Chapter 3

Alternative Food Aid Strategies and Local Capacity Building in Haiti

KATHY MANGONES

Not with corn, but ... with the possibility of being.
                                        —Rainer Maria Rilke

Food aid is one of the most prevalent expressions of humanitarian assistance, and one of its most controversial. It is prevalent because most crisis situations, whether natural or man-made, lead to disruptions in food production and distribution. These disruptions exacerbate existing structural problems and create temporary or more permanent food deficits, which primarily affect the most vulnerable people. Food aid is controversial because many food aid programs, in addition to feeding the hungry, have also led to other problems: increased food aid dependency and a decrease of local production capacity; changes in consumption patterns; increased conflict within areas receiving aid; a politicization of food in conflicts; and the use of food commodities to consolidate status or rank within communities.

During the 1990s, the number of situations requiring humanitarian assistance rose dramatically throughout the North and the South. Thus the persistent and increasing need to provide humanitarian assistance in general, and food aid in particular, has encouraged humanitarian organizations and development practitioners to review how food aid has been organized and to seek improvements. Some organizations have remained firmly anchored in the framework of traditional food aid programs. Others have explored new approaches that can be linked to a longer-term development perspective and that integrate many of the concepts that inform development work. A related possibility, of course, is that

Epigraph excerpt is taken from Rainer Maria Rilke's *Sonnets to Orpheus*, translated by J. B. Leishman, from *Selected Works*, copyright © 1960 by The Hogarth Press. Reprinted by permission of New Directions Publishing Corp.

SUM Incorporated

these new strategies may also limit the negative fallout usually associated with food aid programs, and may even contribute to laying the foundation for greater food security within affected communities.

One of the underlying issues in development work in general and humanitarian assistance in particular is how to ensure that the process helps build the capacities of national actors to address the problems with which they are confronted, and to be owners of the process. Whether this is referred to as capacity building, participation, or empowerment, the fundamental issue is one of ownership, and of ensuring that concerned sectors are the primary actors in their own rehabilitation, reconstruction, or development.

The passage from object to subject, or from victim to actor, is the foundation of all processes of social development. The challenge for organizations involved in providing humanitarian assistance is to take the time and to make the investments—in the midst of what is objectively perceived to be an emergency—to ensure that there is, in fact, ownership of the process and that implementation strategies will contribute to developing capacity and empowering social actors.

This chapter examines the issue through experiences in the provision of alternative types of food aid in Haiti during the critical period following the military coup d'état of 1991. The focus will not be on prevalent critiques of traditional food aid. This has been amply documented elsewhere.[1] Rather, the focus will be on attempts by nongovernmental organizations (NGOs) to create alternative food aid programs that seek to strengthen local food-production capacities, thereby promoting the institutional development of local organizations in a volatile political context, in a country already confronting endemic structural problems.[2]

The perspective of this chapter is unabashedly that of Haitian civil society organizations—a myriad collection that reflects the diversity of Haitian organizational expression and commitment to social change. This approach is a conscious one in that the voices of the social sector are not often heard. Yet Haitians were, in fact, usually on the front lines in confronting the underlying crisis that engendered food shortages, working with local populations to deal with the impact and define coping strategies, and helping other social actors address the underlying issues that aid and abet crisis.

The chapter is structured around the following points: the context, significance, and impact of the 1991 coup d'état; an overview of the major players and traditional food aid in Haiti during the coup; a grassroots perspective on food aid and its impact in Haiti; the search for alternatives; and issues and policy recommendations arising from the Haitian experience that may have broader relevance and application.[3]

Democracy under Fire

During the 1970s and early 1980s, under the authoritarian Duvalier regimes, there were two major trends in community development work in Haiti. The first was characterized by national and international organizations that pursued welfare and limited developmental strategies focused on community development,[4] working through community structures put in place and controlled by the regime (Conseil d'Action Communautaire, or CAC).[5] The second trend was represented by some Haitian NGOs and the church, which had helped communities organize. This work focused primarily on consciousness-raising and mobilization that went beyond welfare and single-community efforts. For these organizations, the major thrust was social change and an end to the regime. Less attention was paid to socioeconomic and technical issues related to livelihood strategies, though there were some exceptions.[6] In addition, there were civil society organizations—founded after the fall of the Duvalier regime in February 1986—that addressed specific concerns within the new political space. These included neighborhood associations, women's organizations, youth groups, and student unions.[7]

This nascent civil society, though fragile, was dynamic and gave voice to democratic demands within Haiti. The common thread among most of the organizations was a focus on protest. Second, they were characterized by a call for social change and the construction of a just and democratic society based on inclusion, respect of human rights, and the rule of law. This was their strength—in that it provided the form and content for denunciation—but it was also their weakness, in that it did not allow them to focus on what to do when and if they were in a position to formulate policy at a macro level.[8] Nevertheless, from Duvalier's fall in 1986 until 1990, when Jean Bertrand Aristide became the first democratically elected president in Haiti's history, through a succession of civilian and military governments, civil society organizations did succeed in gaining greater democratic space and basic civil liberties.

The general elections of 1990, which took place with the support of the international community and in the presence of national and international observers, provided an opening for widespread popular participation in the electoral process. Thus, the 1990 vote was full of significance; it was the first time that the marginalized majority was able to exercise a constitutional right to participate in political processes, and it was also the first time that a candidate embodied the aspirations of the democratic movement and the demand for profound social change. Aristide was elected by an overwhelming majority in what were considered by many to be Haiti's first credible and honest elections.

During his seven and a half months in office, before he was ousted in a military coup on September 30, 1991, Aristide, with a populist discourse, launched a series of actions intended to mark a break from the legacy of the thirty-year Duvalier regime and the previous four years of political instability.

The same discourse which generated support within the pro-change sectors of the population also provoked the opposite reaction among minority sectors. The government underestimated the strength of opposition forces, both within and outside Haiti. On September 30, 1991, the Haitian army, with support from the Haitian oligarchy, forced the constitutional president into exile.[9]

For NGOs, the coup represented a rejection of social transformation. In the days and months following the coup, the Haitian military and paramilitary groups undertook a systematic campaign of repression against civil society organizations and the democratic movement. Targets were easily identified: political leaders, NGO leaders and human rights activists, journalists, community leaders, members of peasant organizations, members of popular organizations.

Indiscriminate repression made it clear that no one was exempt. This led to massive human rights violations: physical harassment, politically motivated rape, arbitrary arrests, assassinations, and disappearances. Between 3,000 and 5,000 people were either killed or classified as "disappeared" during the coup d'état. An estimated 300,000 people were internally displaced. The military also undertook a systematic campaign to dismantle local organizations and to destroy productive collective infrastructure. Organizational headquarters, such as the offices of a national peasant movement (Mouvman Peyizan Papay), were ransacked and pillaged. Records were destroyed, equipment stolen, and funds taken. Far more common was the destruction of crops, animals, seed banks, and silos. The coup d'état thus had a significant impact not only at the political level but also at the social, economic, and organizational levels.

Nevertheless, in the three years following the coup, and despite intermittent but systematic repression, Haitian civil society organizations organized a dynamic resistance. Civil society organizations revised their strategies, adapted to the political context, and ensured minimal levels of organizational support to their membership or partners.[10] Examples include the creation of emergency funds to support the internally displaced and victims of military and paramilitary repression; to purchase seeds and tools, and to replant destroyed fields; to help organizations strengthen their work in human rights; and to strengthen capacities in advocacy. Efforts also included networking at the national level to strengthen popular resistance.

All of these activities were carried out in a hostile environment, under the eyes and guns of a military regime working in close collaboration with a paramilitary organization with members throughout the country. This commitment to carving out space in which to work, mobilize, and organize was often achieved at a high cost to both organizations and individuals: the cost was intimidation, harassment, arrest, and, in some cases, murder. While not all organizations were able to work under these conditions, a surprising number of national and international NGOs and their partners committed themselves to this process, thereby reinforcing their sense of solidarity.

The international community's response to the situation in Haiti was, however, often ambiguous and contradictory.[11] On one hand, political pressures, a trade embargo, and other punitive and intermittent economic sanctions were imposed on the country and its people in an effort to force the military to relinquish power. On the other hand, humanitarian assistance programs were developed to provide help to the Haitian people, who were the primary targets of repression and the victims of the coup. Because of this ambiguity, for many in Haiti the international community prolonged the crisis and, in some cases, strengthened the position of the regime.

Humanitarian Assistance and Food Aid

In the period following the coup d'état, humanitarian programs became the major, if not the sole, expression of international assistance. Constrained by international economic sanctions that prohibited development assistance, both bilateral and multilateral organizations expanded or developed humanitarian assistance programs with a view to alleviating the impact of sanctions on vulnerable sectors of the Haitian population.

There followed a period when actors, both national and international, were obliged to define the nature of humanitarian assistance. The first group to address this issue was the international community. Very quickly, however, discrepancies appeared in how humanitarian assistance was defined by the agencies involved, and these discrepancies continued through the three years following the coup.[12] The second group to respond, in April 1992, were Haitian civil society organizations, through a document prepared by the Commission Permanente sur l'Aide d'Urgence (CPAU).[13]

The guidelines contained in the document helped certain national NGOs in their programming, but they did not necessarily have an impact on the programming of the international community. In October 1992, the legitimate government, though in exile, convened a working group of resource persons drawn from government and the NGO community to prepare a framework or guidelines for humanitarian assistance in Haiti.[14] Whatever the reason, the proposed framework was not implemented and did not guide the international community in its assistance efforts.

The result was that both the form and the content of humanitarian assistance programs in Haiti during the coup d'état were primarily, if not exclusively, designed by the international community in conformity with their own notions of humanitarian assistance and in compliance with their own regulations, even though there were clearly expressed local views on the issue.

Though the focus of this essay is not traditional food aid programs specifically, it is important to examine briefly the predominant approach to food aid and the major institutional actors involved in order to understand the context in which alternatives evolved and in which challenges were addressed. Most international multilateral and bilateral organizations with a humanitarian assistance mandate developed food aid programs in Haiti after the coup d'état. The primary institutional actors were the United States Agency for International Development (USAID), the Canadian International Development Agency (CIDA), the European Union (EU), the French Cooperation Mission, and the World Food Program (WFP). With the exception of WFP, which was directly involved in the distribution of food, all of the others worked through international

NGOs. For example, USAID's food aid program, which was the largest single provider of food aid, was carried out primarily by three NGOs: Cooperative for Assistance and Relief Everywhere (CARE), Adventist Development and Relief Agency (ADRA), and Catholic Relief Services (CRS). These three NGOs were responsible for approximately 75 percent of the total volume of food provided by USAID.[15]

For the most part, all of these organizations used similar approaches. All of the food aid programs were designed to alleviate the impact of the embargo on segments of the population defined as vulnerable. Thus, the objective of the effort was primarily nutritional, and it was focused on the provision of foodstuffs to supplement the daily diet of intended beneficiaries. Reinforcing local capacity was not one of the objectives of these programs and thus was not a criteria for program monitoring and evaluation.

USAID, however, put a monitoring system in place to evaluate the volume of production of certain products in order to assess the projected food deficit. Projections of production capacities were made using satellite photographs. The methodology was criticized by certain sectors of the NGO community because it did not adequately consider social, economic, and political factors, such as the producers and the context in which they worked.[16]

A second monitoring initiative was undertaken by the French, who provided funding to the national association of agronomists—Association Nationale des Agronomes et Agro-professionnels d'Haiti (ANDAH)—to track the agricultural situation throughout the country. These monitoring reports were then used by donors and NGOs. However, according to an assessment of food-distribution programs conducted by Cecile Berut, most implementing agencies did not use these reports to shape their programs, nor did they carry out systematic needs assessments with beneficiary communities.[17] The reasons for this action are not clear. It led, however, to problems in targeting food-deficient zones and beneficiaries.[18]

The primary beneficiaries of food aid programs were children, women, and the elderly. Thus, schools, clinics, hospitals, and asylums were the institutions targeted in food aid programs. Most organizations worked with preexisting partners. Implementation strategies varied from programs that focused on the distribution of dry foodstuffs to those involved in what was called "wet feeding"—in which cooked food was provided to the beneficiary population. Organizations involved in wet-feeding programs in schools or neighborhood canteens saw this as an effective way of decreasing graft and of increasing chances that the intended beneficiaries would indeed benefit. Subsequently, some agencies also began food-for-work projects.

The estimated volume of assistance during the entire three-year period is difficult to assess from existing documentation. However, the total volume of imported food aid during 1993 was approximately 175,000 tons, more than half coming from the United States.[19] Commodities varied from program to program, but included wheat, corn, rice, beans, powdered milk, oil, and fish.

The World Food Program tried to ensure coordination among the organizations involved in food aid. According to the director of a participating organization, the initiative was fairly effective in that it enabled organizations to avoid duplication, to discuss logistics, and in some cases to cover temporary food shortfalls for one another. This initiative, however, did not lead to discussions of strategy, and thus it remained anchored in a traditional approach to food aid, with all of its inherent limitations.[20]

According to a report prepared by the Development Group for Alternative Polices (DGap), food aid programs at the height of the military period were feeding between 600,000 and a million people a day. Other estimates are even higher. This represents approximately 10 percent of the total population in a country where more than 60 percent of the population depends on agriculture or agriculture-related activities for economic survival.

Views from the Field:
Civil Society Perspectives

Haiti's experience with food shortages is not new; however, coping strategies have changed over time. Since its independence from France in 1804, Haiti has confronted periodic shortages as a result of drought, flooding, and other natural disasters. Until the 1950s, the response to such shortages was based on the mobilization of national resources and regional solidarity among communities. In more recent years, however, natural disasters coupled with environmental degradation, demographic pressure, lack of state investment in agriculture and infrastructure, and exploitation of the rural poor all conspired to decrease this capacity and to undermine community solidarity.

Haiti's first experience with traditional food aid was the international relief effort following Hurricane Hazel in the early 1950s. With the exception of a hiatus during the Duvalier years in the 1960s, international organizations since have organized a wide variety of food-distribution programs in Haiti.

The first international organization to develop a permanent food aid program was CARE, operating in the northwest of Haiti in response to food shortages after a prolonged drought in 1975–77. CARE was soon followed by other international organizations that later established permanent offices in Haiti. After the fall of the Duvalier regime in 1986, food aid continued to play an important role in official development assistance. During this period, food aid was most often used in either school feeding programs or in food-for-work projects designed by donors to create short-term jobs, to inject capital into poor sectors of the Haitian population, and to build or repair community infrastructures.

Before the coup d'état, there was already a public critique of food aid programs, and of their negative impact on local production capacities, consumption patterns, community organizations, and the self-image of beneficiaries. The focus of these critiques was on traditional food-distribution schemes and food-for-work, which was likened to the *corvée*—a form of conscription, or work gang, instituted by the U.S. Marine Corps during the 1915–34 American occupation of Haiti, seen as a form of indirect taxation on the rural peasantry.[21]

Food aid was often labeled *manje sinistre*, meaning food of unacceptable quality provided to the victims of natural disasters. Food aid is thus linked to a perception of victimization and loss of dignity. This perception was compounded by the manner in which programs were organized and implemented, with little or no community participation. This was further exacerbated by a perception that food aid was part of what was called in Haiti the "American Plan"—a component of neoliberal development policy. One focus of this policy, promoted by USAID and other donors, was to shift the Haitian economy away from agricultural production for local consumption to an economy based primarily on export agriculture and offshore assembly plants. Food aid was thus seen as a tool to encourage rural farmers to accept short-term labor-intensive jobs in a food-for-work program, rather than to continue to farm small plots of land. This was reinforced by a concomitant lack of investment in agriculture.[22]

The negative perception of food aid was such that in 1986–87, peasant associations in Jean Rabel, an area in the northwest, refused all forms of food aid and food-for-work, with the exception of school feeding programs, for which they requested that only local produce be used. Critics also focused on the misappropriation of food aid and its impact on intended beneficiaries. Examples included assessments of the "profit margins" on misappropriated food. A sack of flour donated for distribution could end up costing intended beneficiaries the equivalent of fifty U.S. dollars, with the "profit" accruing to the various intermediaries involved in the transaction. In such cases, the poor could end up paying more than the rich. In other cases, the poor simply had no access to the food.[23] A third consideration was the incidence of graft and corruption associated with food aid. Access to food aid constituted a privilege, and those with the power to grant access used it to monetary advantage.

In light of these critiques, there were several attempts during the 1980s to develop alternative food aid programs. Objectively there *were* food deficits in certain parts of the country. One initiative undertaken by Co-operation Haitiano-Neerlandaise (COHAN), a Haitian NGO, was based on purchasing local produce, thus stimulating local production and ensuring that food commodities were compatible with the dietary habits of the beneficiaries. Unfortunately, this two-year pilot program, which showed promising results, was brought to a halt because of a shift in the donor's priorities and a lack of interest from other European donors involved in humanitarian assistance.

This analysis provides some insight into the general frame of reference used to assess and evaluate the relevance and appropriateness of food aid programs in Haiti. However, food aid following the coup d'état took on other dimensions in terms of the sheer volume of food aid and in the scarcity of resources for supporting projects for longer-term development. Furthermore, the political context only increased the risk of food aid being used to consolidate power among the few.

The Search for Alternatives: Food Security and Capacity Building

Given the food deficits following the coup d'état and the widespread critiques of traditional food aid, a few national and international NGOs experimented with alternative food aid programs. While responding to urgent humanitarian needs, these new programs would also seek to link emergency aid and longer-term development. For these few organizations, the goal was to create programs that would achieve three objectives and respond to underlying development criteria. They would improve the nutrition of vulnerable groups in a timely and appropriate manner, respectful of human dignity. They would contribute to increasing national production by stimulating production and ensuring the purchase of local crops. And they would contribute to strengthening local capacity by involving communities in the process and providing them with the support to assume responsibility for planning, implementation, and monitoring.

For these organizations, one could not responsibly focus on short-term emergency needs while ignoring the longer-term impact on development. The challenge was to link the two in a manner in which the former would lay groundwork for the latter.

While there were several such projects developed by civil society organizations during this period,[24] the following section focuses on one. This was a long-term project in response to what was perceived as a political crisis that could drag out for an extended period. It was developed by the Haitian staff of an international NGO working closely with community-based partners.

Centre canadien d'étude et de la coopération internationale: Local Production for Food Security

The Centre canadien d'étude et de la coopération internationale (CECI) is a Canadian NGO which has worked in Haiti since the late 1970s, supporting rural development through projects that focus on promoting agricultural production and group formation.[25] CECI staff is composed of Canadian expatriates and volunteers, and Haitians. Funded almost exclusively by the Canadian International Development Agency (CIDA) through a bilateral mechanism, CECI had developed projects in various parts of the country, but with a geographic concentration in the Artibonite, the northeast, and the southwest.

In October 1991, after the coup and the adoption of Organization of American States (OAS) sanctions against the de facto regime, the Canadian government ordered the repatriation of all Canadians working in Haiti and curtailed all international assistance, with the exception of humanitarian aid, until the sanctions were lifted.[26] Over the following two months, all of CECI's expatriate staff departed, leaving only the Haitian staff to ensure basic oversight of equipment and to monitor the limited ongoing activities that might take place. Although asked to close all operations in the field, the Haitian professional staff decided to maintain a minimal presence to continue to work beside their community-based partners and the local field staff. By March 1992, however, it had become apparent that the political situation would not be resolved quickly, and, confronted with the choice of closing all operations or defining a new strategy, CECI decided to do the latter.

This choice was not an easy one. As an institution committed to working on development issues and agricultural production, CECI had no prior experience in humanitarian assistance and had a critical view of this type of intervention. The Haitian professional staff, most of them agronomists, also had great reservations about such a shift in programming. The staff saw several problems with traditional food aid: unfair competition between imported food and local production, which caused prices to fall, decapitalizing local farmers; poor quality of imported food (dumping); risk of demobilization and, in some cases, dissolution of local organizations; difficulties in the management of food aid in avoiding theft; and ensuring that food aid reached the intended beneficiaries. In light of these reservations, they began to define the general parameters of an alternative type of food aid program based in part on purchasing local produce.

The underlying assumption was that certain types of local food could be bought and distributed to vulnerable sectors of the population. Despite the overall food deficit in the country, there were pockets of surplus production that could not be marketed. On top of this, an estimated 25 percent of cereal production was lost in damage after harvest. CECI's Haitian staff carried out a study to identify production zones for cereals and beans, volumes of production, cropping cycles, and marketing circuits. This enabled them to validate their assumption and to define a program that complied with the limitations of humanitarian assistance but did not contradict their commitment to support development and strengthen local capacities.

The project was presented to CIDA's Food Aid Centre for consideration. Despite initial reservations about funding a program based on the purchase of local produce, and after several months of difficult negotiations, CIDA agreed to fund the program for an initial seven-month period. Thus, in September 1992, CECI began its Humanitarian Program (Programme d'Aide Humanitaire, or PAH).

The program was structured around three major themes: the supply of basic foodstuffs, the processing of cereals, and food distribution. Basic commodities for the program came from two sources: imported food from Canada, which represented approximately 20 percent of the total volume and 50 percent of the cost (primarily because of the comparatively high cost of comestible oil), and local production, which represented 80 percent of the total volume and 50 percent of the cost.

CECI determined that cereals (corn, millet, rice) and beans would be purchased locally. In order to establish a reference price for these commodities, CECI launched a bidding process with local producers and suppliers. A number of private sector firms responded to the bid requests, and CECI established a base price that became the reference for a particular commodity.

In order to ensure that the provision of local commodities was not monopolized by private sector firms, and to ensure that small peasant associations could also actively participate in the process, CECI agreed to pay an additional 15 to 17 percent over the reference price to social sector organizations (peasant associations, cooperatives, and *groupement*).[27] The decision to diversify the supply side and to favor smaller contracts with a larger group of suppliers also served to decrease risk and the possibility of distortions of the local market, such as an increase in price and/or a temporary scarcity in a particular commodity.

In order to facilitate community participation in the program and to ensure that the operation would generate a profit for local partners, CECI staff worked with peasant associations and other small producer groups, showing them how to determine their costs of production and how to do a cost-benefit analysis. In addition, agronomists worked with them to improve production processes. CECI also decided to work with *Madam Sara*—women traders who purchase local foodstuffs in village markets for resale in the capital. By choosing to include market women in the supply chain, CECI further reinforced traditional production and marketing circuits in Haiti.

Relationships were governed by contracts that clearly stipulated the rights and obligations of each party. Penalties were included for delays in production and in purchasing. Thus, produce was purchased from three types of suppliers: private sector firms which provided approximately 50 percent of the total, peasant associations (45 percent), and informal-sector market women (5 percent).

Cereals were purchased in bulk to ensure quality and to increase investment in local cereal-processing capacities. Because of the embargo and the stagnation of the local economy, private sector mills were working well below capacity or had stopped completely. This system provided them with a much-needed opportunity to begin working again. A bidding process was launched to establish a reference price, and contracts were then signed with a number of small private mills and one social sector mill. CECI sent technicians to work with the mills to ensure quality. This technical assistance helped the mills upgrade their operations and improve their product. Mill operators were able to rehire staff, to reinvest in equipment, and, in some cases, to expand their operations. An interesting and unexpected benefit was that by-products like chaff were used to make animal feed, which had become both expensive and scarce following the coup d'état. This served indirectly to maintain livestock production for peasant groups and livestock producers who had access to the feed.

In an interview, the owner of one private mill confirmed that the support provided by CECI had enabled him to develop his business and to move from an artisan approach to a professional operation. Based on his contracts with CECI, he was able to leverage funding from the banking sector to help finance operations and equipment. Eight years later he was still in business and had one of the most efficient mills in Port-au-Prince. He continues to work with CECI and has also continued to provide services to the social sector. According to CECI staff, a mill operated by a peasant association also succeeded in consolidating its operations and in upgrading its equipment. This mill is still in operation, providing services to its members and to other producer groups in the region.

To ensure food distribution to the sixty thousand beneficiaries of the program, CECI decided to work exclusively with local truck drivers who were already transporting passengers and goods from the capital to the rural areas. CECI staff met with beneficiaries and asked them to identify truck drivers whom they considered trustworthy and responsible. This approach was in marked contrast to the predominant strategy used by NGOs, based on establishing and maintaining their own fleet of trucks and drivers.

Contracts were arranged with ten truck drivers to deliver food to various schools, medical centers, and hospitals. The contracts specified that payment would be based on the quantity delivered and with respect to the agreed timetable. According to the director of CECI, in more than two and a half years of operation there were only two cases of theft during the transportation of goods. In each case, the driver was identified, obliged to pay for the goods, and removed from the roster of drivers.

CECI also worked with local communities to create participatory management and oversight structures to further ensure the integrity of the distribution system. Management committees were composed of school directors, parents, and schoolchildren. Their responsibility was to control deliveries and to ensure that food was made available to children in the school feeding program. CECI provided training for basic management and reporting techniques. This enabled committees to prepare monthly reports on the evolution of the program. These local committees ensured accountability and provided a legitimate interlocutor for CECI. Food was cooked on the premises of the various establishments. Those that did not have cooking facilities received financial assistance from CECI to set up a kitchen, and contracts were arranged with local artisans to make large cooking pots and metal stoves, further contributing to the local economy.

CECI established a monitoring system using senior Haitian professional staff (agronomists, social workers, and rural engineers). Monitors were responsible for particular areas. They worked with local producer groups, helping them identify and solve production problems. Monthly visits were organized to all of the beneficiaries in order to ensure that operations were progressing normally.

Monthly reports were prepared for the CECI central offices in Port-au-Prince. A review of these reports demonstrates the general caliber of staff members and that their concerns went beyond what one would expect in a humanitarian assistance program. An agronomist who was one of the program supervisors said that, in order to limit graft and corruption, monitoring distribution was perhaps the major focus of the work, but field agents also spent time mobilizing small producers. They worked with local organizations to establish the costs of production, to resolve problems, and to help with production planning and organizational development to strengthen management structures.

Impact of the Program

PAH went beyond the majority of traditional humanitarian programs that seek to alleviate problems but that do not, by definition, seek to address longer-term development issues. The CECI program had tangible impacts in the economic, social, and institutional spheres. An external evaluation carried out by CIDA consultants reviewing all Canadian humanitarian assistance during the period following the coup d'état stated that PAH, as a result of the combination of conditions tied to humanitarian assistance and an expertise in the area of agricultural development, produced an approach that was superior in conception and implementation.[28]

The program was perhaps most visible and successful at the economic level. Over the thirty months of operation, CECI injected more than three million dollars Canadian (U.S.$2.25 million) into the Haitian economy through the purchase of local produce and services. Approximately C$1.2 million worth of cereals and beans were bought from producers. By providing them with guaranteed access to market, CECI stimulated investment and production. Evaluations indicate that peasant associations participating in the program increased the area under cultivation and increased output by using improved agricultural inputs, seeds, and tools.

Approximately five hundred thousand dollars Canadian was spent on the transformation of basic grains and cereals. This enabled mill owners, both in the private sector and social sector, to consolidate or expand their enterprises. During the program, two new mills were built, existing mills were improved, and mills were able to work to their full capacity. New investment resulting from the program was estimated at approximately three hundred thousand dollars Canadian. Additionally, entrepreneurs were able to leverage loans from commercial banks based on the guaranteed sales. For some of the new entrepreneurs, this was the first time they had succeeded in using the formal banking sector.

Cereal by-products were used to make animal feed, providing small producers with a product 15 percent less expensive than other animal feed when it was available. This helped to maintain small livestock producers and to preserve what constitutes an important source of capital and savings in rural communities. More than five hundred thousand dollars Canadian was spent on transportation through the contracts with local truckers, enabling them to remain in business following the coup d'état, thus continuing to ensure transportation of both goods and persons in rural areas.

The program was able to provide food to more than sixty thousand beneficiaries at the worst of the crisis. Beyond this aspect and its related impact on nutritional levels in beneficiaries' diets, the program had other social impacts that were equally if not more important. Beneficiaries and producers mentioned that Haitian food was used to feed Haitians. This was a source of pride in light of the predominant tradition of *manje sinistre*. In a country too often categorized as one of the poorest, demonstrating local capacity should be at the heart of both humanitarian assistance and development initiatives. Intentionally or unintentionally, the project also built on models of traditional solidarity that had characterized Haiti's response to food shortages in the past. The program enabled a number of peasant organizations to continue to function and to carry out productive activities for their membership, their families, and their communities. The experience strengthened their institutional capacities by providing them with an opportunity to develop management skills and to negotiate agreements with an NGO for services rendered.

The program provided CECI with a way of continuing to support its community-based partners throughout a difficult period, when other organizations were obliged to suspend activities in the field. That it maintained contact with community-based organizations contributed to CECI's legitimacy with its partners, laying a foundation for continued collaboration. The program enabled CECI to experiment with a three-way partnership among an NGO, community groups, and the private sector. The linkages between the private and the social sectors were innovative and were an intrinsic part of the program's success. This pilot experience broke down what is often a barrier between the nonprofit sector and the for-profit sectors. It demonstrated that it is possible to develop forms of responsible and responsive partnership with the private sector in the pursuit of social goals. For some observers, this aspect of the program was perhaps one of its most important contributions to furthering reflection on the nature of partnerships for development.[29]

CECI also succeeded to a great extent in reconciling its development mandate with the requirements of an emergency humanitarian program. The experience in Haiti, developed by Haitian nationals, enabled CECI to gain experience in humanitarian assistance and to develop policies and tools that could then be adapted for use in other countries and circumstances.

Finally, the repatriation of Canadian personnel following the coup opened the way for greater Haitian participation in decision-making processes and in program management. What had been an exclusively expatriate domain became a space in which Haitian professionals were able to make a significant contribution in the design and implementation of an innovative program.

For many observers, both inside and outside the organization, this type of program would not have been possible under other circumstances. It was made possible because of a number of factors:

- the Haitian staff were trained and competent professionals;
- they were committed to preserving what remained of productive infrastructure and organizational structures within the country and to seeking an alternative to traditional humanitarian assistance programs;
- they were willing to make the extra effort to conceptualize a program that would build on local capacities and stimulate national production, while at the same time complying with criteria for humanitarian assistance programs;

- they had the knowledge to identify the potential actors who could become partners in the initiative and to adequately defend their idea.

One last factor was certainly significant. The majority of Haitian professionals were new to CECI and were not yet fully integrated into the institutional culture. Thus they were able to bring their own points of view without being constrained. The ability to think outside the lines is what contributes to the development of alternatives.

According to CECI staff, the experience in Haiti modified CECI's institutional policy and practice in other countries, paving the way for greater participation of national staff in decision making. Since 1994–95, there has been a marked increase in the number of national staff within CECI, and a greater number of national professional staff in senior decision-making positions.

Major Constraints

The program was hindered by several constraints that had an impact on its scope, objectives, and impact. Many of these were interrelated and were grounded in a vision of humanitarian assistance as a discreet and distinct activity with no linkages to longer-term development concerns.

From the outset, CECI was obliged to function with short-term CIDA funding agreements. For the donor, a humanitarian assistance program is by definition short-term, even in situations where it is apparent that the program will continue beyond the period defined by the funding agreement. After the first agreement, which covered a seven-month period, CECI was never able to sign an agreement for more than twelve to fifteen months at a time. The result was that a disproportionate amount of time was spent reporting and preparing project proposals for the next phase, in order to decrease the possibility of the program being stopped between funding agreements.

According to CECI's director at that time, the most extreme example of this approach was that CECI once had to spend eight months negotiating a six-month funding agreement. One consequence of funding disruptions was that CECI could not engage in long-term planning. A second consequence had to do with continuity: in some cases, CECI did not have the necessary funds to purchase crops at harvest time, and producers were obliged to seek other buyers as best they could. In some cases, beneficiaries were obliged to sign up with other food-distribution programs because they could not afford to wait for CECI to begin operation again.[30]

PAH was hindered by the fact that CIDA's Food Aid Centre functioned within a logic grounded in projects rather than programs. This short-term perspective is also often coupled with a need to focus on discrete elements rather than a more comprehensive approach. CECI attempted to define a program with interrelated aspects that would contribute to achieving program objectives compatible with development goals. At the same time, its principal donor was functioning with a project mentality, pursuing humanitarian assistance objectives based on criteria linked to short-term results and impacts.

The difference in vision, which is also reflected in the dysfunctional funding cycle, was a major constraint, hindering CECI in its efforts to create greater synergy between humanitarian assistance and development goals, and in making commitments beyond the current project cycle.

The project was also constrained because of differences in vision between CECI and CIDA's Food Aid Centre. According to a CIDA staff member in Haiti, the CECI program was like a minor revolution for the center, challenging it to move beyond the comfortable confines of food aid. The Food Aid Centre is "more concerned with food aid than food security."[31] It is thus apparent that the objectives pursued by each organization were quite different, and perhaps even incompatible. It is important to note that this situation is not limited to Canadian humanitarian assistance. It is representative of institutional practices across the board: organizations—both NGOs and governments—are highly compartmentalized, creating arbitrary and artificial barriers between humanitarian assistance and development.

The constraints limited both the scope and the impact of the program. They affected the scope in terms of the relative size of the program, with a related impact on outreach and possible economies of scale. They affected the program in food production and in the synergies that could have been created by strengthening certain aspects or by strengthening the institutional capacity of local organizations.

What Happened Next

The military regime came to an end in October 1994 with the return of constitutional government and the departure of the military authorities. The return was heralded as a period of reconstruction and rehabilitation, aimed at laying the foundation for longer-term sustainable development. The international community committed itself to a reconstruction and rehabilitation program framework that would guide international efforts to support the return of democracy in Haiti. Unfortunately, as many observers have noted,[32] the Emergency Economic and Recovery Program was defined by the international community with limited input from the Haitian government. There was virtually no consultation with Haitian civil society organizations.

In 1996, CECI was one of ten programs throughout the world recognized by the Food and Agriculture Organization (FAO) as having made an important contribution to improved food security in developing nations. These awards were given as part of FAO's fiftieth-anniversary celebration, and they served to identify organizations doing innovative work in promoting food security and self-reliance.

In this context, CECI geared up to expand the humanitarian assistance program and to develop direct support activities for agricultural production and group formation. Plans included expanding the program to provide support for agricultural inputs such as seeds and tools, rehabilitation and construction of small-scale community-managed irrigation systems, and construction or rehabilitation of silos and drying platforms for grains. Plans included further decentralization of the program, with a greater portion of production by small producers and the introduction of decentralized milling to capitalize rural areas and to facilitate greater small-farmer control over phases of production.

But CIDA decided that CECI could no longer receive funding to purchase local food. As a general rule, 90 percent of the food distributed in Canadian humanitarian aid programs must be of Canadian origin. An exception had been made during the period following the coup d'état, and the Food Aid Centre did not feel that it was necessary to continue in this vein, despite the favorable evaluations, and despite the fact that the new political context in Haiti called for integrating longer-term development concerns into programming.[33]

Given this decision, CECI entered a long series of negotiations and was finally able to get an agreement that would allow it to sell Canadian commodities on the local market to generate funds to purchase local agricultural production. The monetization program was a complicated endeavor, obliging CECI to do surveys to determine which Canadian products had a ready market that would not compete with local production. It finally succeeded in identifying a package of commodities that could be resold for mass consumption, generating sufficient funds to cover the costs of the core program.

It is ironic that at the moment when the program should have been able to expand its operations and systematize its approach, CECI was obliged to do new gymnastics to comply with donor requirements adapted more to the needs of the donor country than the needs of the recipient. CECI succeeded in designing a new strategy, and the program functioned from 1994 to 1999. It was only in 1999 that CECI could begin discussing again with CIDA the possibilities of a multiyear alternative food aid program to explicitly support local agricultural production, food security, and local organizations.

New Directions

Haiti provides an interesting case study on the possibility of linkages between humanitarian assistance and capacity building. But more important, it also demonstrates the need to build such linkages in a systematic manner.

Haiti has often been described as one of the poorest countries in the world, plagued by years of authoritarian and exploitative regimes. Per capita income is the lowest in the region; income distribution and control of assets are highly skewed; access to basic services is limited; and the formal economy stagnates while there is a rapidly growing informal sector. Environmental degradation has compromised production capacities. These characteristics, among many others, are structural problems that must be addressed in order to promote sustainable development processes in Haiti.

While this characterization is true, it is only a partial portrait. It does not show what is happening at the community level. The people of Haiti have struggled to develop their capacities at the family, community, and organizational levels to solve these problems. The myriad civil society organizations, traditional social organizations such as *soldes* and *eskwads*,[34] youth groups, women's organizations, neighborhood organizations, peasant organizations, and cooperatives have developed strategies and gained experience in dealing with their problems.

The coup d'état of 1991 radically exacerbated the preexisting social and economic situation and accelerated decapitalization and impoverishment among the Haitian population. The crisis in Haiti was a combination of structural factors inherent to Haiti and conjunctural factors arising directly from the coup d'état.

In focusing exclusively on the immediate, and treating only the humanitarian and emergency aspects of a problem, outsiders can exacerbate structural difficulties and undermine local efforts to bring about substantive change. In other words, humanitarian action can undermine and compromise possibilities for reconstruction, rehabilitation, and development.

In Haiti, there was a possibility to address humanitarian needs in a manner that preserved local economic, social, and institutional capacities. But doing so would have required a deliberate decision and an institutional commitment to mobilize financial and human resources and, above all, to make a commitment to the process over time.

In reviewing the CECI case, it is clear that there were a number of prerequisites that enabled it to carry out the program:[35]

- knowledge and understanding of the milieu;
- previous experience in development work;
- the availability of, and devolution of responsibility to, professional local staff;
- a network of partner organizations at the field level;

- a willingness to develop new partnerships between social sector and private sector actors;

- a degree of institutional flexibility and relative autonomy at the regional level;

- a willingness to explore and challenge the institutional boundaries imposed on humanitarian assistance; and

- a willingness by the Canadian government to step momentarily outside the parameters of traditional humanitarian assistance.[36]

It is clear, however, that the approach developed by CECI could not have been generalized throughout the country. It could not have been adopted by all donors and implementing agencies, because the primary factors limiting such an approach were economic and organizational. The country's limited agricultural-production capacities could not have completely covered the food deficit. However, local production could have significantly decreased the amount of imported food aid. Not all peasant organizations were able to return to agricultural production following the coup because of the sporadic repression that continued throughout the three-year period. The larger peasant organizations remained targets throughout this period, and certain geographical areas were targeted more than others. Thus the number of potential organizational partners was limited.

The external factors limiting this approach were also institutional—at the level of the international community and at the level of the constitutional government. Political priorities of donors, institutional cultures, and constraints arising from the need to provide a market for donors' own surplus production also would have limited this approach. The government of Haiti, which was in exile, did not play and perhaps could not have played an active role in the definition of policy and practice in humanitarian action.

Despite these limitations, however, the CECI approach could have been expanded, either by increasing the scope of the program (increased funding) or by bringing on other institutional partners interested and capable of adopting a similar approach. The approach could have stimulated critical reflection among government, donors, and NGOs about developing greater flexibility in their programming and about key issues such as humanitarian and development assistance, food aid and food security, and balancing macroeconomic concerns with social objectives. The CECI experience and similar initiatives could have served to develop a policy framework and a program focus that addressed humanitarian issues in a manner consonant with development aims. Critical reflection could have been organized around how to use food aid instruments (direct imports, monetization of imports to purchase local production, and monetization of imports to establish counterpart funds) to meet humanitarian needs, to strengthen local capacities, and to begin laying a foundation for increased food security after a conflict.

Unfortunately, this expansion did not happen. The CECI experience remains a valuable and constructive experience in how things can be done differently. But the impact of the project, however positive, was limited to the micro level. In order to move beyond this stage, concerted efforts are required by

- *government,* to define a framework to guide humanitarian assistance and food aid as one element within an overall policy on food security and agricultural production, and to establish permanent monitoring mechanisms that enable the government to assess food security;[37]

- *international organizations,* to decrease the distance between rhetoric and practice and to reconcile political and economic imperatives with the long-term interests of recipient countries;

- *nongovernmental organizations,* to seek knowledge and understanding in establishing or strengthening partnerships with social actors, and in demonstrating commitment to work outside the boundaries of traditional humanitarian assistance in ways compatible with development principles based on capacity building.

Since programming is often conditioned by policy decisions, it is important that policy makers and donors create an environment in which NGOs have the latitude to develop programs that build the necessary links between humanitarian assistance and development processes. Donors and policy makers should

- develop a more flexible idea of humanitarian assistance and move away from the rigid mind-set that has too often characterized such programs;

- define programs more in terms of the needs of recipient countries and less in terms of the donor countries' needs;

- shift from a narrow focus on food delivery to a broader focus promoting food security, thereby decreasing dependence on donor commodities and promoting greater self-reliance within the recipient country;

- attach greater importance to understanding the local context and processes;

- accord greater priority to working with and through local partners, designing programs in collaboration with local partners and building local capacity;

- redefine the time frame for action and shift the focus from projects to programs and process; and

- develop mechanisms that facilitate donor coordination, creating synergy among the various programs and projects.

In a world where crises and emergencies escalate, where citizens feel increasingly powerless and unable to influence events, where NGOs are being called upon more and more to respond to these emergencies, there is an urgent need to move beyond short-term symptom-oriented strategies.[38] There is a need for new strategies and directions based on the capacity and potential of concerned populations, enabling them to move from object to subject, from victim to actor, *to the possibility of being.* Only then can we hope to see greater synergy between humanitarian assistance and development, and between humanitarian assistance and capacity building at the community level.

Notes

1. See Cecile Berut, *Aide Alimentaire en Haiti* (Port-au-Prince: Action International Contre la Faim and Coopération Française, 1993); Laurie Richardson, *Feeding Dependency, Starving Democracy: USAID Policies in Haiti* (Boston: Grassroots International, 1997).

2. Charles Cadet provides a concise overview of the structural problems confronted by Haiti and their impact on the social and economic development of the country in *Crise, Pauperisation et Marginalisation dans l'Haiti Contemporaine* (Port-au-Prince: United Nations Children's Fund, 1996).

3. For a study of Haiti in the Humanitarianism and War Project during these years, see Robert Maguire et al., *Haiti Held Hostage: International Responses to the Quest for Nationhood, 1986–1996,* Occasional Paper no. 23 (Providence, R.I.: Watson Institute, 1997), particularly chapter 2 "Military Rule." Also available in French.

4. See David Korten, *Getting to the Twenty-first Century: Voluntary Action and the Global Agenda* (West Hartford, Conn.: Kumarian Press, 1990), and Alliette Mathurin et al., *Implantation et Impact des Organisations Non-Gouvernmentales: Contexte (Haiti)* (Arunga and Geneva: SHSE-CIDIHCA, 1989), for a typology of NGOs, and their development strategies.

5. The Conseil d'Action Communautaire (CAC) consisted of community structures put into place by the Duvalier regime with the purpose of controlling the local population. See Maguire et al., *Haiti Held Hostage;* and Mathurin et al., *Implantation et Impact des Organisations Non-Gouvernmentales.*

6. Certain organizations, however, also focused on socioeconomic issues such as understanding the nature of peasant agricultural systems and livelihood strategies and traditional forms of social organization and solidarity. Among them were Madia Salagnac, Groupe de Recherche pour le Developpement (GRD), ITEKA, and Centre Papaye.

7. For a description of the characteristics of popular organizations in urban areas, see Luc Smarth, *Les Organisations Populaires en Haiti: Une etude exploratoire de la zone metropolitaine de Port-au-Prince* (Port-au-Prince: CRESDIP-CIDIHCA, 1998).

8. This observation is developed in Kathy Mangones, "De la Solidaridad a la Cooperación Institucionalizada," in *La República Dominicana y Haiti frente al Futuro* (Santo Domingo, Dominican Republic: FLACSO Working Papers, 1998). This is not a weakness limited to civil society in Haiti. It has tended to characterize community development both in the North and the South. It is only very recently that NGOs and other civil society organizations have linked protest and denunciation with concrete recommendations for policy and practice.

9. Paul Farmer, *The Uses of Haiti* (Monroe, Maine: Common Courage Press, 1994), and James Ridgeway, ed., *The Haiti Files: Decoding the Crisis* (Washington, D.C.: Essential Books, 1994), both analyze the convergence of national and international interests which were behind the September 1991 coup.

10. Regroupement Inter-OPD, in *Aide d'Urgence: Diagnostic, Lignes Strategiques Axes d'Intervention* (Port-au-Prince: Inter-OPD, 1992), defined a humanitarian assistance program that was to guide national and international organizations interested in developing an approach grounded in a development perspective and in strengthening local capacities.

11. Gretchen Berrgren et al., *Sanctions in Haiti: Crisis in Humanitarian Action* (Cambridge: Harvard Center for Population and Development Studies, 1993), and Maguire et al., *Haiti Held Hostage,* raise this issue and its impact on the subsequent evolution of the political crisis in Haiti.

12. Cited in Berrgren et al., *Sanctions in Haiti.*

13. Regroupement Inter-OPD, *Aide d'Urgence.*

14. Comité de Coordination de l'Aide Humanitaire, *Cadre General pour un Plan d'Aide Humanitaire* (Port-au-Prince: Government of Haiti, 1992).

15. Serge Picard, *Aide Alimentaire: Le Cas d'Haiti,* Forums Libre du Jeudi 21 sur l'Aide et Securité Alimentaires en Haiti, Port-au-Prince, 1996.

16. Interview with a member of Association Nationale des Agronomes et Agro-professionnels d'Haiti (ANDAH) and a member of the Haitian Platform for Alternative Development (PAPDA), a coalition of NGOs and popular education organizations.

17. Berut, *Aide Alimentaire en Haiti.*

18. See Berut, *Aide Alimentaire en Haiti,* and Richardson, *Feeding Dependency, Starving Democracy.*

19. Berut, *Aide Alimentaire en Haiti.*

20. Based on a conversation with an NGO director who participated in the coordination meetings.

21. See Mathurin et al., *Implantation et Impact des Organisations Non-Gouvernmentales.* Community "work" projects in fact carried out activities that in theory were the responsibility of the state and for which the state received taxes from its citizens.

22. Josh Dewind and David Kinley, *Aiding Migration: The Impact of International Development Assistance on Haiti* (Boulder, Colo.: Westview Press, 1988), present an interesting and valid, if somewhat dated, critique of what was

then called the "American Plan" and has since been called neoliberal development or the predominant paradigm.

23. Based on an interview with the director of a Haitian NGO who was involved in and evaluated food aid programs during the 1980s.

24. Among the other "alternative" programs developed during this period were those implemented by Action International Contre la Faim (AICF), a French NGO, and Groupe de Technologie Intermédiaire (GTIH), a Haitian NGO.

25. Information is drawn from interviews with Carl Mondé, CECI director when this program was implemented, current and former CECI staff members and program partners, and from program documents, including an external evaluation conducted on behalf of CIDA.

26. In the case of CECI, programs were "frozen" in late 1991 and then curtailed in 1992.

27. *Groupement* are groups of ten to fifteen persons based on affinity and homogeneity (social, economic, and political) of the membership. See Mathurin et al., *Implantation et Impact des Organisations Non-Gouvernmentales.*

28. Alain Boisvert and Henry Hunse, *Vers une Aide Structurante Rapport d'Evaluation des Programmes Finances dans le Cadre de l'Assistance Human-itaire depuis le Début de la Crise Haitienne* (Hull, Quebec: Agence Canadienne pour le Developpement International [ACDI], July 1994), 39.

29. Interview with Phillipe Mathieu, a Haitian agronomist and development consultant who has worked on issues of food security and agricultural production in Haiti.

30. Interview with Abraham Shepherd, a Haitian agronomist and former CECI staff member.

31. Interview with a CIDA staff member in Port-au-Prince.

32. Lisa McGowan, *Democracy Undermined and Economic Justice Denied: Structural Adjustment and the Aid Juggernaut in Haiti* (Washington, D.C.: Development Group for Alternative Policies, 1997), and interview with Phillipe Mathieu.

33. Interview with CIDA staff and interview with Carl Mondé, former CECI director in Haiti.

34. *Soldes* are traditional solidarity loan associations, while *eskwads* are one of many forms of traditional agricultural work groups, bringing together neighboring farmers to carry out labor-intensive tasks such as planting or harvesting.

35. See Ian Smillie, *Relief and Development: The Struggle for Synergy,* Occasional Paper no. 33 (Providence, R.I.: Watson Institute for International Studies, 1998), on the factors that constrain and that facilitate linkages between relief and development.

36. For some observers, this response was in keeping with the Canadian government's clear position against the coup d'état and the de facto regime and in support of democracy in Haiti. Others such as Phillipe Mathieu attribute it to macroeconomic factors.

37. In 1998, the Haitian government established the Commission Nationale Intersectorielle de Securité Alimentaire (CNISA) with this specific mandate. Unfortunately, an analysis of the organization and how food aid has changed as

a result of CNISA is outside the scope of this chapter. According to some agronomists, however, the Haitian government's management of the 1997 drought in the northwest—a management grounded in a preliminary policy framework—would suggest some modifications in how food aid was carried out.

38. See Korten, *Getting to the Twenty-first Century.*

Chapter 4

Rebuilding Local Capacities in Mozambique

The National Health System and Civil Society

STEPHEN C. LUBKEMANN

A people can participate only if they have both the opportunity to formulate their program, which is their reason for participation, and a medium through which they can express and achieve their program. —SAUL ALINSKY

This chapter considers some of the challenges in building local capacity in the health sector in Mozambique between 1990 and 1997, a period that begins with the final two years of a long civil war, immediate post-emergency reconstruction, and transition to longer-term development. The chapter examines the building of local capacity in the health sector in two distinct yet critically interrelated senses.

In a first and narrow sense, the chapter examines the interaction among international actors (donors and operational agencies) and national actors (in particular the Mozambique Ministry of Health) in rebuilding the modern health sector's ability to provide local service after more than a decade of civil war. During the war, the health sector's national coverage atrophied, and the system disintegrated at all levels. The chapter compares a variety of approaches to achieve managerial decentralization and technical capacitation at subnational levels.

In the process, several important questions are raised: Can local capacities in the modern health sector be developed effectively without also developing the national capacities that support them? What are the potential consequences of reconstructing local capacities that cannot be sustained because of conditions on the national level? What project and planning time frames are most effective in meeting the challenges of postemergency reconstruction?

Second, the chapter examines how foreign aid in the health sector has

SUM Incorporated

contributed to the building of a somewhat different and broader sense of local capacity, namely the capacity for civil society. This question is examined in light of Mozambique's historical experience of relations between the central state and local forms of associational life. Colonial and postcolonial government policies prevented nongovernmental organizations from emerging in Mozambique until after the civil war. A long history of heavy-handed state intervention created a political culture in which disengagement emerged as the primary strategy for dealing with the central state. Local associational life often emerged to serve these strategies of disengagement.

This history requires careful consideration of what is meant by *civil society*—as something more than simply private associational life—and what prerequisites must be cultivated for civil society to exist. The chapter considers whether the capacity of the state itself can be ignored in attempting to build civil society where government has historically enjoyed little popular legitimacy. The chapter asks whether, paradoxically, state legitimacy must be reinforced first in order to cultivate a viable independent grassroots force that can engage it.

Finally, the chapter considers whether and how the development of viable public services at a local level (a first form of local capacity) can contribute to changing a political culture from one that privileges disengagement from the state to one that seeks constructively to engage it (a second form of local capacity). It considers whether aid activities in sectors with large public demand, such as modern health, offer a good opportunity for legitimizing the state's local presence.

What changes must be encouraged in central government's views of local participation to open a space where civil society can flourish? What are the consequences of building national public service presence and capacity at a local level without reinforcing old, centralized systems of governance and discouraging local associational life in decision making? The chapter thus considers how and if foreign aid to the health sector in Mozambique has increased the ability of primary stakeholders to engage and influence the political arena and the socioeconomic system in accordance with their interests.[1]

Background

The Mozambican Civil War

Mozambique gained independence from Portugal in 1975, after more than a decade of anticolonial struggle led by the Front for the Liberation of Mozambique (FRELIMO). At independence the Portuguese transferred power to FRELIMO, recognizing it as the sole legitimate representative of the Mozambican people. Shortly thereafter, FRELIMO closed Mozambique's borders with Rhodesia to support the Zimbabwe African National Liberation Army (ZANLA), headed by Robert Mugabe, in its struggle against the apartheid regime of Rhodesian leader Ian Smith. The Smith regime drew on Mozambican political dissenters to establish a military movement. This movement supported Rhodesian efforts against ZANLA guerrillas based in Mozambique and helped destabilize Mozambique politically and economically. That military movement later came to be known as the Mozambique National Resistance Movement, or RENAMO (an acronym for the name in Portuguese). When the Smith regime capitulated in 1980, South Africa's apartheid regime took over the role as RENAMO's patron.

Foreign support remained vital for RENAMO and greatly influenced its strategy and operations throughout the war. However, FRELIMO's own policies of forced villagization (forcing rural people to live in villages), centralized control of commerce and agriculture, and strong-arm measures against traditional social institutions, combined with the economic downturn in the early years of the civil war (1979–82), also fueled popular opposition to FRELIMO among segments of the population in some (particularly rural) areas.[2] By the mid-1980s an initially localized action in Manica Province had become a national civil war.

As a rough generalization, by the mid-1980s a pattern had been established whereby the government forces (FRELIMO) controlled major urban areas and some district-level capitals, while many rural areas fell under RENAMO's military influence. With the assistance of troops from neighboring Zimbabwe and Tanzania, FRELIMO also maintained a tenuous grip on several vital transportation and communication corridors. During the war, most rural Mozambicans were displaced. They fled to FRELIMO-controlled cities or fortified villages within Mozambique, into remote bush areas under RENAMO's influence, or across international borders into Zimbabwe, Malawi, and South Africa. Popular mistrust of centralized authority, already a legacy of Portuguese colonialism, was further aggravated by FRELIMO and RENAMO policies aimed at controlling population settlement during the war.

Wartime Effects on the Health Sector

As part of a broad wave of nationalizations instituted by FRELIMO soon after independence, all health services were made an exclusive public sector responsibility. Centrally planned and directed primary health care (PHC) was adopted as the core of national health policy. During the years prior to the conflict's spread to the national level (1975–82), the health sector was one of the most significant successes of Mozambique's postcolonial government. During this time the number of health posts increased fourfold, the number of inhabitants per health unit decreased from 26,000 to 10,000, and model national vaccination campaigns were carried out.[3]

However, the spread of the civil war ultimately paralyzed public services. RENAMO made a point of targeting the public service infrastructure—roads, administration, communication, schools, and health posts—for destruction. RENAMO also specifically targeted public service personnel, including school teachers and health workers. Under this withering pressure, and with the increased diversion of the national budget to finance military expenditures, Mozambique's modern health sector rapidly atrophied. The lack of funds for health was further accentuated by the imposition of structural adjustment in 1987.[4] By 1992 the rural health infrastructure was virtually wiped out. The only health facilities and personnel that remained, which all were overtaxed, were in the large towns and cities.

The war's intensity and duration also radically affected the capacity, structure, and managerial culture of the national health system. Throughout the war, the health sector became increasingly dependent on a rising flow of external aid, largely channeled through a rapidly growing number of foreign NGOs. With little information on the multiplying number of such projects, donors treated particular programs (such as pharmaceuticals) in isolation from other health-system concerns. A plethora of short-term, on-the-spot projects proliferated without integration into an overarching plan. The health sector became increasingly fragmented along vertical lines. By the end of the war, Durao and Pavignani describe the situation as one in which "Mozambican health authorities were often reduced to passive recipients, even spectators of the relief and rehabilitation show."[5]

Building Local Capacities in the National Health System

Resetting the Postwar Agenda in the Health Sector

During 1991 and 1992, as peace negotiations made headway and a resolution seemed promising, the Mozambique Ministry of Health (MMOH) undertook a comprehensive policy review and formulated a framework for reconstruction and development.[6] Drawn up in consultation with the World Bank (in association with a major loan for reconstruction) and formally launched in 1992, this plan established the primary goal of restoring the national health system to its 1980 level. Key features included reconstruction of physical infrastructure, extension of health services from urban to rural areas (already underserviced and most severely affected by the war), maintenance of a primary health care focus, human resource development, and the decentralization of management systems.

Decentralization in particular was to play a key role within this plan. The policy of decentralization was clearly framed within the more general policy of the decentralization of all state administration that was to accompany democratic reform, reopening space for private enterprise—all part of the move away from a centrally planned and managed economy and society. In all sectors, including health, the building and enhancement of local capacity was seen as a critical component for the success of decentralization.

However, "local capacity" tended to mean different things in different sectors and arenas. In the political arena, discussion of decentralization tended to focus on the election of provincial and district-level officials. Thus framed, creating greater local capacity referred to fostering popular understanding of, and participation in, democratic electoral processes. By contrast, talk of decentralization within the national health system focused on how management systems could be reorganized so that more decision-making power could devolve to subnational parts of what was still clearly a national public system. So defined, local capacity building involved improving subnational management and care-provision systems and expanding these services into a greater number of local settings.

By contrast with other sectors, discussions of local capacity in the health sector focused less on the idea of bringing more nonpublic sector actors into the game and reinforcing their participation, and more on extending the local presence of the public sector and improving its performance at a local level.

Differences in Foreign Approaches to the Health Sector

Durao and Pavignani state that at the end of the war most aid in the health sector was clearly bypassing the public health management system and being channeled through specific emergency aid projects. These were often carried out by international NGOs, the numbers of which mushroomed during this period. This approach carried over into many of the activities that occurred during initial reconstruction, including, for example, the rapid reconstruction of rural health posts by contracted NGOs under the United Nations High Commissioner for Refugees' (UNHCR) Quick Impact Project (QIP). Aid provision in this mode was characterized by multilaterals as donors, short-term commitments, stand-alone packages (as opposed to integration within a larger program), and the targeting of selective problems rather than comprehensive health systems and needs.

Major donors included the United Nations Fund for Population Activities (UNFPA), the World Bank (operating through the World Food Program [WFP] as implementer), the European Union (EU), UNHCR, and Italian Cooperation. During the postwar reconstruction period, some donors continued to operate largely in this mode, providing a large amount of their support via the activities of international NGOs (Italian Cooperation, World Bank). They were joined in this approach throughout the 1990s by other significant newcomers such as the United States Agency for International Development (USAID) and Spanish Cooperation.

No comprehensive, empirically based study has been carried out on the nationwide performance of international NGOs in the health sector. Consequently, most positions taken on their effectiveness are largely reducible to politically motivated opinionating. Durao and Pavignani found that assessments by health officials at the provincial level varied. Sometimes NGOs were seen as highly disruptive of coordination efforts and others as particularly effective in delivering services to inaccessible areas.

They found more consensus at the national level within the MMOH, in which both national and international NGOs were viewed as rivals for funds. Within the ministry, NGOs were an unwelcome but tolerated presence by virtue of their function as vehicles for otherwise inaccessible foreign aid, but the high NGO resistance to coordination mechanisms was not appreciated. This problem was particularly acute in provinces such as Zambezia, where intense wartime devastation most severely reduced public health system capacity and where an unusually high number of international NGOs was present.

Other former advocates (European Union) of the short-term project/NGO approach have gradually moved closer to the advocates of another school of thought that focused throughout the 1990s on reinforcing the capacity of the ministry of health and on channeling aid more directly through it.

In the early 1990s a number of these donors began to provide direct budget support, in part unrestricted, managed directly by the MMOH and channeled via the Ministry of Planning and Finance (MPF). The most significant problems experienced in this approach were the lack of capacity for managing such funds in the MPF, and a resistance to transparency. Often referred to as the "like-minded donors," this group includes Swiss Cooperation (SDC), the Norwegian Agency for Development Cooperation (NORAD), the Canadian International Development Agency (CIDA), more recently Irish Cooperation and in many respects Finnish Cooperation (FINNIDA), and the Danish International Development Agency (Danida).

The last two members of this group (FINNIDA and Danida) have implemented a third, somewhat hybrid, approach that combined some project elements with a program philosophy. Both of these efforts targeted an entire province (Danida in Tete and FINNIDA in Manica). From the outset both projects saw their activities as framed within the National Health Sector Recovery Program (NHSRP) and as long-term commitments that would last more than a decade. These programs set out to address the reconstruction of the health sector in each province in an integrated fashion—physical infrastructure, human resource development, health systems support, and management capacitation.

When they started in 1991 and 1992, these projects differed significantly from national-level approaches that focused on specific subcomponents of health being organized vertically from the national level down (such as pharmaceutical supplies), and from approaches that focused on subprovincial, short-term relief projects, often implemented by international NGOs. FINNIDA and Danida were informally appointed by the MMOH as the focal donors for their respective provinces. Particularly at the provincial level, the provincial directorate of health (PDH) and the focal donor worked together to informally coordinate the activity of all actors in the health field to ensure that all efforts contributed effectively to the recovery program.

This approach has been particularly successful when measured in terms of the reconstruction results achieved. By 1997, NHSRP's rehabilitation and expansion program was judged to be roughly halfway complete when viewed at a national aggregate level. Forty percent of the population was estimated to have access to the most basic services.[7] By contrast, in Manica Province, under the FINNIDA-financed Manica Province Integrated Health Project (MPIHP), the indicators were much better. By 1997, 90 percent of reconstruction of physical infrastructure and restaffing had been achieved.

In terms of most major health service provision indicators (consultations per head, deliveries coverage, measles coverage, service units per head), Manica scored approximately 50 percent over the national average in 1997. The percentage of qualified health staff increased significantly. Management capacity development included computerization and training in accountancy, human resources planning, construction and maintenance supervision, and medical supply and health information systems, according to national-level protocols.[8]

Less measurable accomplishments of great importance in Manica were the degree to which professional identity among Mozambican health workers had been cultivated and the degree to which the project had been integrated into the MMOH, cultivating a sense of national ownership of results.[9]

With its growing success, this model became increasingly influential throughout the 1990s. By 1997 other foreign agencies had begun similar "adopt-a-province" approaches: the European Union in Zambezia, the Italian Cooperation in Sofala, and Dutch Cooperation in Nampula. Although the FINNIDA and Danida projects were generally seen in a positive light, the projection of this model at a national level began to raise some questions about what conditions and donor qualities might be necessary to ensure its success. These included how to ensure that local authorities rather than foreign project managers "owned" the projects; how to ensure adequate coordination mechanisms between the provincial and national levels to prevent provincial-level activities from contravening national policy; and the fear that national imbalances among different provinces (some adopted by such projects and others still "orphans") might result.

The FINNIDA Case

Commitment to a time frame spanning emergency and development. Although designed during the emergency, FINNIDA's MPIHP was conceived within a long-term development perspective. At its inception in 1991 (a year before the war ended), the MPIHP was unprecedented in its planned seventeen-year time span. From the outset the project was envisioned as spanning the termination of the conflict, emergency reconstruction, and transition into peacetime development. This long time frame had a vital impact on both the project's planning and its implementation. Conceived during the wartime emergency phase but with a view to the conflict's resolution and postconflict transition, the project was designed to address the different problems specific to each phase, so that achievements in earlier phases contributed to goals in subsequent phases. Consequently, accomplishments in the health sector in Manica were cumulative to a degree not achieved elsewhere.

Much has been made in recent years of reconceptualizing humanitarian relief work so that its accomplishments contribute to a successful transition to postemergency development. This idea also figured prominently and was experimented with in Mozambique.

With longer-term goals shaping the project's orientation, more time and care were allocated to a baseline study.[10] The baseline study and planning carried out by the first consultant team involved approximately one year of work in the field. This allowed the project to be incorporated more thoroughly into the sector's national-level strategy.[11]

The long-term time frame also enabled the project to reap the benefits of relationship-building at both the national and local levels. To the MMOH, the long-term framework represented an unusual sign of commitment on a donor's part, and encouraged the establishment of stronger informal relationships. It also removed the idea of "outlasting the other party" and thus contributed to a spirit of seeking and negotiating solutions.

The longer time frame also allowed for necessary adjustments in vital dimensions of the project. A private, for-profit consulting firm called FINNCONSULT was hired to implement the project, a departure from the usual practice of using NGOs for such work. The first team of technical advisers (TAs) recruited by FINNCONSULT accomplished the baseline survey and planning, but it was marred by internal tensions and technical shortcomings. Once these came to light, FINNIDA and the MMOH jointly pressured FINNCONSULT to change its team. The success of the MPIHP program owes no small debt to the technical capacities and managerial diplomacy of the team that replaced the original one.

A second major adjustment that occurred during the first years of the project involved the expansion of activities to the whole province. From the outset, the project envisioned activities in areas where security could be assured. This had limited the initial planning primarily to the Beira corridor area, which was protected by Zimbabwean troops. With the advent of peace, expanding coverage became vital, both from the technical perspective of health care provision (lessening pressure on urban facilities and reestablishing broad local access to primary health care) and from a political perspective (making rural areas more attractive to potential returnees and demonstrating willingness to rebuild in areas under the nominal control of RENAMO). Such adjustment would not have been feasible in a short-term project given the high technical requirements involved.

It is hard to overemphasize the departure in donor thinking involved in this long-term time frame and in the commitment to development while still in emergency, particularly in the early 1990s. With hindsight and an apparently lasting peace in Mozambique, it is easy to underestimate how much uncertainty characterized the environment in which these decisions were made. It is important to recognize that the late 1980s and early 1990s offered, if anything, food for the cynic rather than nourishment for the optimist.

As a project conceived and initiated during the conflict itself, and grown through the rocky negotiation of de facto peace, what properties enabled FINNIDA to foresee and negotiate the challenges and opportunities of this trajectory successfully? Was FINNIDA just lucky?

Pragmatism: Choosing the "doable." The Mozambican civil war imposed varying degrees of intensity on different parts of the country. Relatively favorable conditions characterized the situation in Manica compared to the total disarray experienced in other areas. A modicum of health service infrastructure and administrative apparatus was still functioning in Manica's corridor area. Precarious as it might have seemed, the corridor was one of the more stable and safe areas in the country. Furthermore, it provided access to Zimbabwe and to a source of technical skills, raw materials, and the technological resources needed to reconstruct the health sector. The corridor population represented a significant part of the province's population in a concentrated and more easily accessible state.

Manica was by no means the neediest or most troubled province in the country at the time. However, rather than choosing a province for urgency or degree of need, FINNIDA took a more pragmatic approach. It sought to guarantee minimal conditions of military security, stability, and infrastructure on which to build its work during the war in order to increase the likelihood that these had a decent chance of surviving and being built upon. Manica was chosen because it was a potentially "doable" area rather than because it was the most needy area.[12]

The project's ability to take advantage of opportunities as they emerged can also be traced to atypical structural features. These included the statement of a mandate in very general terms, which left its concrete operation relatively unspecified and thus open to development, modification, and reconceptualizing.

Substantial changes were made during annual planning-adjustment exercises in light of improved understandings of a fluid situation. Thus the project was able to respond well to the development of peace because its mandate was not overspecified. As peace became a concrete reality, and in what constituted a gradual geographic "creep," the provincial-level PDH/TA team availed itself of its liberty to redefine concrete objectives, proposing the reallocation of funds to cover what eventually became a provincewide rehabilitation of the entire health network. This gradual process allowed for adaptation to postwar demographic developments as refugees returned from abroad, the corridor population diminished, and rural populations grew.

The focal-donor role. FINNIDA's focal-donor role on a provincewide basis provided a perspective from which it could see how its activities fit with those of others in the health sector. Its flexibility gave it the power to adapt its funding and activities to fill in the gaps left by more rigid programs and organizations, so that it could best contribute to provincial health objectives. Furthermore, the financial weight of both FINNIDA in Manica and Danida in Tete was such that they were able to influence other organizations toward coordination. From 1994 to 1996, FINNIDA accounted for almost 40 percent of all foreign aid provided for the health sector in Manica Province. The two other major donors (United Nations Children's Fund [UNICEF] and Swiss Cooperation) provided support primarily channeled through national-level, vertically structured programs.[13] Finally, FINNIDA's commitment to the provincial plan's larger objectives gave it the will to adapt and to leverage its own influence with other organizations in order to fulfill the plan.

Provincial level as an advantageous intermediary scale. FINNIDA's and Danida's focus on comprehensive sectoral intervention at the provincial level had clear comparative advantages over a solely national or a more localized approach. This intermediary scale allowed for attention to the intricacies of local context not possible with a national focus. At the same time it required attention to macro-level issues, albeit grounded in a concern with how these translated into operations on the ground. These projects have remained attuned and responsive to national directions and local concerns without becoming the prisoner of one and ignorant of the other. Accordingly, interventions at district and local levels could be coordinated with sufficient understanding of the larger picture to counteract excessive localization of interests while also allowing implementation of national policies in local terms. The provincial level of operations was also sufficiently large to give the project a voice in influencing national policy that it, in turn, had to live with.

A final positive aspect is the balance between a foreign presence sufficiently large for the aforementioned purposes and the ultimate national ownership of activities. Coordination and intrasectorial integration have proven difficult to realize in provinces in which smaller and less dominant donors have taken the focal-donor role.

Concerns have nevertheless been raised within the MMOH about the risks of having a dominant donor operating under the adopt-a-province model.

Private consultants or NGOs? Perhaps the most distinctive structural aspect of the MPIHP program is that a private, for-profit consulting firm (FINNCONSULT) was hired to implement the project rather than an international (or national) NGO. This is an innovative and unusual position relative to the larger field of humanitarian and development practice in Mozambique, where NGOs have predominated. This consultancy was tendered internationally, with bids subject to joint review and consensual approval by both FINNIDA and the Ministry of Health.[14]

Most NGOs have a particular philosophy of humanitarian aid, and they are organized around such an idea. Many NGOs construct a public image tied into funding and constituency concerns based precisely on this organizing philosophy. They remain highly responsive to these philosophies even if contracted as implementers of projects funded by donor or national organizations that have their own philosophies, which may conflict with those of the NGO. By contrast, a private consultancy's organizational culture and strategy for survival are organized around the imperative of accomplishing goals dictated by its clients.

Furthermore, NGOs were seen as having less interest in imposing standards on employees, being less willing to fire them, and even sometimes obscuring incompetence to protect the image of the NGO. By contrast, professional consultancies were felt to be more demanding in ensuring standards in employee performance. FINNCONSULT was under pressure to deliver the services on which it had bid to preserve its professional reputation in an increasingly competitive market.

Rethinking assumptions among health-sector donors. Mozambique's economic situation serves as a monumental constraint to the possibilities for reform and development in the modern health sector. The salary paid by MMOH is increasingly small by other nations' standards, even when compared to the growing opportunities in the private sector and among NGOs. The public health sector will increasingly lose the most qualified officials to private sector activities if the wage issue is not addressed. In particular the imbalance that favors urban over rural areas is likely to be aggravated. Under donor pressure, MMOH is also trying to reduce the level of corruption that characterizes the provision of health services to the population. Success in these measures will ironically reduce one of the concrete incentives that these positions hold for health workers. Without replacing these informal incentives with formal ones (that is, better salaries), the health profession will become less attractive.

As of 1997, the policy of some donors (such as USAID) was to avoid increases in Mozambican salaries. Other donors, led in particular by the

Swiss, began to revisit this problem, recognizing that low salaries lay at the root of many of the sector's problems. In 1997, donors sought a compromise that avoided paying direct salaries but that provided other direct benefits to make jobs more attractive. In the FINNIDA case, this involved the rehabilitation, improvement, or construction of new housing for health workers. These houses are generally several notches above standard quality; they represent an increased level of comfort as well as a mark of social prestige. They were therefore a powerful incentive for health workers at the most basic level.

Rethinking sustainability and investment in recurrent costs. Throughout the 1990s, and as a consequence of a realistic assessment of Mozambique's foreseeable macroeconomic future, a different idea of sustainability has gradually emerged among the so-called like-minded donors. This view holds the potential for reorganizing the possibilities of sustainability and dependency in humanitarian and development operations. The original documents of the MPIHP project envisioned three project periods of five years each. The initial project did not conceive of a significant role for FINNIDA in recurrent costs after the first five-year reconstruction phase. Maintenance and the payment of salaries were to be assumed by the government of Mozambique.

What has become obvious is that the MMOH is structurally unable to assume these responsibilities. Increasingly through the 1990s, the like-minded donors opted in practice to modify their approach. In practice they have opted to measure accomplishment in more relative terms. Rather than focusing on whether certain preset milestones have been passed, evaluation focuses on whether measurable, relative improvement has occurred, given emerging contingencies. The focus is whether progress is being incrementally and yet noticeably made, rather than whether progress has attained a certain level by a particular time.

This approach is based on a fundamental shift in like-minded donors' thinking about sustainability. These donors accept that it will be two or three decades before Mozambique may be able to sustain the health system at the basic level envisioned in the national Health Sector Recovery Plan (1992). They have committed themselves to this sector for the long haul, and they have increasingly been willing to reconsider the possibility of contributing to recurrent-expense support.

Within this mind-set, FINNIDA acknowledges that the MPIHP may not be a final solution for the health sector in Manica. It is acknowledged that in twenty years another project may be necessary as the final push that establishes a self-sustained infrastructure in a recovered and developing Mozambique. Is such an approach pragmatic or fatalistic? Should lower levels of service be guaranteed at sustainable levels first, or should minimal levels of service be ensured as a matter of basic human rights?

These are broader questions that involve difficult negotiation between political and moral considerations.

Conclusions on Building Local Capacity

This section has focused on building local capacity in Mozambique in a specific sense of this term. It examined how different foreign aid approaches to partnership with the Mozambican Ministry of Health contributed to reestablishing the national health system's coverage at a local level and to decentralizing key aspects of management, so that critical decisions could be vested in provincial and (eventually) district-level health structures.

The success of the FINNIDA (and Danida) cases offers several new directions for other contexts. A longer time frame, intermediary scale of activity, focal-donor role, the use of a private consulting firm rather than an NGO as an implementing partner, a genuinely practiced commitment to national ownership, a flexible mandate, and a different view of sustainability were all innovative features that distinguished this project and contributed to its success between 1991 and 1997.

Consideration of even these successful programs clearly raises other important questions about what goes into successful local capacity building. Specifically, to what extent is the building of local capacity dependent on simultaneous attention to building supporting capacities at the national level? Similarly, can a sectoral approach (at either a national or local level) work when health, for example, is so dependent on other sectors, and on larger macroeconomic trends?

Health-Sector Aid and Local Capacity

Defining Civil Society in the Mozambican Context

The following section considers the relationship between reestablishing the local capacity of the Mozambican national health system, and building a different local capacity—namely, the capacity for civil society. As analysts such as Young, Harbeson, Chazan, Azarya, and Guyer have pointed out, the concept of civil society experienced a phenomenal resurgence in humanitarian conflict resolution and in development analysis in the 1990s without, however, being defined in precise or consistent ways.[15] It has been argued that Mozambique is representative of a society with a weak, virtually nonexistent civil society.[16] Yet at the same time, that it has a rich and diverse cache of associational forms with local grassroots (rather than state) origins and legitimacy makes it important to consider carefully this civil society that Mozambique may or may not have.[17]

Political sociologist Victor Azarya notes that what is often referred to by *civil society* is nongovernmental associational life. In Mozambique this would include all manner of associational life, including traditional authorities, churches, unions, burial societies, and nascent national NGOs. Yet as Azarya points out, what we refer to when using such definitions is simply society at large. In what way does civil society become distinguishable from society in such a formulation? Azarya rightly states that "if civil society just means society, then we should call it society without superfluous attributes. If we insist on referring to *civil* society, then we have to explain what makes society 'civil' or at least what part of society is the 'civil' part."[18]

Political scientist John Harbeson may provide an answer to the second part of this question in his claim that individuals, associations, or groups are participants in civil society to the extent that they seek to define, generate support for, or promote changes in the basic political order. He defines *political order* as the arena within which processes for the authoritative allocation of social values takes place. By this definition, "civil society is not simply synonymous with associational life; rather it is confined to associations to the extent that they take part in rule-setting activities."[19]

Azarya himself provides a useful answer to the first part of his own question. He argues that what makes society "civil" is a set of attitudes toward the public sphere. More specifically,

> Civil society is a sense of reciprocal expectations that prevail among groups in society that involves a commitment to take part in the establishment of a common order and a voluntary compliance to abide by its rules (though without relinquishing the right to act within those rules to promote one's interests). This public domain is distinct from the private sphere but also from the state. In this formulation the characteristics of civilness involve the degree of legitimacy attributed to this public sphere.[20]

Drawing on Hirschman,[21] Azarya argues that one of the major characteristics of a robust civil society is that "discontented actors prefer to exercise 'voice' options rather than 'exit' ones. 'Voice,' in essence, is a participation option even in criticism and opposition to the established order. It involves an engagement, a willingness to risk the retaliation by the opposite side.... 'Exit,' conversely, is ... an avoidance of the risks of involvement, a withdrawal or disengagement from public action."[22]

We can combine these answers to define civil society more specifically as forms of associational life involved in negotiating the political order with the state (and among actors) *premised on the degree of legitimacy granted by all of these players to that process of negotiation itself* and thus on the commitment to exercising "voice" as opposed to "exit" options. Perhaps the most basic prerequisite for making society "civil" in the sense that Azarya proposes is that the players grant that the presence of other players and their right to exercise voice is also legitimate.

Legitimizing the State's Local Presence from a Grassroots Perspective

This problem warrants examination in the Mozambican context from the perspective of local, nonstate actors. In other words, have Mozambicans developed a historic tendency to engage the state through strategies of voice or exit? Furthermore, how do local forms of associational life relate to these strategies? Does the basis for their credibility and legitimacy among local people result from how they enable a more effective participation in voice strategies or from how they facilitate exit strategies?

Throughout Mozambique, the historical record argues largely in favor of a mass political culture that has favored exit to voice options. Through much of the twentieth century, the weakness of the Portuguese colonial structure—both in administrative and financial terms—led to practices that were sporadically intrusive and heavy-handed, rather than comprehensive and incrementally systematic. Rather than employing overt resistance or forming grassroots political movements to change the state's policies, Mozambicans reacted to colonial rule through mass, illegal labor migration across international borders, flight from forced labor, evasion of tax collectors, and a multitude of other passive-resistance strategies: noncompliance, absenteeism, and petty vandalism.[23] These strategies of exit proved highly effective in defending local interests against the far more powerful colonial state, particularly since that power was not so great that its exercise could be sustained in a uniform manner through space and time.

In this environment, the central state increasingly came to be seen as an actor that usually pursued interests opposed to local ones, and as a source of unwanted attention. In parts of the country, this perspective on centralized authority carried over from precolonial experiences with the powerful indigenous Gaza state, and it was strongly reinforced throughout the colonial period. The elite urban intellectual movements and the ethnically based, northern, rural economic interest groups that coalesced in the early 1960s to form FRELIMO and to carry out the armed anticolonial struggle represented use of voice, an exception to the more prevalent exit pattern.

FRELIMO's association with the end of colonial rule briefly opened the possibility for reversing this exit pattern and for relegitimizing the presence of centralized government in local lives. In some areas, particularly in the far north and, to some extent, in the far south of the country, this did occur. However, FRELIMO's own radical attempts to create not only a centrally planned and managed economy but a command society soon alienated large portions of the Mozambican population, particularly in rural areas. Increasingly these populations reverted to historically effective strategies of exit, as FRELIMO's ever more heavy-handed intrusiveness (further aggravated by wartime conditions) reawakened and reinforced long-established assumptions about the state's detrimental presence.

As a result of this history, one of the most basic ingredients or preconditions for civil society is found wanting throughout rural Mozambique: namely, the willingness of society to accept state intervention and the state's right to voice, or to engage the state with its own voice. Thus, in Mozambique, one of the basic preconditions for civil society's establishment and growth must be recognition of the government as a legitimate presence and player. Capacity building that aims to build civil society in Mozambique arguably must start first by developing this most basic prerequisite.

The process involves revolutionizing deeply ingrained understandings of how power and political processes work, and of what they should consist. It also involves changing the implicit criteria used in evaluating the legitimacy of much local associational life. Instead of placing value on associations' effectiveness in facilitating exit options, value would shift to how well associations facilitate options of voice, that is, engagement with the state in defining the political order. Ironically, the pathway toward building local capacity for civil society in Mozambique may require creating a local presence for the national government that local people see as valid and desirable. Presumably this presence would meet needs that local people see as important. How might the health sector be a vehicle for starting this process in postconflict contexts?

One of the modern health sector's advantages in reintroducing and validating the state's presence in Mozambique resulted from the high demand for these services, which cut across virtually all segments of the population. Under both Portuguese colonialism and postcolonial rule, modern medical services were in high demand. In some remote districts, colonial records show significant popular subscription to the limited medical services offered, and a high rate of better services being procured across borders, such as in southern Rhodesia.[24] Some of the FRELIMO policies that met with the least resistance and most success were its immunization campaigns.

Health Services: A Focus for Civil Society

Although the Mozambican peace accord was signed in 1992, the following three years brought several critical developments that enabled peace to become a reality on the ground. These included the demobilization of armed combatants, the demining and reconstruction of major thoroughfares, the repatriation of refugees, the movement of internally displaced populations, and the holding of national elections. The most critical of these processes was probably demobilization. Despite the successful (if often touch-and-go) demobilization of the bulk of the military forces in 1993 and 1994, RENAMO retained a number of forces in the field, informally organized and in unknown numbers. Particularly in areas where RENAMO had strength, armed contingents remained, and the potential for the conflict to reignite was high. Establishing a legitimate government presence in these areas proved a monumental challenge.

In several cases, health projects represented the first government-related attempts to establish a desired or even tolerated presence. Whereas RENAMO had often established parallel administrative and, in fewer cases, educational structures, it had rarely established a parallel health structure.[25] Thus, unlike other forms of government presence, health services were in demand among RENAMO-area and returning populations, particularly those coming from refugee camps in Zimbabwe and Malawi under UNHCR auspices. In some cases, health projects could thus piggyback onto UNHCR projects as a way of aiding returnees, and thus represent themselves in a relatively depoliticized way.

Having a highly visible foreign element was very important at this stage in many of these projects. In Manica Province, many health officials mentioned how they tended initially to identify themselves as associated with "the FINNIDA project" rather than with the provincial directorate of health. In parts of Manica this emphasis was initially very important in guaranteeing access into RENAMO-held areas, where people were more receptive to projects identified with foreign entities. Over time, such identity strategies became less necessary. The health department's presence as a recognized aspect of the central state came not only to be accepted, but it experienced high demand. In some areas with particularly strong ties to RENAMO, health services often proved to be the only services received with little ambiguity or opposition.

In order to achieve this legitimacy, foreign support of the government's local presence in the health sector, rather than competition with it, was needed. Even when working in collaboration with Mozambican health officials, many NGOs have promoted their own identity. By contrast, projects, such as FINNIDA's MPIHP, that have been most successful in promoting the legitimacy of the national health service in their own right have taken an approach that differs in small, often intangible ways, but with significant results. MMOH and PDH officials were quick to note how well the identity of the MPIHP was subsumed within the framework of national, rather than foreign, institutions.

There was a concerted effort *not* to make distinctions between the MPIHP as a FINNIDA project and as a project of the provincial directorate of health. Personnel, whether FINNIDA or PDH, made a point of distinguishing themselves as affiliated with the PDH. None of the project's vehicles was labeled FINNIDA or FINNCONSULT; they were marked instead as Department of Health vehicles. This stood in sharp contrast to the practices of many other bilateral donors with provincial-level projects (even in Manica itself), and to the practices of NGOs. How vehicles were labeled may seem a small thing but symbolically it was not.

Fostering a sense of ownership of the health system and of MPIHP among the PDH cadres was also manifest in important managerial practices such as the provision of technical assistance. It would have been easy for a system to develop in which the technical advisers allowed informal channels that bypassed PDH counterparts. However, this has not occurred. In the chairing of regular planning meetings, in the setting of agendas, in the organization and submission of reports, TAs have purposely reduced their responsibility over time, encouraging PDH counterparts to take the initiative. In short, the philosophy is that national counterparts should be encouraged to take as much responsibility as possible—ironically, often more than they want—and simultaneously to provide full accountability for that responsibility.

In many places throughout Mozambique, health services (with the possible exception of education) are the state's only significant local presence, and in many more areas these services are the only local form of state presence in high demand. This reality may help enhance the capacity for civil society by improving public attitudes toward state legitimacy through an extension and improvement of the local delivery of these services. At the same time, however, this opportunity, if it is not sustained or if it becomes corrupt, could reinforce the long-standing views that delegitimize the state's local presence.

It is no secret that "informal costs"—meaning corruption—constitute the most significant portion of out-of-pocket health costs borne by the average health service user. There is a vigorous black market sector in the sale of pharmaceuticals. Many drugs are reportedly available from health service staff when these staff are at home and not on duty. Interviews in the city of Chimoio verified that chloroquine sold at a rate ten to twenty times higher than the official price at a health post. Many interviewees also reported the need to bribe teachers for their children to make progress in school and health workers in order to receive a consultation.

However, as Durao and Pavignani correctly observe, "The most obvious, pervasive, and influential [problem in the civil sector] is the extremely low remuneration of staff.... [M]ost survival schemes are used by decent people and have been forced on them by necessity."[26] The issue of petty corruption in social services is an even larger and more intractable problem than that of sustainability, given that public-wage reform involves far more than the health sector. Such reform extends into structural adjustment policies that are reinforced by an international political and economic climate in which Mozambique has a negligible voice. Without a resolution of the salary question, it seems doubtful that the corruption problem can be addressed adequately. Meanwhile, the growth of this type of petty corruption threatens to hijack attempts to legitimize the state's local presence and to encourage new attitudes toward engaging the state through strategies of voice.

Legitimizing Local Strategies of Voice from the State's Perspective

Developing an effective local presence for national government in a widely demanded service is only half of what must be considered in examining how foreign assistance helps establish preconditions for civil society. This section deals with the equally important other half: how aid programs in the health sector encourage government to recognize and legitimize local voices other than its own and their right to engage in the political and social order.

Both colonial and postcolonial regimes strongly discouraged local strategies of voice. They lamented and fought strategies of exit while seeking to promote their own solution which, simply put, was compliance—understandably not an option eagerly received by local actors. Sogge neatly summarizes colonial perspectives in this respect and their effect on local associational life:

> The colonial rulers tried to arrange civil society along the lines of the Portuguese metropole, guided by the principles of corporatism: the representation of business, labor, farm, and other group interest *in ways designated by the state.* In the corporatist system, the state used non-governmental bodies to propagandize and gain adherence to *its* policies; in return, members of those bodies received state protection and patronage. Corporatism in Mozambique was uneven and never realized.... [L]ate in the colonial era it [the colonial state] assembled small numbers of African rural producers in agricultural cooperatives. But these were for *colonial political purposes,* not for the promotion of producers' interests. The state regulated the associational life of proprietors through *gremios* [government-sponsored and controlled "cooperatives" under the Portuguese dictatorship]. These were restricted de facto to Portuguese settlers.... According to one observer, in the mid-1960s there were no more than twenty indigenous civil organizations, including football clubs.[27]

Sogge goes on to describe the even more restrictive policies pursued by FRELIMO immediately following independence:

> FRELIMO "colonized" associational life, preserving the spirit of colonial-era laws and patterns of supervision. Organizations of wage earners, teachers, journalists, women and youth, ostensibly

based on membership, were subject to dirigiste control. The space for autonomous political action in civil society remained small until around 1990.[28]

Historically, therefore, the state itself has been unwilling to permit a space in which local actors can exercise voice options. It has worked actively to discourage forms of associational life with independent grassroots legitimacy that target that space. Until 1990, only three Mozambican service organizations or NGOs existed: Caritas Mozambique (founded in 1977); the Mozambican Red Cross (founded in 1981 at FRELIMO's initiative); and the Christian Council of Mozambique (founded in 1948).[29] The constitutional reform of 1990 guaranteed freedom of associational life, and some new national NGOs have since emerged. According to Kulima and Sogge, by 1996 approximately thirty-five national NGOs existed.[30]

In their 1997 review of the Mozambican social sectors (health and education), van Eijs and da Silva found virtually no Mozambican NGOs dedicated in practice to health or to education activities exclusively. They wrote: "Although they [Mozambican NGOs] may limit themselves in their constitutions to health or education, in their work with the communities, they end up involving themselves in activities in other areas."[31] Like most Mozambican NGOs, those involved in the health sector were active in physical reconstruction during the postemergency phase. One survey conducted in Zambezia Province in 1996 found that seven of the eleven Mozambican NGOs with activities in health and/or education had facility construction as their principal activity.[32] Small in scale, thoroughly dependent on foreign funding, and with activities largely limited to reconstruction, many of these NGOs vanished when the reconstruction projects that gave them birth ended.

Van Eijs and da Silva are critical of how the few international agencies that work through local partners relate to these partners. Relationships are usually a matter of subcontracting for services to implement projects designed by the foreign agency, or, less often, of providing financial support for projects presented by the Mozambican partner. Van Eijs and da Silva argue that, in either case, the agenda of the foreign agency dictates which activities are carried out, and how. This influence makes itself felt through the specification of activities or through the selection of national partners who present projects that fit the agency's agenda, and through the rejection of projects that do not. Local partner organizations must often make themselves "fit" other agendas to survive financially. Foreign-agency intervention and pressure is evident in all projects, whether designed and carried out or only implemented by Mozambican partners.

An alternative approach would be based on the idea that most national

NGOs have a well-developed mission, other than that of serving as local partners for foreign NGOs, and thus should benefit from a piece of the aid pie. While there are undoubtedly exceptions, this is the general case as seen by members of the national and local Mozambican government, by foreign donors and NGOs, and, perhaps most important, by the few members of the Mozambican population who come in contact with these organizations.

It is clear that by far the most enduring and successful national NGOs are the handful based in the capital and that run as high-level consulting firms, operated by Mozambican elites. Often these individuals have close connections to, or simultaneous positions within, the state apparatus itself. Without disparaging the excellent consulting work that a number of these organizations have performed, it is nevertheless incorrect to argue that national NGOs in Mozambique are an expression of broadly representative local demands for voice.

This is not to say that more grassroots-based national NGOs might not emerge, especially in the health sector. However, apart from limited private health practices catering to elites in the urban areas, it is unlikely that these NGOs will have the capacity for large-scale intervention in, and impact on, the modern health system.[33] Many generalist foreign NGOs also fail in this respect.

Despite the dearth of national grassroots NGOs whose capacities might be built, particularly in the modern health sector, there are clearly candidates in larger society that might build capacity for civil society. A series of associational forms grounded in broad grassroots interests and locally legitimized already are of relevance to the modern health sector. However, the state has actively discouraged Mozambicans' use of these associations to exercise strategies of voice. These associations include church groups, traditional authorities and community elders, and traditional medical practitioners (TMPs).

The following section focuses on three questions: Are there opportunities for enhancing the capacity of civil society in the health sector by reforming the state's perspective on local associational forms? Conversely, what are the dangers of continuing to ignore or of alienating these associations? In what ways has foreign aid in the health sector encouraged the state to undertake these reforms?

Articulations between Modern and Traditional Medicine

Generally speaking, illness in Mozambique is interpreted within a moral-religious framework and is attributable to action by spirits of the dead. The spirits' activation may be attributed either to failure in upholding social norms between the living and the dead or to witchcraft generated as a result of tensions between living actors. Traditional healing is associated with the diagnosis and treatment of these spiritual/social problems. This perspective does not necessarily stand in opposition to modern medicine's explanations of illness, and in fact may often complement it. The average person may be willing to accept a modern explanation of how an illness has been contracted. But this does not prevent a social/moral explanation for why that illness was contracted. The answer to this second question is sought through TMPs.

Traditional medical practitioners are, and most probably will continue to be, used as a healing recourse, *despite* increases in the use of the modern medicine. In other words, there is no trade-off between use of the modern health sector and use of the traditional health sector. People may increase use of the modern health sector to seek cures while continuing to avail themselves of a traditional healer to treat what they perceive as the moral root of a problem that will recur or worsen if left unattended.

This culturally constructed view of health has important implications for the modern health sector and for any project that aims to improve the modern health sector's capacity to respond. Beliefs may affect choices about the priority attributed to modern and traditional sectors in time and financial resources. Furthermore, ethnographic evidence supports the notion that traditional healers are generally the first recourse. Factors such as cost may also influence the sequence of people's health care choices.

Modern medicine's position as second stop in the curative health chain implies both risks and opportunities for modern health practices. One risk is that modern health services may have to cope with traditional practices that are detrimental to health, increasing the modern health sector's curative burden. Such practices may increase the incidence of HIV—such as through the use of razors in ritual aspects of traditional healing—or they may simply bring delay and deterioration in a patient's health before the patient approaches modern health services.

Another problem in the relationship between modern and traditional health sectors is the historical antagonism between government and traditional practitioners. The postcolonial government's relationship to traditional healers was to minimize, if not to eliminate, their role in public life and health. Although this policy changed to one of passive tolerance during the conflict itself, the vigor with which initial anti-TMP policies were pursued has left TMPs with general mistrust toward the formal health authorities. Furthermore, when TMPs see the modern health sector as direct competitors, market rivalry can produce antagonism. TMPs play important leadership roles in local communities, especially in curative health. If TMPs do, in fact, constitute the culturally constructed first option in the curative-health chain, the TMP attitude toward modern health may have a serious impact on modern health services.

However, the TMP position as first link in the curative health chain also poses major opportunities for the modern sector. If TMPs are trained to cope with basic diseases and prevalent maladies, such as diarrhea, burdens can be lessened for the already overextended health care system. Such a first line of defense would also extend health coverage to a far greater proportion of the population. This could be done at minimal expense, because TMPs are not salaried by government. Earlier referrals would bring patients to health posts in better condition, when treatment is easier and less expensive. Furthermore, preventive health and health education among the population as a whole could be improved substantially by inculcating new understanding among TMPs.

The Ministry of Health has shown little orientation to the ways in which the modern health sector should relate to the traditional health sector. At the most general level, the MMOH has, since 1992, sought to find forms of collaboration with TMPs. More specific MMOH policy in this respect is being discussed, but there is no indication as to whether or when change might be forthcoming. Apart from the history of ideological antagonism to traditional life, another source of reluctance among health officials is that TMPs' misapplication of knowledge could result in worse health outcomes for those they treat. However, this view ignores that TMPs are constantly evaluated by local people in light of the TMPs' healing record. Those who systematically produce undesirable results quickly gain a bad reputation and lose their clientele.

As of 1997, neither national nor foreign actors in the modern health sector had conducted a comprehensive study to examine the possibilities for building relationships and articulation between traditional health and modern health services—despite the fact that at least three preliminary studies commissioned by foreign NGOs recommended such measures.[34] Big players among the foreign donors, such as FINNIDA and Swiss Development Cooperation, have left the initiatives in this area to a handful of international NGOs. At best, when not apathetic donors have reacted to initiatives generated by NGOs, responding with limited funding for sporadic and ad hoc rather than systematic activities.

The cultural distance between Western medicine and traditional practices has also been a factor producing skepticism about this issue, leading to it being ignored by most foreign actors in the health sector. The relationship between the modern health sector and the traditional thus remains unclear, and it is in need of further examination at a national level.

One initiative that successfully used an existing local institution was the National Training and Capacitation Program for traditional birth attendants (TBAs). This program was supported at a national level by Swiss Development Cooperation, Redd Barna, and UNHCR, and at a provincial level by focal donors (such as FINNIDA). The TBA or midwife role already existed within local communities. The program sought to improve TBA technical capacities and hygienic practices and to link TBAs and modern health services to enhance reproductive health services, particularly with respect to maternal health care (MHC). TBAs were trained to diagnose and triage cases for referral to modern health facilities instead of treating all cases themselves, and to use improved methods, information, and hygienic practices in cases they did treat. The TBA program also emphasized prenatal and postpartum aspects of MHC, expanding the notion of care related to pregnancy. TBAs received no compensation for their services from government or from project sources. Any compensation or incentives were negotiated and legitimized within the local community.

Two hundred TBAs were trained in Manica Province during Phase I of the MPIHP, with positive results. In 1993, TBAs attended 3,517 deliveries, with the number climbing steadily to 4,861 deliveries in 1996. This result exemplifies the possibilities in pursuing greater integration between the modern health sector and grassroots social institutions.

Cultivating Other Forms of Community Participation

The Conselhos de Lideres Comunitarios (Community Leadership Councils, or CLCs) program was developed by the International Health Committee (a small foreign NGO active in Manica) as a way to involve community leaders in the dissemination of health information and education. It also sought their involvement in the organization and implementation of health service programs (such as vaccination campaigns), and in identifying and troubleshooting health problems and local difficulties in health service delivery. This novel initiative involved monthly meetings at local health posts. CLC members were leaders from different local bodies, including churches, traditional authorities, TMPs, the Organization for Mozambican Women, and the Mozambican Youth Organization. These groups were invited to send representatives to participate in the CLCs. The approach was therefore based on voluntary participation and on local concerns about health. CLC members were not paid for their participation, an important factor in ensuring long-term sustainability.

According to a 1995 evaluation, members generally conceived of the CLC as a preventive-health education channel (90 percent), and as a mechanism for mobilizing people to use health services and to partake in health programs (80 percent).[35] Only 15 percent saw the CLC as a channel for making local views about health problems known to health services or for finding solutions, although these issues have increasingly become viewed as part of the CLC role. A fairly high proportion of community members was aware of the existence and activities of the CLC, and, significantly, an overwhelming majority registered a desire for a CLC when its purpose was explained to them.

The CLC program began in 1992 in the Gondola district. By 1996, fifty-five CLCs were functioning in eight of Manica province's nine districts. In several cases, individuals who had experience with CLCs in one district mobilized and organized CLCs in districts to which they later moved, reflecting the value they saw in the program.[36]

Clearly, community willingness to participate in such programs is a prerequisite for their success. And as the growth of CLCs in Manica has shown, there is openness to this type of local participation in Mozambique. Despite this promise, the International Health Committee received little support and even some hostility from the MMOH in continuing its initiatives in Manica and in exporting them to neighboring Sofala Province. At the provincial level, the PDH remained moderately enthusiastic about the value of this work, particularly given that the activities had been carried out in collaboration with the Community Health Section of the PDH, and that they were integrated into its programs and objectives.

In encouraging the government to grant space for the participation of other local voices, foreign aid programs in the modern health sector arguably have made the least effort. In the best of circumstances they have contributed only minimally to the building of local capacity, in the sense of creating and expanding space for nongovernment actors in the health sector. There is a long way to go in encouraging government to acknowledge the legitimacy of other players, or to be engaged by local players through strategies of voice.

Conclusion

Efforts to cultivate civil society in Mozambique require an understanding of how a specific colonial, postcolonial, and wartime history structured relationships between the state and society in ways that sustain exit over voice. Under Portuguese colonial rule, policies of social exclusion based on race amplified the deliberate effort to restrict voice by minimizing and monopolizing all forms of nonstate associational life. Intrusive and oppressive colonial policies led most Mozambicans to view the state as something to be avoided. In this context, Mozambicans evaluated the legitimacy of local forms of associational life in terms of their ability to facilitate strategies of exit—avoidance, noncompliance, and disengagement with the central state.

FRELIMO's Marxist ideology and its history of internal struggles during the anticolonial war contributed to its paradoxical view of local associational life: on one hand, the energy of local participation was viewed as important for producing social change. On the other hand, this energy was viewed as susceptible to reactionary corruption and to the "obscurantism" of traditional beliefs. Popular participation thus had to be controlled by a leadership with the "correct" ideological vision. This view informed FRELIMO's attempts to monopolize local associational life.[37]

In the context of the deteriorating economic and security conditions resulting from foreign aggression, these intrusive social policies eroded FRELIMO's legitimacy as anticolonial liberator, reinforcing the colonial-era preference for avoiding engagement with the state. Population control by all combatants during the civil war further entrenched this view. At the same time, the exigencies of the emergency understandably reinforced the state's top-down modus operandi. Despite ongoing attempts at decentralization and democratization, the political culture, along with the incentive and administrative structures of the Mozambican state, still militates against opening space for nonstate actors genuinely to engage in voice.

In general, the government of Mozambique is far more open to decentralization of management than to opening space for people to negotiate social or political change. The public sector is still structured so that health service workers at all levels are almost exclusively responsible to those higher in the bureaucratic structure, rather than to their local constituents. Foreign actors in the modern health arena consequently face a paradox when considering how to build local capacity in both of the senses considered in this chapter. The Mozambican government seeks to be viewed as the only local entity as a means of channeling aid resources in its direction, and to delegitimize initiatives that support other forms of associational life that aspire to that label.

It is important to support the reconstruction of national systems of social service in order to cultivate legitimacy for the state, particularly in light of a history in which little legitimacy has existed. At the same time, however, it is important to encourage government engagement with local (i.e., subnational) voices—an attitude it resists, in collusion with foreign actors. In Mozambique many voices that might help the modern health sector are found in traditional forms of associational life rather than in the nascent national NGOs.

Building civil society is not as closely associated with the modern health sector as it is with aid initiatives in other sectors, such as education or political administration. This chapter has argued, however, that improving and extending services in an area of felt need, such as modern health, particularly when the population historically has viewed government's local presence as intrusive and detrimental, may play an important role in establishing the most basic preconditions for building civil society. Building local capacities in the sense considered in the first section of this chapter—in coverage provided by the national health care system and in decentralization—may hold exceptional possibilities for legitimizing the state as a local player, thus changing local political culture. Conversely, if issues of sustainability are not addressed, and if the state itself is not encouraged to recognize the legitimacy of other local actors as participants in negotiating change, the political culture may simply reinforce exit over voice.

Notes

1. An analysis of the interaction between international humanitarian actors and Mozambican civil society is included in an earlier study of the Humanitarianism and War Project. See Antonio Donini, *The Policies of Mercy: UN Coordination in Afghanistan, Mozambique, and Rwanda,* Occasional Paper no. 22 (Providence, R.I.: Watson Institute, 1996).

2. Jocelyn Alexander, "Terra e Autoridade Politica no Pos-Guerra em Moçambique: O Caso da Provincia de Manica," *Arquivo* 16 (1994): 5–94; Mark Chingono, *The State Violence and Development* (Aldershot, England: Avebury Press and Ashegate Publishing, 1996); Christiaan Geffray, *A Causa das Armas: Antropologia da Guerra Contemporânea em Moçambique* (Lisbon: Afrontamento, 1989); Margaret Hall and Tom Young, *Confronting Leviathan: Mozambique since Independence* (Athens: Ohio University Press, 1997); Harry West, " 'This Neighbor Is Not My Uncle!': Changing Relations of Power and Authority on the Mueda Plateau," *Journal of Southern African Studies* 24, no. 1 (1998): 141–60; Stephen Lubkemann, "Situating Wartime Migration in Central Mozambique: Gendered Social Struggle and the Transnationalization of Polygyny" (Ph.D. diss., Department of Anthropology, Brown University, 2000).

3. Hans Abrahammson and Anders Nilsson, *Moçambique em Transição* (Gothenburg, Sweden: Peace and Development Institute, Gothenburg University, 1994), 44.

4. In 1987, Mozambique became the first country to assume structural adjustment under wartime emergency conditions (Abrahammson and Nilsson, *Moçambique em Transição).*

5. Enrico Pavignani and Joaquim Ramalho Durao, *National Coordination of External Resources in the Health Sector: The Mozambican Case Study* (Maputo: Swiss Cooperation, September 1997), 10.

6. The first part of this phase focused primarily on rehabilitation and reconstruction. This was later subsumed under the second phase, known as the National Health Sector Recovery Program (NHSRP), approved in 1995. The NHSRP took a more comprehensive approach, including direct budget support and institution building in addition to construction and development.

7. Pavignani and Durao, *National Coordination of External Resources,* 3–4.

8. Manica Province Integrated Health Project, *Manica Province Integrated Health Project Mid-term Review* (Helsinki: Finnish Cooperation [FINNIDA], April 1997).

9. MPIHP, *Manica Province Integrated Health Project Mid-term Review,* 58–61. Less information was available on Danida's work in Tete than on FINNIDA when materials were gathered for this analysis. By 1998 only one early review had been conducted on Danida's work (1995), and it did not allow for evaluation of results comparable to the six-year perspective available from the MPIHP 1997 midterm review.

10. These studies examined prewar service levels and under less than ideal data-availability conditions.

11. Informally the FINNIDA initiative also encouraged the MMOH to think in more strategic terms about the sector's organization and direction at a national level.

12. This raises the paradoxical question of whether agencies should just choose "easy" or "doable" projects, particularly when it is in the least-"doable" places that aid is most needed.

13. MPIHP, *Manica Province Integrated Health Project Mid-term Review*, 56. By contrast, at the national level the admittedly strong influence of Swiss Cooperation was mitigated by the fact that other major donors contributed at similar levels or, in a few cases, even more extensively.

14. There were no Mozambican consultancy groups or national NGOs with the technical capacity for carrying out this scale and type of program in 1992 (and as of 1997 there still were none).

15. John W. Harbeson, "Civil Society and Political Renaissance in Africa," in *Civil Society and the State in Africa*, ed. John W. Harbeson, Donald Rothchild, and Naomi Chazan (London: Lynne Rienner, 1994), 1–32; Naomi Chazan, "State and Society in Africa: Images and Challenges," in *The Precarious Balance: State and Society in Africa*, ed. Donald Rothchild and Naomi Chazan (Boulder, Colo.: Westview Press, 1988); Crawford Young, "In Search of Civil Society," in Harbeson et al., *Civil Society and the State in Africa*, 33–50; Victor Azarya, "Civil Society and Disengagement in Africa," in Harbeson et al., *Civil Society and the State in Africa*, 83–100; Jane I. Guyer, "The Spacial Dimensions of Civil Society in Africa: An Anthropologist Looks at Nigeria," in Harbeson et al., *Civil Society and the State in Africa*, 215–30.

16. Carlos Fumo, "ONGs Moçambicanas: Sua identidade e Papel No Desenvolvimento do Pais," in *Faces e Contra-Faces na Identidade Civil Moçambicana*, ed. Ana Piedade Monteiro and Alexandrino Jose (Maputo: Centro de Estudos Africanos-Universidade Eduardo Mondlane, 1995), 35–45; Pavignani and Durao, *National Coordination of External Resources*.

17. David Sogge, "The Civil Sector," in *Mozambique: Perspectives on Aid and the Civil Sector*, ed. David Sogge (Amsterdam: Gemeenschappelijk Overleg Medefinacierig, 1997).

18. Azarya, "Civil Society and Disengagement in Africa," 88.

19. Harbeson, "Civil Society and Political Renaissance," 4.

20. Harbeson, "Civil Society and Political Renaissance," 3, citing Azarya, "Civil Society and Disengagement in Africa," 91.

21. Albert O. Hirschman, *Exit, Voice, and Loyalty: Responses to Decline in Firms, Organizations, and States* (Cambridge: Harvard University Press, 1970).

22. Azarya, "Civil Society and Disengagement in Africa," 98.

23. Allen Isaacman, *Cotton Is the Mother of Poverty* (Portsmouth, N.H.: Heinemann, 1996).

24. Southern Rhodesia only gained independence as Zimbabwe in 1980, five years after the end of colonial rule in Mozambique in 1975.

25. Ken B. Wilson, "Cults of Violence and Counter-Violence in Mozambique," *Journal of Southern African Studies* 18 (1992): 527–82.

26. Pavignani and Durao, *National Coordination of External Resources*, 10.

27. Sogge, "Civil Sector," 11.

28. Sogge, "Civil Sector," 12.

29. Sogge, "Civil Sector."

30. Kulima, *Directorio das Organizações nao-govermantais em Moçambique* (Maputo, 1995); Sogge, "Civil Sector."

31. Tinnie van Eijs and Terezinha da Silva, "Entitlements to Health and Education: Guaranteed by the State, Defended by Civil Society?" in Sogge, *Mozambique*, 132.

32. Guy Mullin, *National NGOs in Zambezia Province, Mozambique—Inventory of NGOs and an Analysis of Their Work and the Potential for Investment in NGO Coordination and Capacity Building* (Maputo: LINK Forum Report, 1996).

33. If encouraged to emerge, these organizations are likely to become involved in less-technical activities such as general sanitation, nutrition, and health education—areas critical to primary and preventative health care.

34. Carolyn Nordstrom, *African Health Care Systems and the War in Mozambique, a Six-Part Study* (Maputo: Mozambican Ministry of Health, 1990–91); MPIHP, *Manica Province Integrated Health Project Mid-term Review.*

35. Silvia Gurolla-Bonilla, *Avaliaçãao dos Conselhos de Lideres Comunitarios* (Chimoio, Mozambique: Mozambican Health Committee, 1995).

36. Diana Auret, *An Analysis of Community Contribution and Self-Help in the MAARP Infrastructural Project* (Chimoio and Maputo: GTZ, 1993).

37. Hall and Young, *Confronting Leviathan.*

Chapter 5

Means without End

Humanitarian Assistance in Sri Lanka

ARJUNA PARAKRAMA

The challenge [is] to create a civil society where the government is empowered to govern and the people are empowered to demand accountability in governance. —SAAVITHRI GOONASEKERA

This chapter investigates whether humanitarian assistance provided by international aid agencies in Sri Lanka's Northeast Province during a protracted seventeen-year civil war has enhanced local capacity in these areas. Faced with the human devastation and economic debilitation in war that appears intractable, it is crucial that the communities caught in the middle—whether in refugee camps or shattered villages—should be supported, not merely to sustain life, but to take control of their future. This study examines how well international humanitarian agencies fulfill this role.

The first part of this chapter describes and analyzes the historical and political context within which this conflict takes place.[1] This is followed by an analysis of humanitarian assistance to the internally displaced and war-ravaged communities in Sri Lanka's Northeast Province. The historical underpinnings of the conflict, as well as the most recent internal refugee displacements, present the essential backdrop. The chapter's third component examines the role of humanitarian assistance in building local capacities, paying particular attention to the contemporary phase of interaction. Most of the international agencies have gained more than a decade of invaluable experience working in these areas. Hence, it is fair to assume that they have evolved systems and processes that they consider optimal under the circumstances. This is not to deny that all such processes are continuously evolving, but merely to assert that these agencies have had sufficient time to work out the systems most conducive to them. A final section examines some of the theoretical issues

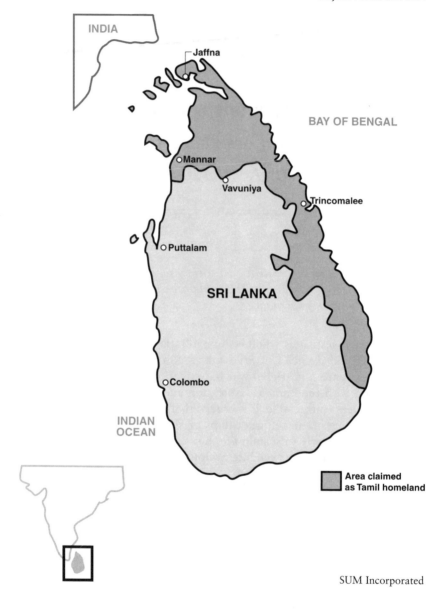

INDIA

Jaffna

BAY OF BENGAL

Mannar

Vavuniya

Trincomalee

Puttalam

SRI LANKA

Colombo

INDIAN
OCEAN

Area claimed
as Tamil homeland

SUM Incorporated

for which the study has laid the groundwork, and which transcend the immediate Sri Lankan context, with possible applicability to other conflicts. This reiterates the attempt made throughout the chapter to present sets of generalizable principles that may be used in the analysis of similar contexts elsewhere in the contemporary world.[2]

The Sri Lankan Conflict

Early History and Context

The island country of Sri Lanka (formerly Ceylon) lays claim to a recorded history of more than 2,500 years, in which migrations, invasions, and commercial and cultural exchanges have taken place with India and occasionally with other nations in the region. There is controversy over when the ethnic groups we now identify as Sinhala and Tamil began to see themselves in these specific terms, but it is accepted that distinct identities based on language, religion, geographical location, economic activity, and culture have coexisted in the island for hundreds of years. At present, three-quarters of Sri Lanka's eighteen million people are Sinhalese Buddhists, living mainly in the southwest of the island. Eighteen percent of the population are Hindu Tamils living in the north and east, and approximately 6 percent of the population forms a distinct Muslim minority. Ethnic tensions between Sinhalese and Tamils have simmered for much of the twentieth century.

Colonial Legacy and Postindependence

The centuries of varying colonial control—1505 to 1948—transformed the feudal subsistence agrarian economy that had existed for centuries into a mainly derivative export-oriented economy dependent on fluctuating prices for its tea, rubber, and coconut. Coffee was first grown in the central hills of Ceylon, only to be replaced with tea in the 1860s after a coffee blight devastated the plantations. The British were the only Western power to control the entire island (1815–1948). One of the strategies of control employed by the British was to create an urban, educated, anglicized, and Christianized elite drawn from both the Sinhala and Tamil communities. This elite was able to amass considerable wealth and to enjoy substantial power in the colony. The Buddhist Revival in the late nineteenth and early twentieth centuries was inflected by anti-Tamil sentiment. The groundwork was prepared at that time for a majority Sri Lankan identity that was exclusively and intolerantly Sinhala Buddhist.

Tamils from South India were indentured to work on the vast tea estates, and some of their descendants are still tied to the tea plantations under appalling conditions. The predicament of this group of landless workers, numbering nearly one million people and mainly confined to the central mountain zone, was compounded when, through a series of bilateral agreements with the Indian government, a decision was made to repatriate a large proportion to India. The Citizenship Act of 1948 clearly discriminated against Tamils by denying them the right to citizenship "by descent" as was the case with other groups in the country. Instead, they had to be "registered," selectively, as citizens. Pacts drawn up with India in 1954, 1964, and 1974 dealt with repatriation of Tamils to the Indian state of Tamil Nadu, but conditions there were abysmal for those forced out of Sri Lanka. It was only in 1984 that all those remaining were granted citizenship rights upon application, but there was still an administrative lag in implementation.

In the postindependence period after 1948, the inability of the majority Sinhalese to come to terms with the power-sharing aspirations of the minority Tamils led to a decision by Tamil youth that they could claim their legitimate share of power only through violence. They have justified their adoption of violence by pointing to a history of frustrated attempts by Tamil politicians to negotiate with majority-dominated Sri Lankan governments. The Sinhala-Only Act of 1956 is often cited as the cornerstone of discriminatory policies, but this is, in fact, only the most obvious instance of a series of actions that systematically marginalized Tamils and other minorities.

At the other end of the spectrum, the inability of successive governments to address basic issues of employment and equity fueled disenchantment in the Sinhalese-majority south as well. This led to the Maoist Janatha Vimukthi Peramuna (JVP) insurrection in 1971 (and again in 1987–89, but this time in a more nationalist/chauvinist garb), whose perpetrators were mainly disaffected Sinhala youth drawn from the universities. This insurrection was ruthlessly crushed in under six months at the cost of an estimated thirty thousand deaths.

For the Tamils, legitimate grievances that derived from the denial of citizenship rights, discrimination against the Tamil language, and the limiting of access to employment and higher education were exacerbated by widespread and brutal attacks on Tamils in 1958, 1960–61, 1977, 1981, and 1983. In the 1990s and thereafter, in the face of a civil war and atrocities on both sides, Tamils continued to fear for their physical safety, and hence the claim of equal rights has taken second place to an even more urgent need to ensure basic security.

1977 to 1994

The United National Party (UNP) assumed power at the general election in 1977 and pursued a policy of economic liberalization that included establishment of free-trade zones, the reduction of welfare subsidies, and the dismantling of protectionism measures such as tariffs and the privatization of state-controlled industries. This dramatically reversed the quasi-socialist policies of its predecessors. With liberalization, however, disparities between the richest and the poorest widened further. Competition heightened and the ever-present antagonism among ethnic communities was exacerbated. University admission, always a contentious issue, because only 10 percent of qualified candidates can be accepted, became inflamed as a bone of contention. Thinly disguised ethnic quotas appeared in the form of admissions allocations based on language, and these enhanced the proportions of Sinhalese entering the university. This proved extremely frustrating to Tamil youth, whose only means of upward mobility was higher education.

Simmering Sinhalese paranoia, which had been fueled for short-term political gain, led to an orchestrated nationwide attack on Tamils in July 1983. The immediate pretext was an ambush by rebels in the north that had killed thirteen soldiers. As a direct consequence, the militant groups were able to recruit large numbers of young men and, later, women, even though earlier intelligence reports had claimed that there were only sixty or so Tamil separatist guerrillas.

The UNP administration proved insensitive to Tamil grievances, and successive UNP leaders waged what can only be described as a war against the Tamil people of the north and east; no distinctions were made between armed militants and the unarmed civilians. Bombing, shelling, and wanton destruction of property as well as looting and rape were common occurrences. Virtually every casualty among the military provoked a reprisal attack on civilians.

The Liberation Tigers of Tamil Eelam (LTTE),[3] which demanded an independent state for Tamils and had ruthlessly eliminated all other militant groups by 1986 or so, began to deliberately provoke such atrocities. The LTTE attacked religious targets as well as civilian and economic targets. The state military decimated entire villages, torturing and mutilating their inhabitants in retaliation. Neither the military (including the police) nor the numerous vigilante groups and paramilitary outfits were held accountable, even though detailed evidence of culpability often was available.

On the economic front, employment for Tamils in the state sector was virtually nil, since security clearance was required and this was unobtainable in most cases. Tamil recruitment to the armed forces has been confined to statistically negligible numbers of officers, with impeccable credentials, from outside the Northeast Province.

The severity of the government war effort in the north led to Indian intervention in 1987, and to the entry of the Indian Peace Keeping Force (IPKF). The force left Sri Lanka on March 25, 1990, at which time there was a brief truce between the government of President Premadasa and the LTTE. Hostilities resumed soon after, in what has been described as Eelam War II, and low-intensity conflict persisted throughout the last four years of the UNP regime.

1995 to 2000

In the decade up to 1994, the nationwide emergency was lifted only for a few months in early 1990. The UN Working Group on Enforced and Involuntary Disappearances has recorded that the number of "disappearances" in Sri Lanka between 1983 and 1991, related to both the war and the JVP insurrection, was the highest for any country in the world. Moreover, the per-capita deaths by violence during the latter part of this period were the highest for any comparable time frame in any country, with the single exception of El Salvador during the height of the repression there.

It was in such a context that the People's Alliance (PA) government led by Chandrika Kumaratunga was ushered in, in August 1994, with the hope from many concerned groups that the impasse would be resolved. The new government had pledged to resolve the ethnic crisis through political means, by devolving maximum power within a united Sri Lanka. A measure of its initial success was the sharp decline in deaths and disappearances during its first year in office. Amnesty International recorded fifty-five cases of disappearance and approximately forty extrajudicial executions in 1995, which is orders of magnitude lower than those recorded for previous years.[4]

The initial phase produced a cease-fire in early January 1995, and for the first time a government on its own initiative was sponsoring negotiations in the northern Tamil city of Jaffna. The initiative, however, was naive in conception and implementation, notwithstanding its good intentions. The LTTE preconditions for the commencement of political talks could not be met, since some of these demands were of a military nature. The cessation of hostilities was broken by the LTTE on April 19, 1995, a hundred days after it had begun.

Thereafter, both sides pursued the war with a vengeance, though accusations and counterclaims of secret talks occasionally surfaced. It is clear, however, that neither the Kumaratunga government nor the LTTE has demonstrated any real commitment to a negotiated settlement. The Kumaratunga government prosecuted what it called a war for peace, attempting to capture more and more territory—first the Jaffna Peninsula and thereafter the sixty-mile road connecting it to the south—but it met with major military setbacks in November 1999, which virtually nullified its strategy over the previous three years.

The government is pursuing a self-defeating and self-contradictory policy toward the ethnic crisis. On alternate days it appears to be for war or for peace, but its actions indicate an unshaken will to wage a brutal war, thus playing into the hands of its sworn enemy, the LTTE. Also, it has chosen to brazen its way through scandals and alleged fraud of huge proportions, and there appears to be a systematic attempt to undermine the judiciary and gag the press. All this is coming from an administration that received an overwhelming public mandate to wipe out corruption, usher in peace, and reconstruct a democratic framework.

It would appear that, like its predecessor, the People's Alliance government may wish to use the war and the exigencies of the crisis to deflect criticism against its mismanagement and corruption in the south. This is a dangerous trend, because military "victories" would have to be manufactured in order to preempt other issues.

Internal Displacement and Civilian Victims of War

Seventeen percent of the country's population lives in the Northeast Province, of whom more than one million face the continual threat of displacement and dislocation as a direct result of the fifteen-year conflict. Reliable numbers of refugees in camps, as well as those living with relatives, are not readily available because the issue is politically fraught. But in June 1999, 683,266 persons belonging to 186,528 families depended on the government's free dry rations for their survival.[5] At the beginning of 2000, an estimated 585,000 civilians were internally displaced by the war, in addition to approximately 250,000 international Sri Lankan refugees and asylum seekers who span the globe. Of those internally displaced, roughly 300,000 live in areas outside government control.[6] Widely accepted estimates place the death toll at 65,000 in the conflict thus far, with hundreds of thousands injured, and internal displacement affecting a million people.

Human rights violations attributable to the military were common in the first phase of the war, which lasted from the massacres of civilians in 1983 up to the Indo-Lanka peace accord in July 1987. The Indian occupation of the northeast, which lasted for two and a half years, constituted the second phase of the conflict. Both this phase and the next, the so-called Eelam War II, saw further human rights violations by the state machinery in the form of retaliatory massacres, arbitrary arrest and torture, rape, extrajudicial killings, and extensive damage to property. The main guerilla group, the LTTE, was involved in attacks on unarmed civilians, destruction of religious and cultural sites, and extortion.

In the wake of the military offensive in the north and the 1995 taking of Jaffna, the government still has not reestablished its credibility with the Tamil civilians who have been displaced, harassed, and made to suffer greatly in makeshift refugee camps. Some Tamil refugees in the east may even be worse off than those in the Wanni, which is the area north from Vavuniya to the Jaffna Peninsula and the region in which the conflict has been greatest and the suffering most severe. Often these refugees in the east do not have camps or even semipermanent locations to spend the night. Many of these people have lived a nomadic existence, carrying all their belongings in plastic bags, since 1990. Muslim refugees from

Mannar and the north have been in the refugee camps in Vavuniya and Puttalam since their eviction by the LTTE in 1990.

The freedom of movement of Tamils from the north to the south has been severely restricted in the most recent phase of the war. All those who wish to travel to the south (mainly Colombo) must pass through the Thandikulam checkpoint north of Vavuniya. It is reported that of those who throng the checkpoint each day the vast majority are turned back without receiving adequate reasons. New transit camps were set up at Thandikulam in 1996, and nearly two thousand persons a day were reportedly turned back after the 1996 Central Bank explosion in Colombo. The situation is further exacerbated by the need to obtain a pass from the military and paramilitary groups operating in and around Vavuniya. This is carte blanche for bribery and corruption on a huge scale. In February 2000, attempts were being made to introduce a similar pass system in the east on the argument that suicide bombers came from that area.

The systems in place to prevent attacks on civilian targets in the south systematically discriminate against and even criminalize the Tamil population. At military checkpoints (which number in the hundreds within Colombo), the determining factor for passage is whether a person is a Tamil or not. Detention without charges, repeated arrest even after security clearance, and restrictions on mobility add to a climate of fear and insecurity among underclass Tamils who do not have recourse to local human rights groups or political patronage.

The irony is that the desired result—minimizing the threat of a suicide attack—will not be achieved by this approach. In fact, it is only by winning the trust and cooperation of the overwhelming majority of innocent Tamils that LTTE cadres will be identified. The disillusionment of the Tamil people can be seen clearly in the voting patterns at the 1999 presidential election, when President Chandrika Kumaratunga was reelected despite a significant Tamil vote against her—the same Tamils who voted en bloc to bring her into power in 1994.

The nettle of Sri Lanka's problem is that military logic is slowly but surely taking over the entire fabric of governance. The government appears to be unable or unwilling to act on its claim that it is committed to maintaining a distinction between the LTTE as a terrorist group and ordinary Tamil people. Claims based on exigency and expediency, not to mention the invocation of public opinion, ring hollow. What is required, if the crisis is to be resolved, is not a set of fine-tuned excuses for inaction, or the maintenance of the status quo, but a serious attempt to identify those responsible and to prosecute them. Only then will a clear message be sent to the Tamil people who are the victims of these atrocities as well as to the psychopathic minority within the military who are its perpetrators.

Humanitarian Assistance to War Victims
in Sri Lanka

Possibilities and Constraints

International and local humanitarian agencies have been instrumental in providing emergency assistance since 1983 to victims of the war and atrocities. Emergency rations and other assistance were provided by foreign governments in 1958 and in the 1970s as well, but there was no sustained administration of such aid, nor is there adequate documentation of its modalities. Hence, the issue of humanitarian assistance in Sri Lanka can be meaningfully studied only in the last sixteen years of virtual civil war. Here, too, the response to the carnage of 1983, which was ad hoc and piecemeal, lies outside the scope of this essay. The conclusions in this analysis are based on the most recent, post-1994 humanitarian intervention programs, although a continuity exists with programs of the immediate past.

By this time, the main international agencies had gained nearly a decade of field experience in working with internally displaced persons (IDPs) both within and outside refugee camps in the conflict zone. Emergency supplies have taken the form of food, roofing equipment, essential medicines, and medical care. Aid agencies work in both government and rebel-controlled areas, and they depend on the goodwill of both sides to work in these regions. Obtaining government clearance in particular often leads to delays and frustration, which is compounded by arbitrariness and lack of transparency.

Rajasingham-Senanayake observes, "As the Euro-American world pays more money to stem the tide of refugees and contain refugee populations within refugee-generating states, the growing humanitarian industry, which seeks to mitigate war's effects on displaced civilians, also creates various economies of dependency that structure the internal dynamic of Sri Lanka's armed conflict."[7] Rajasingham-Senanayake, who claims extensive knowledge of the border-village areas, adds, "Often conflicts between impoverished sectors of the host population and internally displaced persons arise as a result of humanitarian interventions,"[8] though she provides neither details nor sources, which prevents verification and makes the statement susceptible to the charge of overgeneralization.

Tensions between displaced populations and local communities nearby are understandable and well known. The competition for scarce resources, changes in the ethnic ratios and hence the political base, and the overburdening of the infrastructure cause the tensions. The long-term Muslim refugee camps in Puttalam (for people displaced since 1990 from the north) are oft-cited examples of this predicament. Humanitarian assistance dispensed for more than ten years by all the major international donor agencies active in Sri Lanka has been unable to address this issue, which lies beyond the agencies' scope. However, donors working through a monopolistic community-based organization in the area also have been unable to address issues of participation and power-sharing within their organization, and they are unable to shake off a deadening dependency.[9] Rajasingham-Senanayake and others have made the point that displacement itself is traumatic, and strategies for coping with this trauma require the attention of humanitarian agencies that have hitherto ignored this aspect entirely.[10]

Humanitarian Assistance by Organizations within and outside the UN System

The United Nations High Commissioner for Refugees (UNHCR) remains the lead agency within the United Nations system in dealing with the war areas, but the United Nations Development Program (UNDP), the United Nations Fund for Population Activities (UNFPA), and the United Nations Children's Fund (UNICEF) run substantial programs in the Northeast Province. Typically, their dealings are with state-sector officials and they remain substantially within the bilateral framework. Individual projects may vary as to the level and extent of capacity building, but monitoring and evaluation remain top-down in approach. Working with the provincial administration and central-government bureaucracy militates against enhancing local capacities.

The Sri Lankan state sector remains hierarchized, archaic, and riddled with vested interests. In such a context, individual commitment cannot achieve sustained results in strengthening local capacities. Overlapping jurisdictions of the civilian administration and the Ministry of Defense (MOD) result in much confusion and buck-passing. Specific cases have been cited in which the transport of essential items, approved by the Ministry of Health, was indefinitely delayed by the denial of MOD clearance. That these decisions appear arbitrary and capricious does nothing to help the situation.

All in all, the strengthening of local capacities does not appear to be a key focus in the United Nations system within the war areas. For example, doctors and nurses on transferable service may not provide a sustainable enhancement of local capacity. UNICEF's work with midwives in their own communities is hampered by the fact that the programs themselves are conceived, drawn up, and evaluated by persons who have nothing to do with the community. The tendency with UNDP projects in the region is to opt for tangible outcomes that can be measured quantitatively. However, such projects tend to focus on the outcomes per se, and not on the processes that enable the development of local initiatives and skills. Projects that emphasize process have less-quantifiable outcomes, take longer to accomplish, and require a much more intensive donor involvement.

UNHCR in Sri Lanka has a major focus in facilitating the repatriation of approximately fifty thousand refugees who have returned to Sri Lanka since the beginning of 1992.

> [U]ntil recently little effort has been made to develop a systematic approach to reintegration. UNHCR assistance in voluntary repatriation programs focused on individual returnees rather than on the communities to which they returned. However, it has become clear that there exists a serious gap between this individual reintegration assistance and development programs aimed to develop the region to which people return. This gap not only threatens the successful reintegration of returnees, but also jeopardizes the viability of their communities. Thus the initial response should bridge the gap between individual reintegration assistance and development needs.[11]

By UNHCR's own analysis, this situation is far from satisfactory in the long term. UNHCR's strategy has evolved into a three-pronged intervention that, unfortunately, has been seen as sequential, not concurrent. Thus, the first intervention provides immediate assistance for those in reception and transit facilities on their arrival from India. The second takes the form of presettlement assistance allocated on a family basis for those who wish to move out. The third encompasses community-oriented microproject assistance in returnee villages.[12]

Coordination of humanitarian efforts in Sri Lanka has been hampered by overt and covert political interference, as documented by Koenraad van Brabant and others.

> Most documented experiences of the coordination of humanitarian action relates to situations in which government is weakened, collapsed or not in control of significant parts of its territory. Sri Lanka provides an example of a government that has exerted its sovereignty and simultaneously pursues political, military and humanitarian objectives. Throughout the period in question, humanitarian agencies not only needed to coordinate for program effectiveness, but also to advocate for humanitarian space and access. . . .
>
> [There are] a number of constraints to effective coordination, including the absence of professional and methodological knowledge, the usual institutional resistance to coordination and contextual constraints, such as outbreak of war. However, the single most important obstacle remained the absence of an effective institutional

link between the humanitarian efforts of the government and those of specialized agencies.[13]

Institutional Strengthening

The Sri Lankan civil war is unique to the extent that the general formulas said to be applicable to emergency and postemergency humanitarian intervention do not seem to apply.[14] The commitment to strengthening local capacity in the war areas of the Northeast Province is both difficult and dangerous. Neither the state military nor the separatist guerillas will allow an independent network of local communities to flourish in the areas under their control. This situation has remained virtually unchanged since the beginning of the armed conflict in the mid-1980s. Successive regimes have presented different public images of this issue. However, the ground realities have changed little, though the political rhetoric has progressed from overtly racist and majoritarian to conciliatory and rights-oriented.

The exigencies of war militate against many of the capacity building strategies available in a postconflict situation at the organizational and sectoral level. International humanitarian agencies and large foreign donor organizations, however, still retain sufficient bargaining power with both protagonists to ensure that emergency assistance could become a means of facilitating some capacity building in Sri Lanka. But the means and mechanisms of this process require creative conceptualization, which unfortunately these agencies appear unable to provide.

Humanitarian agencies working in Sri Lanka's war zone tend to work with three categories of communities: those in established refugee camps; those living in partially destroyed homes and ravaged villages; and those fleeing the mortars—either in temporary abodes or forced into a nomadic situation. Mid- to long-term associations are built up between these agencies and the communities in the first two categories. Those in the worst condition, who belong to the third category, find their way either to camps or back to their home areas, and in any case they, too, come to occupy an identifiable territory, even if more transitorily than the others.

Displacement to the camps can vary in duration and distance. Some Muslims in the camps in Puttalam have lived there for more than a decade, with little hope of returning to homes that in many cases are a hundred miles away. Others are constrained to live in camps in the Wanni, only a few miles from their villages. In this context, capacity building would involve the strengthening of these communities—which most often remain segregated by ethnicity—so that they could deal with their predicament in the short and long terms. This means that the exclusive focus on enhancing their capacities to deal with short-term or immediate needs, such as food and medicines, would be inadequate, even counterproductive, however efficiently it is achieved. They would still remain dependent on the continuing supply of these resources.

What is needed is an integrated approach that addresses refugees' long-term needs and concerns. This approach should not stop at their access to goods and services, but include the articulation of their political and social rights, gender sensitization,[15] and the realization of their economic potential. In this sense, capacity building would encompass full participation for refugees in the wider society they inhabit.[16] Unfortunately, in Sri Lanka, humanitarian assistance has been, by and large, uncoupled from any of these longer-term concerns, and it has been left to the specialist development agencies to tackle capacity building outside the delivery of essential supplies and services.

The ongoing war has, in this sense, served also as an alibi to block attention to the larger causal and other issues in the lives of the internally displaced. Some of the concerns and obstacles to capacity building strategies in Sri Lanka's conflict area are detailed below.

- It is difficult to obtain approval on a continuing basis from either the government or the LTTE for programs that seek to organize local communities through open nonhierarchical groups that are willing to take the risk of questioning entrenched authority. From the LTTE point of view, only organizations and communities that subject themselves to its total control and who operate within its dictates are acceptable. While this tight rein has proved effective in some instances to expose, curtail, and even prevent individual corruption, it also annihilates independent thinking and democratic values. The state military, too, encourages only groups that help extend its authority and assist it in the war. Thus, both these groups use civilians as human shields, bargaining chips, and sources of unpaid labor and information. This predicament confounds aid agencies, which are continually negotiating the middle ground between emergency relief and development in the conflict areas. It appears that by 2000 the eastern areas, which were relatively free of direct pressure, were becoming arenas in which both protagonists jealously guarded their hegemony. As a result, some agencies face the difficult choice of continuing to work in a situation in which they have to remain accountable to the whims of local military and/or LTTE leaders, which often involves open corruption, or whether they will pull out and go elsewhere.

- Access on a regular basis is difficult due to ongoing offensives, land mines, and other military obstacles, and the absence of infrastructural and other resources. Many areas in the war zones become inaccessible, and the populations living in these areas continually face displacement and dislocation. Focal areas such as schools, community centers, and places of worship are unavailable or unsafe. In an increasing number of regions, this lack of even basic infrastructure, combined with drastically restricted access, has resulted in the inability to implement even the simplest capacity building agenda. Moreover, these are often the areas of greatest need, and the result is the perpetuation of abject dependency and apathy.

• Even in relatively structured environments such as refugee camps, community organizations are looked upon with suspicion by the combatants. Individuals who take leadership roles in such organizations are at risk unless direct lines of patronage are maintained, and unless purely logistical and managerial functions are undertaken. It is crucial that the combatants controlling an area perceive no threat. The LTTE has allegedly dealt summarily with community leaders whom it has accused of spying for or working with the Sri Lankan military. Similarly, prominent leaders in "uncleared" areas are viewed with suspicion by the government as LTTE sympathizers and front men. This demonstrates the risks inherent in empowering individuals within the community, because they become targets when they are perceived as a threat. This has had serious repercussions because of the community's unwillingness to take on responsibility and the agencies' reluctance to place members of the community at risk. Moreover, the individuals concerned are subjected to intense pressure that seeks to influence and control decision making at the community level. On the positive side, however, there are a few exceptional instances when an entire community has risen in support of its representatives and has been able to force the military or LTTE to back down.

• The widespread corruption in the allocation and accounting of emergency supplies, generally but not exclusively at the local level, creates powerful disincentives to capacity building of any kind at the recipient end, since this would inevitably lead to exposure and reduction of such corruption. Mismanagement, waste, and incompetence at any point in the organizational chain, from expatriate chief executive to local assistant, also militate against the ability of recipient communities to question these inadequacies in the delivery of humanitarian assistance. The discussion of theoretical concerns below bears out this thesis. That systems of accountability remain focused on inputs and deliverables rather than on impact points to the inability of humanitarian agencies to make the shift to complete transparency and openness.

The foregoing four reasons are widely understood. The following two remain undocumented. Attempts to strengthen local capacity may appear to obstruct the efficient delivery of emergency relief supplies, and certainly this is true in the difficult early stages. Hence the higher management levels of the international NGO or aid agency often see only the short-term disadvantages in capacity building. In the interest of efficient delivery and accounting, initial experiments with the local resource persons are deemed failures, and more qualified, better-trained outsiders are put in place in the name of providing the best systems of support at the moment of greatest need. Documentation, accounting, and reporting systems, which are invariably imported from First World contexts, are seldom modified or made appropriate to the exigencies of the local situations.

The failure of imported accounting and reporting systems in a given community is a failure precisely of these systems and not of the community's ability to use them. Sri Lanka is singularly plagued by the inability of its donor community to understand this simple truth, and to work toward creating user-friendly systems, compatible with conditions and skills available within the communities themselves. Reinventing these systems can also be a powerful exercise in capacity building if the communities themselves are involved in the dynamics of this process.

Without exception, however, the systems of recording, reporting, and monitoring are already in place, even before the communities or the assistance programs have been identified. The point is that capacity building at the organizational level and more so at the sectoral and the institutional levels is not a linear, incremental development. In fact, the initial period may record slower progress and greater inefficiency in the more conventional yardsticks than hands-on, donor-centered, nonparticipatory relief work that is oblivious to enhancing local capacity.

- The use (and abuse) of expatriate staff in Sri Lanka, usually more prevalent in an emergency than in a development setting, works against capacity building at the community level, since the expatriates seldom, if ever, acquire fluency in the language and culture in order to function as effective conduits of structural change. The typical scenario in Sri Lanka is of both headquarters and regional expatriates who require translators and intermediaries in order to function in the field. Intermediaries are not specialists in devolving responsibility and strengthening local capacities, nor is it in their best interest to do so. The hierarchies created by the very visible presence of nonlocal expatriates, given Sri Lanka's cultural deference to foreigners, is counterproductive to this end, though it may have useful side effects in providing a measure of security and status to the programs. In addition, the context of the ongoing war, taken together with the modalities of conflict employed by the rebels and the response by the military, has led to a further problem that militates against the generation of local capacity and the potential for leadership.

- The use of suicide bombers and the earmarking of economic and civilian targets by the LTTE have led to increased suspicion of Sri Lankan Tamils working in the war zone. Meaningful change in local capacity can derive only from increases in responsibility and control of humanitarian programs within the communities themselves. Yet the employment of locals in positions of authority brings danger for the credibility of the project itself. This situation creates a dilemma for international relief agencies, and more than one organization has suffered huge losses to its credibility and, indeed, to its ability to function at all as a direct result of local staff being caught assisting the guerrillas with supplies or information. The suspicion and tension are so great that the leaders of these local organizations do not desire positions of visibility and status because this may spark animosity from the defense forces. Moreover, state and guerrilla interference in every aspect of the relief activity is debilitating to the nurture of local leadership.

In November 1995, a meeting planned by the NGO Forum, an umbrella group of international agencies working in Sri Lanka's war zone, was forcibly disrupted, and many prominent journalists were assaulted, allegedly with the concurrence of a faction within the government. The campaign against foreign-funded NGOs has gained momentum in recent years, with Sinhala extremists alleging that the NGOs are secret supporters of terrorism. In March 1998, the government suddenly brought back a bill it had shelved two years previously curtailing the activities of NGOs; it passed through parliament during an opposition boycott.

The controversial new law comes as an amendment to the Voluntary Social Service Act, and it provides the minister in charge with wide powers to investigate, monitor, and control local NGOs. Although these provisions do not cover international agencies based in Sri Lanka, in the same month Peace Brigades International was forced to close its offices in the country due to Defense Ministry demands that its situation reports be submitted for "editing" before circulation, and that the names and addresses of all clients and contacts be provided. This climate of interference does not bode well for relief programs with capacity building components, and many agencies see a low-key minimalist approach as the easiest way to survive.

A recent work by Jonathan Goodhand and Nick Lewer suggests that NGOs "have only a limited impact on the local dynamics of conflict, and [the situation] point[s] to a need for NGOs to understand in more depth the complex historical and social aspects of protracted and violent conflict."[17] Notwithstanding the problem of intention, this posits a minimalist role for Sri Lankan NGOs. Goodhand and Lewer's methodology remains unspecified, and the claim itself cannot be supported by the minuscule survey they have conducted. But the minimal impact of NGOs on local communities, for whom they have provided humanitarian assistance continuously for well over a decade, is indeed food for thought.

Humanitarian Assistance: A Means without an End?

In the context of civil war and internal displacement, the strengthening of local capacity can take many forms and variations. It is important to analyze this variety and range in order to assess the contribution such assistance makes to long-term empowerment.

Levels of participation and the building of capacity can be identified along the following scale, in ascending order:

- *Top-down approach:* Humanitarian assistance that is planned, delivered, and distributed with no input from the communities involved, and with no feedback afterward. Assessment, evaluation, record keeping, and accountability are functions of the humanitarian agency, which may employ local people to perform some of these tasks. The language of the field agency in its reporting, accounting, and evaluation functions is English.

- *Directed decentralization approach:* Planning and delivery of emergency rations and so on are head-office and regional-office functions, though distribution is implemented through a local committee, which is a combination of elected representatives and appointed members. Full-time employees from among the community are still selected by and accountable to the agency. The community "leaders" who monopolize the allocation and distribution remain in position year after year.

- *Directed devolutionary approach:* Although overall allocations are determined at the head office, international humanitarian agencies work through local organizations formed through the groundwork of the agency's regional or local representatives. Constitutions are drawn up on the basis of a provided model; regular meetings are held and office bearers selected, but the agency's representatives remain in "advisory" capacities. This process enables the community, through the veneer of participation, to arrive at decisions most acceptable to the agency.

- *Limited-participation approach:* The agency's representatives in the field work with community organizations that they have helped establish to prepare project proposals and needs lists (according to a predetermined format designed for international uniformity) that will be suitably modified and amended at the head office in Colombo. At this level, capacity building will take the form of skills training in maintaining accounts and registers, project writing, basic management, and employment training. It is important to note, however, that the managerial and accounting skills are geared toward the systems adopted by the agencies concerned, not as part of a process to design appropriate reporting and documentation for the individual community.

- *Participation approach:* Emergency humanitarian assistance is coupled with awareness programs that focus on access to rights and services, and that are fundamentally participatory in nature. However, program design, implementation, and targeting remain agency functions, broadly speaking. Community organizations tend to represent elites within these underprivileged groups. Therefore, the identification of needs does not percolate down to the poorest people, who tend to be marginalized from the activities sponsored by the external agencies.

- *Full-partnership approach:* The rare context in which transparency and accountability cut both ways, and in which the community organizations are genuine partners with the international agencies. Essential to this relationship is long-term, stable funding, community-friendly reporting and documentation systems, and programs that are not limited to skills training but that also involve raising awareness regarding access to rights and services. The language of interaction is the mother tongue of the community, and full-time employees should be equally accountable to both program partners. Programming should be a collaborative effort with top-down processes eliminated. The relationship between the partners should be seen as mutually beneficial; hence, the terminology *humanitarian,* which implies charity and a patronizing attitude, is subjected to scrutiny. In this perspective the common condition of displacement does not lead to a homogenizing of diverse peoples, but differences are respected in programming.[18]

International humanitarian aid agencies in Sri Lanka tend to operate within the first four categories. Humanitarian agencies that also are development-oriented (such as Oxfam) may demonstrate some of the characteristics of category five. However, in general,

The staffing profiles of international relief and development agencies operating in the Wanni reveal a predominance of upper caste Jaffna Tamils among the local managers and senior program staff. Staff from the Wanni region itself and from other social groups are under-represented in these positions. Difficulties arising from this situation have been noted by both aid agency staff and displaced or resident communities. The issues of hierarchy inherent among the communities of displaced are similarly reflected within the agency-constituency relationship.[19]

Sri Lankan Issues in Theoretical Perspective

Debates within humanitarian assistance appear to have set up a false dichotomy between neutrality/impartiality and the empowerment of local communities. This false dichotomy can be laid bare through an analysis of the Sri Lankan context. The slippage can be seen clearly in the following citation from Joanna Macrae, one of the most influential and prolific scholars in the field:

> Should health and food interventions strive to be neutral in their relation to conflict, or should they rather aim to influence its course? Equally, should the aim be to prioritize rapid and impartial delivery of effective services, or rather to contribute to long-term capacity building? It [the paper] concludes that while relief should be delivered in a manner which is politically *informed* it should not be politically *driven*. In other words, it argues that the core principles of humanitarian action—neutrality and *impartiality*—should be safeguarded.[20]

The building of local capacities is posited as a wholly long-term activity as opposed to the rapid and impartial delivery of effective services, as if these objectives are mutually incompatible. Implicit to the juxtaposition of questions raised by Macrae is that capacity building *is* somehow a politically driven activity.

However, Macrae herself uses terminology proposed by Duffield[21]—"complex *political* emergency"—in order to underscore the "deliberateness of disaster creation, and the political obstacles to mitigating conflict-induced disasters.... As such, war-related humanitarian crises are symptomatic of strategies of warfare which seek to inflict not simply a military defeat, but to disempower the opposition, to deny it an identity and to undermine its ability to maintain political and economic integrity."[22]

This would surely imply that all humanitarian assistance in such a context is a political act, and, moreover, one that should run counter to hegemonic power relations within the area in question. Macrae herself highlights this issue powerfully, pointing out that

> Humanitarian interventions frequently run counter to the logic of war. For belligerents, undermining the capacity of opposition military and political actors to sustain and protect populations under

their control is critical. Conversely, capturing relief can serve an important function for warring parties, enhancing their own political legitimacy and their military capacity. Thus, while international actors may seek to portray their interventions as essentially neutral in intent, in other words designed only to respond to suffering of civilians, for warring parties, relief is anything but neutral.[23]

The dilemma of humanitarian assistance, at least as it is practiced in Sri Lanka, lies here. The donor agencies and international humanitarian actors do not see themselves as taking sides in the war, much less as siding with the dispossessed against both warring protagonists. Hence, their "neutrality" is purchased at the expense of forfeiting an engagement with the broader political issues that the war engenders. This translates on the ground to a strict adherence to logistical and narrowly humanitarian issues—admittedly crucial in a time of terrible suffering—which leaves no room for the more overtly political concerns that affect the lives of the displaced communities with whom actors work.

This version of humanitarian assistance does not run counter to the logic of war. On the contrary, in this case humanitarian assistance minimizes the cost of war—helps pick up the pieces or clear the battlefield—and it serves as an essential component of the grammar in which the logic of war is embedded. Humanitarian assistance can be said to help the LTTE as they help themselves to a good proportion of the supplies; it assists the government's image locally and internationally by easing civilian suffering. True, humanitarian agencies advocate against atrocities and campaign unwaveringly to ensure basic food supplies, but they do not take sides against the war itself. The Sri Lankan example would indicate that Macrae is making too much of the radical potential of humanitarian assistance per se, unless and until it is explicitly linked to a wider agenda.

Yet if the protracted Sri Lankan conflict demonstrates the need for "an approach which conceptualizes humanitarian work as part of a development continuum with postconflict intervention," this "major approach of the 1990s" has itself become "widely recognized to be ineffective as a model for dealing with complex humanitarian emergencies."[24]

Macrae also identifies a common failing among international relief agencies that focus primarily on the delivery of supplies as opposed to impact on affected communities. That agencies in Sri Lanka follow the dominant pattern identified by Macrae, Duffield, and others in equating logistical performance with community impact may also be strategic. It is reported informally and confidentially that more than one-third of all emergency supplies goes to the LTTE, but this is not put on paper anywhere for fear that the government will use it as an alibi to curtail hard-fought "concessions" further. Moreover, the risks involved in the compilation of such data in the field cannot be underestimated. The government uses the fact that the LTTE is skimming off the top to justify its bureaucratic delays and foot-dragging on emergency supplies. The idea is that fewer supplies would suffice, because the LTTE is taking some. The argument goes: "Why should we (the government) be feeding the LTTE?" Caught in the middle of the question, ordinary people suffer from what is perceived as their collusion with the LTTE to defraud the government.

The preoccupation with "pragmatic and palliative approaches to ongoing complex humanitarian emergencies"[25] is nowhere more clear than in the Sri Lankan context, where, after a decade of work, little substantive change can be seen on the ground.

Sri Lanka is also an arena in which the minimalist ("do no harm") perception of humanitarian assistance requires further investigation.[26] That most IDPs and the local communities that are assisted come from minority ethnic groups has fostered an antipathy in Sri Lanka toward even purist humanitarian organizations such as the International Committee of the Red Cross (ICRC). Even the government has on occasion criticized the alleged partisanship of this agency, which is the most visible in rebel-controlled areas. UNHCR and, surprisingly, even Médecins sans Frontières (MSF) have maintained a lower profile and are consequentially less controversial among chauvinist Sinhalese critics. Yet in 1999 the role played by the ICRC in establishing the crucial Civilian Safety Zone (CSZ) is a remarkable achievement by any standard.

> Although technically the ICRC was playing the "postman" (it has now been revealed that the LTTE and the military had exchanged 16 letters through the ICRC during the period June 26 to August 4 [1999]), a column in one of the weekly papers quoted an ICRC field-worker as saying that considerable "imagination" was used to "persuade" both sides on the need for compromise in view of the deteriorating humanitarian situation.... The singularity of purpose with which it approached the supply-route deadlock in the Wanni is a classic case study of the possibilities and problems relating to the methodology of work of humanitarian organizations in conflict situations.[27]

The relationship between humanitarian assistance in the northeast war zone and the strengthening of the institutional capacity of affected communities remains tenuous at best in Sri Lanka. The complexities of the ongoing conflict have provided both the rationale and an excuse for the rejection of a fundamentally participatory relationship between the donor agencies and the people with whom they work. In place of a mutually beneficial partnership, the relationship tends to degenerate into a more superficial and mechanical system, by which accountability and transparency, where they exist, operate only at the grassroots. This allows humanitarian assistance to cease as a threat to the socioeconomic pathologies; these pathologies have created the terrible conditions that required humanitarian interventions in the first place. Humanitarian assistance, in this sense, is not a means to end human suffering by addressing its causes as well as its effects, but a means that has no end in both senses of the term. It is endless in time, and it has no end or goal for itself.

Notes

1. Such an account can only amount to an impressionistic sketch and should not be relied upon as either exhaustive or nuanced. For an analytical commentary on the ethnic conflict on the ground, readers are directed to the work of the Jaffna-based University Teachers for Human Rights (UTHR), notably R. Hoole et al., *The Broken Palmyrah: The Tamil Crisis in Sri Lanka—An Inside Account* (California: Sri Lanka Studies Institute, 1989), and the special reports published by UTHR over the last decade. There is a vast body of material on the subject.

2. At the same time, the dangers of overgeneralizing and homogenizing differences, described by Sunil Bastian as part of working in conflict areas ("Development NGOs and Ethnic Conflicts," in *Culture and Politics of Identity in Sri Lanka* [Colombo: ICES, 1998]), have been kept in mind throughout. In fact, the entire debate on complex political emergencies requires precisely this kind of differentiation and nuance.

3. The Liberation Tigers of Tamil Eelam (LTTE), led by Velupillai Prabhakaran, has been, since the 1990s, the sole surviving separatist group waging war against the Sri Lankan state. See Hoole et al., *Broken Palmyrah*, and University Teachers for Human Rights (J) Reports 1–22 for a critical account of the philosophy and modus operandi of the LTTE, both in its relationship to other militant groups and to the Tamil people it claims to represent. Typical of the sycophancy and partisanship that the LTTE appears to generate among some prominent expatriate Tamils, on the other hand, are Nadesan Satyendra's writings.

4. Amnesty International, *AI Index*, ASA 37/04/96 of February 13, 1996.

5. Commissioner General of Essential Services, Government of Sri Lanka, Colombo, *Report of Issue of Dry Rations*, June 1999.

6. These data are derived from Arjuna Parakrama, "Global Lessons from the Margin: The Real Cost of War and the Price of Just Peace as Seen through Sri Lanka's Ethnic Conflict" (work in progress), and build on United Nations High Commissioner for Refugees (UNHCR) and U.S. Committee for Refugees estimates. The Ministry of Rehabilitation and Reconstruction in Sri Lanka estimated in 1995 that internal displacement stood at 1,017,181.

7. Darini Rajasingham-Senanayake, "The Dangers of Devolution: The Hidden Economies of Armed Conflict," in *Creating Peace in Sri Lanka: Civil War and Reconciliation*, ed. Robert I. Rotberg (Washington, D.C.: Brookings Institution Press, 1999), 62.

8. Rajasingham-Senanayake, "Dangers of Devolution."

9. Rajasingham-Senanayake writes about Puttalam (and Vavuniya), "Humanitarian aid appears to have generated its own economy of dependence among the poorer refugees who remain in camps six and more years after they arrive" ("Dangers of Devolution," 63). That these refugees live in the camps for more than six years is a function of the fact that their homes remain in the war zone. The issue of permanent relocation is a vexing one that cannot be laid at the door of humanitarian agencies. However, the apathy and dependency created by humanitarian assistance in the form of handouts needs to be acknowledged.

10. The reader's attention is directed in particular to the pioneering work by Professor Daya Somasunderam, *Scarred Minds: The Psychological Impact of War on Sri Lankan Tamils* (New Delhi: Sage, 1998), for its account of both individual and collective trauma suffered by these victims of the war.

11. United Nations High Commissioner for Refugees, *A Primer on Micro-projects in Sri Lanka: A Formula for Consolidating Durable Solutions* (Colombo: United Nations High Commissioner for Refugees, 1993).

12. UNHCR, *Primer on Micro-projects in Sri Lanka.*

13. Koenraad van Brabant, *The Coordination of Humanitarian Action: The Case of Sri Lanka*, Network Paper 23, Relief and Rehabilitation Network, which details the situation during the Eelam War III between 1994 and 1996. No significant changes have taken place to improve matters since then.

14. There are, of course, parallels with the post-Rwandan assessment of relief aid in general, such as those contained in G. M. Sorbo et al., *Norwegian Assistance to Countries in Conflict* (Oslo: Royal Ministry of Foreign Affairs, 1998); and in "Linking Relief to Development, United Nations Development Program Rwanda (1998)," cited in *Humanitarian Assistance: Breaking the Waves of Complex Political Emergencies: A Literature Survey*, ed. Joakim Gundel, Center for Development Research Working Paper (Copenhagen: Center for Development Research, 1999), 40.

15. The strengthening of women's roles in society through enhanced responsibility and participation in decision making, albeit at the level of the delivery of essential goods and services, is a notable general achievement of humanitarian intervention in Sri Lanka. See subsequent sections for a discussion of this phenomenon.

16. That this agenda is neither platitudinous nor overly unrealistic is borne out by the fact that some communities in the east have been able to achieve, albeit at great cost, tangible victories even over military oppression. These victories have been achieved in situations of overt injustice, through collective action and intercommunity solidarity. There is vast anecdotal evidence of such examples of empowerment, but no systematic documentation that I am aware of. This is a fruitful area for further inquiry.

17. Jonathan Goodhand and Nick Lewer, "Sri Lanka: NGOs and Peace-Building in Complex Political Emergencies," *Third World Quarterly* 20, no. 1 (1999): 69–87.

18. The negative effects of such homogenization in Sri Lankan humanitarian intervention has been persuasively argued in Simon Harris, *Homogenising Humanitarian Assistance to IDP Communities (A Cautionary Note from Sri Lanka).*

He shows that, in some refugee camps in the north, the "community" is not merely diverse and disparate, but it is also one in which the members do not see themselves as an integral part of the whole.

19. Harris, *Homogenising Humanitarian Assistance*, 3.

20. Joanna Macrae, "Purity or Political Engagement? Issues in Food and Health Security Interventions in Complex Political Emergencies," *Journal of Humanitarian Assistance* (March 1998).

21. M. Duffield, "Complex Emergencies and the Crisis of Developmentalism," *IDS Bulletin 25*, no. 4 (1994): 37–45.

22. D. Summerfield, "The Psycho-Social Effects of Conflict in the Third World," *Development in Practice* 1, no. 3 (1991): 159–73, cited in Macrae, "Purity or Political Engagement?" 3.

23. Macrae, "Purity or Political Engagement?" 4–5.

24. Rajasingham-Senanayake, "Dangers of Devolution,"65; Gundel, *Humanitarian Assistance*, 40.

25. Gundel, *Humanitarian Assistance*.

26. See Bente Hybertsen, Astri Suhrke, and Gro Tjore, *Humanitarian Assistance and Conflict: A State-of-the-Art Report* (Bergen, Norway: Chr. Michelsen Institute, 1998), for an account of the four main positions vis-à-vis the nature and extent of humanitarian intervention in complex political emergencies.

27. Kethesh Loganathan in *Peace Monitor I*, Centre for Policy Alternatives, Colombo, 1999.

Chapter 6

Women's Organizations in Guatemalan Refugee and Returnee Populations

MIKE LEFFERT

They returned with a very highly developed consciousness regarding their rights. . . . But regarding their development, this is more or less a vacuum. . . . [T]hey have had an experience of dependency rather than one of self-management. —Padre Beto Ghiglia

This chapter is based on an investigation into relationships created and capacities generated during the fourteen-year period in which forty-five thousand Guatemalans took refuge in camps in Mexico. The study focuses on international support for women's organizations in the refugee camps and the awareness of gender-related issues that Guatemalan men and women acquired while there.

The Guatemalan refugees—mostly indigenous, mostly campesinos (meaning laborers or farmers)—were forced to flee their country in the early 1980s because of military counterinsurgency programs, which, by the army's own count, led to the destruction of 440 rural communities. Following the election of a civilian government in 1986, negotiations began between the leftist insurgent forces on the one hand and the government and army on the other to end a conflict that had begun in 1961. On December 29, 1996, nearly eleven years and four government administrations after the start of negotiations, a final peace accord was signed.

The refugees' stay in Mexico constituted a prolonged and complex "emergency" that required direct, extensive, and continuous international assistance to sustain the refugee population. This lengthy period in refugee camps was characterized by dependence on material assistance and tremendous uncertainty regarding the expected length of stay. It resulted in the reconfiguration of traditional social relations, affecting individuals, families, and whole communities.

The Guatemalan refugee camps in Mexico became, for many, a hotbed of learning. Conditions at many of the camps bore little resemblance to everyday life, and for some people—especially women—this was not altogether a negative thing. For women, there was some relief from the routines that had consumed every waking moment of their arduous previous lives. Some work the women had previously done was now taken over by donor institutions, and many women took advantage of the time to organize, meet, discuss, and learn. What they learned could not necessarily have been predicted from what was taught.

To begin to understand the extent of these changes in the lives of the Guatemalan refugees, one must first consider the situation that had brought them to Mexico and the evolution of the rules and conditions under which they lived, returned, and live today.

The psychological impact of a war on a population cannot be underestimated. In this case, everyone was drawn into the conflict, their agendas set by one side or another. That meant that decisions and strategies were driven by considerations that could not be stated—in other words, by hidden agendas. For instance, for many if not most international players, the state was the enemy. But when the refugees returned, they would have to work with the state. Some refugees understood that, but many international nongovernmental organizations did not. For many NGOs, development meant creating infrastructure, but providing infrastructure also meant augmenting the state's capacity to oppress the people.

By way of background, the indigenous population of Guatemala began suffering incursions of outsiders with the Spanish conquest in the sixteenth century. Under Spanish rule, these linguistically and ethnically diverse groups were enslaved and robbed of their religion and lands. Independence from Spain in 1821 only worsened their situation. The independent country became even more oppressive than before, as the ruling class of New World–born Spaniards, *criollos,* became free from what little constraint the crown had imposed on descendents of the Mayans. By the mid-twentieth century, 3 percent of the population owned 70 percent of the arable land in this agricultural nation.

The single historical hope for redress came in 1944, when a civilian government took over from a beleaguered dictator to begin a period of democratic change. The change, however, which included land reform, proved to be more than the *criollo* oligarchy, the church, and, most important, the United States–owned United Fruit Company could tolerate. United States policy toward the region was now energized by anticommunism and the Cold War. That, together with Secretary of State John Foster Dulles's family interests in the United Fruit Company, prompted a Central Intelligence Agency–led coup in 1954 that toppled the socially conscious Arbenz presidency, returning the country to military government. By the late 1960s, a Marxist guerrilla movement had formed. While the movement was small, the government murdered about ten thousand peasants in quashing it.[1]

Nevertheless, armed opposition persisted. The guerrillas began organizing indigenous peasants in the highlands, and by 1978, when General Lucas Garcia assumed the presidency, they had become a credible threat to the status quo. By 1983 the army had adopted a scorched-earth policy to extinguish the insurgency. In the highlands, the military massacred thousands of peasants and razed more than four hundred villages. Elsewhere throughout the country, nonindigenous leaders, students, professors, and priests were killed by military and paramilitary groups. An entire generation of dissident leadership was killed.

A final accounting of the terror would show that two hundred thousand had died or disappeared; just short of a million and a half people had been forced from their homes and lands. Guatemalan refugees, mostly indigenous, were scattered from Honduras to Canada, and everywhere in between, including Guatemala itself, where thousands who would not or could not cross borders found themselves hiding in forests, always on the run from the pursuing army. These would come to be known as the Communities of Populations in Resistance (CPR). Because the refugees were for the most part indigenous, it follows that the river of fleeing people had as its source the northern and northwestern part of the country, the highland departments of Huehuetenango and Quiche, the steaming Alta Verapaz, and the vast Péten.

The experience of women's organizations from the establishment of the refugee camps in southern Mexico to the present is the focus of this chapter. It examines the complex interactions of foreign and national institutions, the genesis of ideas about gender equality, and the influences of economics, ideology, and politics in the larger sphere in which a historically fractured culture was further sundered. Since the refugee population living in Mexico returned to Guatemala in the mid- and late 1990s, there has been a notable dispersion of women's organizations along with a widely documented decline in efforts at organizing women in the returnee population, and a regression to traditional gender roles.

The findings of this chapter bring to light three central conditions that bear directly on the possibilities of building long-lasting capacities in complex emergencies:

- International cooperation, and the values that this transfer of resources carries with it, occurs today in a world in which the globalization of ideas is taking place at a rate that far exceeds the globalization of material conditions;

- This transfer of ideology, which takes place in a world dominated by market relations, often fails because "suppliers" of the ideas have failed to study the material and historic roots of their own ideology.

In this context, ideas become a transferable but subsidized commodity, with complex emergencies functioning as opportunities for promotion or "marketing" around a "universalized" yet imported agenda;

* Emergencies, by definition, mark a break with noncritical periods of a population's history, often accompanied by shifts in environment, production, community ties, and relations with outside actors. The exceptional nature of these shifts creates severe limitations on efforts at long-lasting changes in a population. In fact, the social relations created by new dependencies during the prolonged emergency often disguise underlying realities and give false readings on the perceptiveness of people and on the sustainability of new ideas.[2]

Social Organizing during the Emergency

Refugees flooding into Mexico soon found themselves in a world quite different from the one they had left. Mexico welcomed them sympathetically for the most part, and there they found relief not only from the terror of pursuit, but also from hunger and sickness. The Mexican government, with funding from the UNHCR, set up a refugee commission. COMAR—the acronym in Spanish for Mexican Commission for Aid to the Refugees—began establishing temporary camps. By the end of 1981, 2,000 refugees were registered; a year later there were 30,000; and by the time the return began in 1993, there were about 45,000. The number of unregistered Guatemalans in Mexico has been estimated at around three times this number.

Women and their children held a special place in the scorched-earth policy with which the government had attempted to halt the insurgency. Women were targeted for rape, torture, and murder, because, as one woman put it, paraphrasing a pronouncement of General Efraín Ríos Montt, "our bellies only produce guerrillas." With this as incentive, the motivation to leave was extreme. Recounting their history, members of Mamá Maquín, the women's organization that emerged in the camps, date the first flights to Mexico at 1980, with the first of these coming from Petén, the northernmost, largest, and most isolated of Guatemala's departments.

The trickle of exiles became a flood around 1982, when mostly indigenous people from Ixcán and Huehuetenango joined the exodus. The indigenous included Kanjobal, Mam, Chuj, and Jacalteca, as well as Spanish-speaking nonindigenous people, a point worth noting since each of these ethnic groups speaks different languages. Among the indigenous women especially, few spoke Spanish.

Some of the women who arrived at the camps were not strangers to the idea of organization. With the help of the Catholic Church's liberation theology, many rural Guatemalans—especially in the Ixcán region—already had the experience of meeting and learning together. In a rudimentary attempt at development, women gathered to learn dressmaking, baking, catechism, and family planning, and they were exposed to techniques of social-consciousness raising. An organization of midwives also developed.

Not until the end of the 1980s did the Mexican government allow international NGOs into the camps. The NGOs had no opportunity to plan for the long term. Most women did not read or write. There was little probability of instilling anything in the way of technical capacity. For most of the time in the camps, there was nothing that could even remotely be thought of as capacitation or training. Mobilization for return was the one issue overshadowing all others. Even before the 1992 agreements that provided for an organized return, people had started going back.

In May of 1990, forty-seven women from refugee camps convened in Palenque, in Chiapas, to talk about the discrimination they were experiencing as women, as indigenous, and as poor people. They talked about their marginalization and lack of voice within the camps and their exclusion from participation in decisions that affected them. Their isolation was palpable; not even visiting journalists thought to talk to them. It was there in Palenque that they decided to form an organization to deal with these problems, and they named the organization Mamá Maquín, after Adelina Caal Maquín, a woman killed in the Panzos massacre in 1978 for daring to claim her right to land. Their original objectives, translating from their own words, were:

- to defend the right we women have to organize and educate ourselves and to participate equally with the men;
- to struggle for the defense and rescue of our indigenous culture;
- to defend the right that our voice as women refugees be heard in all those aspects that might be in the interests of women, and of refugees;
- to defend our right as women to express our will in the return;
- to recognize all activities that support organizations of refugees and those in solidarity with Guatemalans.[3]

The organization grew quickly. By August 1993, Mamá Maquín reported a membership of more than seven thousand women in the camps. According to its figures, 84 percent were indigenous, of whom 57 percent were Kanjobal, 10 percent Mam, 10 percent Chuj, and 7 percent Jacalteca. Sixteen percent spoke only Spanish. Of these, 81 percent of the Chuj could neither read nor write, nor could 74 percent of the Kanjobal, nor 67 percent of the Mam. Most had never been to school. Even among the Ladina and Jacalteca, who often came from urban areas, 42 percent were illiterate.[4]

International Support for Women's Organizing

There can be little argument that without outside support, there was not much chance that rapid growth in Mamá Maquín could have taken place. The refugee women's circumstances coincided closely with a UNHCR institutional commitment to gender rights. Significantly, one Mamá Maquín national leader interviewed for this study credits UNHCR workers with introducing her to the concept of rights. The agency also took the initiative to coordinate the work of individual NGOs with the aim of making the women's organizations flourish.

The linchpin of the effort was education, with literacy and language of primary importance. Spanish would become the lingua franca in the camps and in meetings, since there were many monolingual speakers among the different ethnic groups. The strategy was, according to UNHCR documents, to promote literacy by channeling the activities through Mamá Maquín, to train a literacy team and female promoters from the refugee population to teach the women in their camps, and to link literacy education to awareness-raising on women's roles, conditions, and rights.

This was a three-phase program. During the first year, a needs assessment was undertaken by refugee women; women's literacy groups were formed in the camps; and NGO support was secured. The second phase lasted two years, during which teachers were trained for literacy education; schoolbooks were produced based on the first-phase experience; and Mamá Maquín became the administrating and contracting agency for the program. During the final phase, of one year's duration, there was an evaluation of the results. That evaluation indicated the following effects, taken verbatim from the report:[5]

- women's self-esteem increased due to greater awareness of their rights;

- full literacy in Spanish of a small group of women was achieved and several hundred were making headway in the literacy process;

- by the time of the evaluation, more than half the literacy teachers had returned to Guatemala, which provided an opportunity for continuity, subject to the availability of support for these activities;

- the women's organization had grown in numbers, presenting other women with an alternative they previously did not have;

- the women in mixed groups advanced more slowly than the men in these groups, and many abandoned their classes;

- the women's organization acquired the technical capacity to negotiate with NGOs regarding terms for the consultancy and the administration of the project.

A report commissioned by UNHCR[6] noted that the strategy of integrating literacy education with "reflection on everyday experiences and basic rights provided women with a powerful source for self-esteem and motivation. It permitted them to learn Spanish while simultaneously learning to read and write." It also concluded that literacy "proved to be the one road initially most open to the participation of women since it was of little threat to men." Another important finding was that child care is essential to the process, discouraging dropouts and the distractions of having children in the class. The evaluation also confirmed that having men in the classes "was neither appropriate nor successful."

Shoring up the educational effort was a project on time-saving and domestic work, designed to free up women's time by providing corn-grinding mills for the women's organizations to manage, and gas stoves, which had the added benefit of reducing smoke contamination and deforestation. A rise in the price of gas eventually scuttled the stove idea, and the corn mills served as time-savers only when the women had money to pay for the service. Another problem was that the mill management tended to fall into the control of men, because women lacked technical skills related to the operation of the mills.

Literacy education with ancillary projects was not the only way UNHCR carried rights education forward. Together with participating NGOs, the agency's protection and program teams trained women in awareness and defense of their rights as women, as refugees, as indigenous people, and as a social class. Along with this emphasis, a pilot committee of men and women refugees was formed in one camp to provide victim support. The overall project included workshops on women's human rights and rights training for women leaders that covered domestic and sexual violence, reproductive rights, rights to land, and other issues. This, in turn, was supported by publicity campaigns that took advantage of a women's radio-broadcasting project. Finally, the program arranged for public denouncement of aggressors.

Negotiating the Return

A key part of the civilian government's efforts to win credibility with the international community following the genocidal counterinsurgency and repression was the creation of conditions for the return of the

Guatemalan refugees. Their voluntary and organized return would be an important sign of progress in demilitarizing the countryside and restoring the rule of law. The principal documents defining the terms of this return were the accords signed on October 8, 1992, which became known simply as the October 8 Accords. The accords set forth the right of the refugees to a collective and organized return, individually and voluntarily expressed. They reaffirmed the human and constitutional rights to life; personal integrity; free association, organization, and movement; personal-identity documentation; and the civil and pacific character of the return and returnees.

These accords, the outcome of more than a year of negotiation by the government, permanent commissions, and international advisers, formed the legal basis and guidelines for the return. The first point of the document sets the tone: "The return of the refugees must be a voluntary decision, expressed individually, brought about in a collective and organized manner, in conditions of security and dignity." In brief, the accords guaranteed the rights of freedom of movement, freedom to associate and to organize, the right to life and personal as well as community integrity, and the right to be accompanied by national and international organizations in all phases of the return. The introduction affirms that all provisions pertain to female as well as male returnees, and that any agreement outside the accords to which the government was party, and that is more favorable than the accords themselves, supersedes the accords.

The October 8 Accords were by no means the last word in the return negotiations. In 1992 an agreement was reached on the Regulation for the Concession of Credit to Return Groups Larger Than Fifty Families, which established a revolving credit system for cooperatives.

A general definition of the cooperatives is that the property is held cooperatively, but individual co-ops then decided whether everything would be held in common, or whether individual families would receive land assigned to them, which they then could use for their own purposes. Various sharing arrangements could include all land held in common, shared and marketed by the whole community; all land held in common, with families allowed to use individual fields at their discretion; no land held in common, but produce marketed cooperatively. Under the revolving credit system, a loan was to be arranged for the co-op, but repayment of the loan would go into the operation of the co-op and would become the working capital of the group.

On the revolving credit system, the accords stated: "The reimbursement of credit will be made to the associations or entities that the returnees form, with the object of establishing a revolving fund that can become a permanent and social source of investment to the benefit of the return communities and those of neighboring populations."

There is general agreement that the work of the Mediating Body (IM, for its initials in Spanish), and of the International Group of Consultation and Aid to the Return (GRICAR), was crucial to the overall return and its success. In July 1998, IM/GRICAR sponsored a workshop seminar to document the experience of the accords. Attending were forty-six people representing nearly all of the organizations that participated at any level in the return. Additional information was compiled from a questionnaire distributed to these organization representatives and others involved.

The forum was no mere exercise in self-congratulation. Perhaps the most crucial contribution of the invited outsiders—that is, the international consultative group—was the establishment of a culture of dialogue and negotiation. If such a culture ever existed in the history of Guatemala, it had certainly atrophied over the previous thirty years of warfare and strife. Even within sectors, there was serious division. The government put on a show of unity, but it soon became apparent that the government was not the army; that the army was used to being in control; and that the army still regarded the returnees as subversive, as a potentially belligerent force of politicized, organized people whose return was to be tightly controlled, if not entirely discouraged. It largely fell to the outsiders to provide a negotiating forum in the midst of this, and they did.

In the end, it can now be said that everybody who wanted to did return to Guatemala. The process stumbled and fell here and there, and one of the stumbling places was the participation of women. Were they used and later cast aside in the return operation?

IM/GRICAR, in discussing lessons learned in the process, asserts that "the participation of the women is indispensable." Indeed, as will be detailed elsewhere, women were mobilized in the nuts and bolts of the return, and they had important influence on the process. Nevertheless, despite protestations of indispensability, IM/GRICAR qualifies its affirmation of women by stating:

> While reaffirmation of the basic rights of women at the level of certain of the accords signed was achieved (in the preamble of the accords...and in relation with the right to land on equal terms with the men in the Regulation for the Concession of Financial Resources of 1996), in practice these basic rights were ignored in many cases if the women were not disposed to struggle for them specifically, or if they didn't have the necessary backing to make themselves heard. It is necessary, therefore, to point out that the participation of the women did not achieve all that it should have, nor did it satisfy the expectations generated among these same women.

Women's Role in the Return

UNHCR's direct action on rights extended beyond domestic and sexual violence to land rights. UNHCR Guatemala consultant Paula Worby stresses that "demanding direct access to co-own land was an outgrowth of women's learning and organizing to affirm their rights in general, and would not have gone forward without the existence of organizations of refugee women."[7] Women's inclusion in ownership of the lands they would soon be calling home was clearly one of the destinations on the long road outlined above, but they were not alone in seeking this gain.

Worby also emphasizes that male leaders not only permitted, but promoted, women's organizing in what she calls "a moment of political opportunism." She notes that women's demands to return home, to land, and to restraints on the army made for good press, and impressed international organizations and embassies. Further, for those male leaders linked to the insurgency, for whom the return had major strategic repercussions, manipulation of the women in facilitating the return was also opportune.

Men's self-serving manipulation of the women's activism was soon laid bare: a rollback in the women's march to equality was in the offing. An early indication of what was to come followed the first step over the border into Guatemala. Women took that step with the expectation of signing the legal document listing beneficiaries, but they found that only men and widowed women were listed. And when a community formed the cooperative to which the land title was to be transferred, women with partners were excluded.

Mention must be made of what Guatemalan law had to say about the possible consequences of this exclusion. At first blush, the Guatemalan Constitution asserts women's equal rights, but the law, which famously veers from the constitution at its leisure, is equivocal. Worby demonstrates contradictions in the family code, in which, for instance, Article 79 states "matrimony is founded on the basis of equal rights and obligations of both spouses," while Article 109 takes away the meat of it by giving household representation to the husband and giving equal authority and considerations only "within the home."

In practice, debate about the law is somewhat hypothetical since, apart from the gamble of going before judges accustomed to following the money rather than the law, most indigenous couples are joined according to traditions recognized by their communities, rather than the law. With the signing of the peace accords in December 1996 came some hope of an amelioration of this dilemma, since several sections of the agreement explicitly obligate the government to eliminate any legal or de facto discrimination against women in their access to land, housing, or credit. There is, however, no time frame attached to these otherwise laudable sentiments, so in practice they have no force until the government says they do.

With this initial disappointment came, for some, an early indication that there is nothing absolute about having a right. Without a means of exercising the right, it is little more than an attractive concept. And there can be negative consequences of exercising a right, even in the absence of opposition. In communities in which women were included in land titles, they were shocked to find that the cost of registering their title was more than the cost of a one-name title, already expensive. To this day, many have been unable to come up with the fees. Where money *is* found, in the form of a donor contribution, communities can be split between those who get the money and those who don't. But even those who do raise the legal fees are not finished. There are still the cooperatives.

Most of the returning people were organized into cooperatives, both for historic reasons and also because of the revolving-credit aspects of the funding arrangement. It is the cooperative that receives an individual family's payment of the original loan, and this is the working capital of the co-op. In order to exercise a "right" to land ownership in practical terms, one must have the "right" to get access to it and to work it. That right comes with membership in the cooperative. Again there is a fee. A woman must be a member in her own right to be eligible to enjoy the fruits of her proprietorship, another hurdle that many women have been unable to surmount.

The accumulated experiences of empowerment and organization in the camps were severely tested following the return and settlement into the new communities. Some writers have attributed women's waning influence to a desire to return to normalcy after the camp experience, but this ignores the fact that the camp experience lasted for fourteen years. Many returnees had never known a way of life that would evoke nostalgia for the pre-refugee-camp days.

A less speculative view would take as a point of departure the observation that negotiators for the return had manipulated women from the beginning. Their need for high-profile, self-actualizing, participating women would now be subordinated to the demands of the return itself. Absent the vigilance of the internationals, more traditional models of governance would resume. In Ixcán in 1997, in the community of Nuevo Pueblo, in the department of Quiché, men denounced organized women for having positions closely aligned with the guerrillas, and this denouncement came despite the fact that the final peace had been signed months before. The Unidad Revolucionaria Nacional Guatemalteca (URNG) was now a legal political party, no longer a guerrilla force. This same male leadership then declared that any meeting it did not specifically approve would henceforth be illegal.

There is no question that women's interests and the organizations they created to promote them have suffered severe reversals in Guatemala. The women's efforts could have been regarded as very successful if the purpose had been simply to return to Guatemala and settle in new homes. In fact, that viewpoint has some currency among workers in the field. The problem is that the women themselves had expectations of carrying on with the learning they had begun in Mexico, regardless of how anyone chooses to frame their objectives.

Carolina Cabarrus has been studying this issue as an NGO consultant. She has concluded that regardless of the time in the camps spent on learning, the women had lived in an environment of massive moral support for their goals, and in which they had learned to *receive*—that is, to meet their needs by just asking. They learned to think in terms of "projects," and they were schooled in the mechanisms of proposals, solicitations, assessing needs, and so on. In effect, says this longtime observer, herself an avowed feminist and a Guatemalan, "they learned to function like NGOs."[8] The shift from an environment in which largesse is given to one in which one must work for everything one gets is enough, in this worker's view, to account for much of the fallback.

This way of looking at things has found agreement among those concerned about the situation. Santa María Tzejá is a community that has been extensively studied and discussed in Guatemalan development literature. It has uniqueness as a return community because those who returned to Santa María had actually come from there; they were coming back to their former homes, unlike most returnees who found themselves in new places. Not everybody from Santa María Tzejá left, and there was a reuniting of those who stayed and those who had left.

Clark Taylor wrote a book about Santa María Tzejá, *Return of Guatemala's Refugees: Reweaving the Torn.*[9] Clark visited the town twice yearly after 1987 for a total, at the time of publication in 1998, of twenty-one visits. Besides giving a detailed picture of the community, Taylor introduces local thinkers who bring an interesting perspective to the subject. Padre Beto Ghiglia is parish priest in Cantabal, the urban center of the Ixcán, and has long experience with the returnees. He has a rigorous view of "development" and divides the subject into three categories, roughly summarized as

- that which emanates from the community itself, along the lines of Paulo Freire, a Brazilian community development revolutionary. In this category, people are subjects, participants in, and authors of their developmental plans. The URNG and the Communities of Populations in Resistance are Ghiglia's examples of organizations developing primarily around this concept;
- that which is offered by NGOs—more about building things and offering services. It is a kind of intermediate development. Exam-

ples include provision of latrines, potable water, efficient stoves, and "projects that benefit women";

- that which is linked to the global economy. Examples are large-scale electrification, roads, and water projects. In the Ixcán, these are linked to international oil drillers, hardwood companies, and the army. They need these developments for their own interests and share them with others at a price. In these examples, the price includes extracting community cooperation over environmental damage, access to co-op lands, and similar considerations.

Ghiglia considers the first sphere the most difficult to promote with donor agencies. In his world, this would have meant beginning with studies to sort out problems regarding the reintegration of returnees with those who stayed along with problems relating to demobilized guerrillas. The work would have identified the kind of development the people themselves desired. But funding agencies need to promote something that produces quicker results. Taylor offers a critique very much in line with the discussion up to this point:

Clearly the culture of learning they experienced in Mexico failed to offer an understanding of the pitfalls of development. In all the conversations I had with returnees in Santa Maria, regarding the culture of learning in Mexico, none referred to courses or workshops on issues related to development. Everyone described learning about human rights and the training they received for various trades and skills. No one mentioned development. When asked about it specifically, two men in separate interviews said there was no anticipation of the issues of development. One of them remembered one workshop on quick-impact projects[10] they would have available to them, but that was all. The other man remembered only that they were told that they would have to work hard. No workshops were offered in how to sort out development priorities or in how to plan for the development of their own communities.

Now that the former refugees were back in Guatemala, the contrast between their treatment of human rights and development issues was striking. Leading individuals were named to serve as human rights promoters, to educate their community about this very important aspect of their lives. But there was no equivalent interest in naming "development promoters." No such term appears in their vocabulary.[11]

This critique juxtaposes the concept of human rights with that of development. Development encompasses human rights only in the first category of Ghiglia's schema, which is development that emanates from the community itself. Otherwise human rights and development can be seen as separate. In the camps, there was a coincidence of interests between the women refugees and UNHCR, whose agenda centered on women's inclusion as a matter of rights (empowerment vis-à-vis men). But it was not necessarily in the interest of the agency, given its emergency and refugee-related responsibilities and its contractual relationship with NGOs to encourage a questioning of development. The NGOs were under time-limited, "must-spend-it" budgetary constraints, and they frequently knew what they were going to do before they began. In Ghiglia's second category, the issue is not whether the projects are necessary but how extensively agencies are engaged with the people's visions, plans, initiatives, and desire for full participation. With this as the criterion, most of this development objectifies the population.

Additionally, there were the development agendas of the military (infrastructure, roads, bridges), and of international private enterprise with oil and timber interests. In other words, women were trained to strive for participation, but not to analyze what it was that they were to participate in. It is important to take note of another of Ghiglia's observations, regarding the work of Paulo Freire. Oppressed people often appropriate an oppressor's way of life as an ideal. This dynamic operated not only among the refugees themselves but even among dedicated UNHCR personnel. The interests of the dominant classes remained, albeit hidden under a different rubric.

Ghiglia sums it up this way: "They returned with a very highly developed consciousness regarding their rights, regarding their position against the army, for example. But regarding their integral development, this is more or less a vacuum.... [T]hey have had an experience of dependency rather than one of self-management. We see that as a limitation."[12]

In a July 1999 interview in Santa María Tzejá,[13] Florencia, leader of the women's organization, presented a picture of the women's situation that reflects the previous discussion. The returning women shared their learning experiences with those who had remained, and many of the latter eagerly joined the organization. For Florencia, getting her name on a land title was not an issue. The property to which she and her family returned had been left to her by her father. Nor was it an issue for most of the returnees to this community, since they were returning to their former homes. Most women there belong to the organization and try to meet weekly. Their major concern at the time was a corn mill.

The community was divided into two sectors, and each had a motor-driven corn mill. A mill of this kind means that women do not have to grind corn with a primitive stone implement, a process that consumes hours each day. But the mill in Florencia's sector was broken. Many women walked about fifteen minutes carrying the corn to the second mill. Both mills charged less than a U.S. penny per pound for the service.

The amount was based on the ability to pay rather than on actual costs of operation. As a result there was no money to fix the broken mill. They did not know how much it would cost, but they thought it would be in excess of a thousand quetzals, about $130 at the time. They had received the mill through the Canadian agency Centre canadien d'étude et de la coopération internationale (CECI), in cooperation with UNHCR. Asked to list in order of importance the priorities of the women's organization, the first three related to getting the mill fixed. The conversation went like this:

Q. What would be first priority?

A. The mill.

Q. Second?

A. The motor.

Q. Third?

A. Fixing the motor.

Next on the list was a set of pots. They had been given improved stoves, but traditional cooking vessels did not fit on them. The fifth concern was for a chicken project. Florencia said that the women's group was looking into asking agencies to get these things.

The interview fits with Ghiglia's analysis and Taylor's critique, at least insofar as it is clear that the women's organization was functioning more as an NGO than as an advocacy group. It fits with a comment made by another interviewee, Carolina Cabarrus, a consultant with Project Counseling Services, who was in the midst of compiling a survey of women's issues among returnees. "There was no time to reflect. They went straight from the camps to the new situation without time for consolidation, for what they learned to become part of them. In time, they will forget."[14] There is at least one other way of thinking about the conversation with Florencia: she was also saying that she and her neighbors had basic infrastructural and economic needs that preceded more abstract ideological activities, and until those infrastructure needs were met ideas would have to wait. Meanwhile, they would pursue the filling of those needs in the way they had learned in the camps.

Learning to function like NGOs in the camps, together with other inferentially learned habits in an atmosphere of scarcity, has other consequences. In another return community visited in researching this chapter, a major women's organization suffered from an organizational style learned and encouraged in the camps: NGO competition. This had become a source of divisiveness within the community.

Nueva Libertad is a community of returnees near Fray Bartolomé de las Casas. Unlike Santa María, this cooperative is representative of those described earlier. The land was purchased and the revolving-credit arrangement utilized. Among women's organizations, it had the advantage that three of the founding members of Mamá Maquín returned there. It was also the first of the co-ops in which women became members in their own right. Around 1997, some women began to express discontent about the structure of Mamá Maquín, which had grown nationally as an organization. It had obtained legal standing, loosely the equivalent of a nonprofit institution. It had local chapters throughout the return areas and a central office in Guatemala City.

For many of the women of Nueva Libertad, this was a disadvantage. They expressed discomfort with what they saw as a large bureaucracy with the potential to interfere with their autonomy. Moreover, the women of this community wanted to work with women of surrounding communities who were not returnees, and Mamá Maquín had a policy of working only with returnees. For these reasons they decided to form another group. Two of the three original leaders sided with the dissenters, and one remained with Mamá Maquín. The membership clustered around one or the other pole, but many women exercised their right to join both. The new entity was named Adelina Caal after the same woman for whom Mamá Maquín was named.

They drew the attention of some resident-volunteer accompaniers from the Basque country, and they received funding from their parent organization. The Basques had witnessed the downside of bureaucracy and costly mediation, and were philosophically aligned with the splinter group. Their assistance came at a cost, however. Most of the women in Nueva Libertad were struggling to find money for cooperative membership. So much so, in fact, that some sold some of their property to get the money. The Basques gave money for this purpose to Adelina Caal, creating severe divisions within the cooperative. This was a paradox. In the words of a Mamá Maquín national leader, "I can't deny the influence of outsiders in creating the awareness of the right to land."[15] But there could be no denying the influence of outsiders in the division of a community.

The exercise of a woman's right to have her name on land titles has its genesis along two axes. One is ideological and political; women's self-esteem is elevated by ownership. The other is political and economic. Women are protected against economic loss as a consequence of the dissolution of their marriage or partnership. But gains along these axes are reciprocal with their corresponding losses. That is, if self-esteem is enhanced by ownership, it can be, and in this case was, reduced by the lack of it. By the same token, if women are protected against loss as a consequence of ownership, they suffer opportunity loss through the reduction in the value of lands that, because they are parceled out in smaller plots, are no longer available for more productive use, such as grazing of cattle. In the absence of a judicial system that enforces the advantages of property ownership for women, only the losses are evident. In most of the cooperatives, conversion to individual ownership has indeed weakened cooperativism, to the point that most are now dysfunctional, leaving behind a structure through which the state can continue to exercise control through the credit agreements, and through which authoritarianism rather than cooperation flourishes. Co-op leaders have power, but no economically useful way of exercising it.

Xamán is another community in which the cooperative no longer functions. It had worked for a time as a marketing co-op, but that fell into disuse, according to informants, because of a widespread belief that co-op officials were misrepresenting prices received for the agricultural products of parcel holders. There was no requirement that these leaders present documentation of transactions. They just left with the produce, and they paid off the campesinos when they got back, with nothing more than their word for an accounting.

The community has a Mamá Maquín chapter. The women have been involved in efforts to reduce family violence, and they have been successful in getting alcohol sales—which they identified as being a major cause of the problem—prohibited in the small stores, although there is still a thriving bootleg market. The women have made no progress on issues of ownership or participation. Only men are co-op members. Although women want land registered in their names, they have not been able to raise the money to do this. In this case, exercising their rights would mean separate payments for surveying the parcels, joining the co-op, and registering the land in both spouses' names. The local Mamá Maquín leader is hoping that the national office can get the money. According to that office, there have been no developments along these lines.

Mamá Maquín is hampered in its organizing efforts by lack of money. The organization would like to attend educational and assembly activities at Fray Bartolomé de las Casas, but it has no money even for transportation. A bus to take them there and back would cost about 600 quetzals (U.S.$77). They list their priorities as follows:

1. A child-care facility.
2. A motorized corn mill.
3. A clothes-washing facility.
4. Potable water.
5. Travel money for women's educational and organizational purposes.
6. Help with marketing of crafts.

This list is similar to that of other communities. It makes the most concrete kind of sense. Without satisfying their labor and personal timesaving needs, they do not see any hope of reaching goals of self-improvement, or of redressing gender imbalances. Consistent with the acquisition paradigm learned in the camps, returnees expect to gain these benefits through donation rather than by an integrated production strategy. But the installation of infrastructure does not guarantee these benefits. A mill saves time, but if it breaks and there is no money to fix it, the mill becomes a net consumer of time and energy, or it falls into the more capable hands of men, whereby imbalances of power are exacerbated.

The final place of note among cooperatives is Primavera. This is not a return community, but a community of CPRs. The Communities of Populations in Resistance are people who were internally displaced during roughly the same time that others were in the camps. That they did not have the camp experience, but did experience the same antecedent events, might qualify them as a control group for identifying behavior among returnees attributable to the camps. While no rigorous scientific assumption is made here, there are notable differences between the two populations.

One of the structural differences is that, among the returnees, the trend is for co-ops to be cooperatives in name only, or at best to function as marketing cooperatives while allowing the land to go private. Among the CPRs, however, the land truly is held cooperatively. The CPRs themselves, as well as most writers on the subject, attribute the survival of the cooperative concept to the profound interdependence and enforced trust relationships formed during the years of living together in the forests, on the run from the pursuing army. While returnees were learning to receive, these populations were learning to organize for survival. They have had to call on their survival instincts and skills even in relation to the returnees.

When the political climate seemed to permit it, the CPRs—many of whom had been members of the Ixcán co-ops—openly settled on co-op lands. They were subsequently caught in a political cross fire, however, when the permanent commissions, in an attempt to extend their mandate, challenged their right to remain. The CPRs, rather than allow themselves to be dispersed, chose to leave. The Catholic NGO Caritas financed the purchase of a farm for them, which is now known as Primavera. In general, the financing arrangement is similar to that of the returnees, in that members make land payments into a revolving fund.

The women's organization is called, appropriately, the Organization of Women in Resistance. The absence of problems related to private property rights does not mean that they have no rights problems, but such questions are confined to questions of the right to participate as citizens within the cooperative structure. The women distinguish rights and power. They have the right to participate but lack the power to do so, attributing this imbalance to resistance among the men. Resistance is a word *they* use to describe the dynamic, the word inextricably woven into their community self-concept.

There is a significant difference among the CPR women in the way they characterize the goals and priorities of their organizations. Despite having less infrastructure than returnees' communities, cooperative productive enterprises appear more frequently, and at higher priority, than basic needs. The list of their priorities reads:

1. Funding for meetings and start-up projects.

2. A means of buying yarn for weaving.

3. Family planning.

4. Training in methods of developing the community.

5. A chicken farm.

While this list might not seem fundamentally different than those of the returnees, this list is economically oriented, rather than "rights" oriented. The women have the same problems as the returnees, but they see solutions embedded in a production strategy. There is a different order to their thinking, compared to the returnees. They are saying that power is economic rather than legal, and they do not view the exercise of their rights to be based on outside institutions. They are as much in need as the returnees, if not more so.

They do not have improved stoves; in fact, they have no stoves. They make fires on dirt-covered platforms, putting up with the traditional smoke and wasting wood, a waste that translates into accelerated deforestation and additional time spent gathering wood. They have wells but lack fuel for the engines, so when diesel is in short supply it is used for boat motors and mills, and the women must walk half an hour to haul water. Such priorities discriminate against women, but the discrimination tends to be economic. The underlying question for CPR women is, "How might we get these things for ourselves?" This outlook was implicit in the interviews, and it is explicit in the fourth item on the list, training in methods of developing the community.

The CPR women do not seem particularly moved by a rights orientation, but they are not strangers to it. As early as 1994, while the CPR women were still in their original community in Victoria, rights trainers, themselves newly trained, were visiting the CPRs with a you-have-a-right-to-your-opinion message. This writer was there, along with a photographer, and remembers it like this: The women were asked to gather in an area used for meetings. There were no men around. The speaker, Juana Ramírez, a twenty-three-year-old NGO worker, began a talk, the essence of which was, "You have a right to your opinion. You have a right to express yourselves." Juana went on in this vein for about half an hour in the heat of the day, while her audience stood or sat in bored silence. Juana called for comments from the women. Not a word. She waited a really long time, maybe half an hour, until a buzz started among the women. They were saying sotto voce to each other, "What about the pigs?" The buzz got louder, and one woman addressed Juana: "You promised us pigs, what about the pigs?"

Discussion with the participants revealed that the women had understood that they were to be given a pig project. That, together with a marked tendency toward politeness, was why they were sitting there in the heat. Their take on rights was that the men worked in the field and they worked in the compound, and that was how things were. If they had some pigs to take care of, that would improve nutrition all around. They never got the pigs. Whether they got their rights or not depends on how one looks at it, but by 1999 they were interested in neither pigs nor rights. They seemed able to stand on their own feet and to look after themselves within the community and way of life they had chosen.

Juana was trained to give pretty much the same presentation wherever she went, without regard to the history of the specific community. Common elements of the presentation were boredom and trainers pressing for responses that never came. There is even a film taken in the camps, in which an instructor guided women through an exercise in which she asked them to bend over as if burdened by a weight on their backs, and then to name their oppressors. The women named the army, soldiers, colonels, the government, and the rich, but they did not seem able to spit out the answer: "men."

This reluctance on the part of women to identify men as the culprit in their struggle suggests that the women were capable of a more comprehensive political analysis of their circumstances than their instructors. They were able to see men in the act of grabbing power and of refusing to share it with women. But they repeatedly insisted on an organizational approach to overcoming the problem, rather than letting the situation degenerate into a male-bashing paradigm for which the cure would be to depend on the state to pass laws to protect them. Whether they see through to the faulty psychology of passing from one "daddy" to another or simply distrust a state that has only oppressed them is a matter for another inquiry. But the evidence points to a conclusion that more thought ought to have been given to a rights-based ideology to overcome the oppression of women.

This "more thought" might have begun with the planners themselves, and with a recognition of the vast social gap that exists between them and the population for whom they plan. Those differences are in play even when the planners are themselves Guatemalan. Ana Grace Cabrera is in charge of UNHCR's women's issues, and she offers her personal history as an illustration. She grew up in the southeastern part of Guatemala, where there are very few indigenous people. "I grew up not knowing a thing about the indigenous, much less did I have interest. I didn't know about the reality of the war until the return."[16] She goes on to explain that what she knows about feminism she learned at UNHCR. She acknowledges that she knows more about these women's rights than she does about their history.

Guatemala is the most socially stratified country in Central America; it is a living colonial museum. One Guatemalan cannot be asked about another without first asking about race, class, and geography. These divisions are also fault lines in understanding identity issues. If the question "who are we?" had been asked, and the answer was "not them," then it is important to find out who "they" are. And that would not be a simple matter of asking. The refugee women had already learned that humanitarian relief agencies functioned on a project basis—one year's funding at a time, within predetermined guidelines. Give the wrong answer and someone else gets a project that, regardless of its long-term relevance, will in the short run ameliorate today's poverty. Fierce competition among groups in the camps was an important element of unintended inferential learning.

Conclusion

Women as a class are probably the most vulnerable members of Guatemalan society. If something bad is looming, it will likely hurt women first—like frogs in nature. Women have been hurt after repatriation by expectations encouraged in the refugee camps. Their social and political evolution has regressed, in part because of the methods they learned to employ. Specifically, they learned to further their interests as a matter of "right" where there is no institutional or cultural means of establishing rights, and to expect that their material needs could be satisfied by donations from outside sources.

A person cannot step into the same river twice, or so the old saying goes. In returning from Mexico largely ill-equipped to deal with new opportunities, refugee women were, in effect, stepping back into the same river. The political realities, the hidden alliances and agendas of the major actors during the time of refuge, make it difficult, if not impossible, to suggest what ought to have been done. There is some likelihood that over time the inefficient strategies that the women adopted will fall away from lack of reinforcement, and that they will be replaced by more effective strategies.

The organizations and/or the communities may well have found themselves in similar circumstances today without the foreign intervention. Cooperatives may not be the best form of organization; a rights orientation may be the best theoretical basis for women's development. The overarching issue is the way they got here. Had these been their own decisions, had they arrived at them through a process like that described by Padre Beto Ghiglia, the priest from Cantabal, they would at least be in control of the process, conversant with its history, and able to pick it up where they left off, a little wiser.

The women are victims of the Golden Rule. They have been done unto as those who did would have others do unto them. There was no discernible effort on the part of their benefactors to ask, "Who are we doing this for anyway? Is there a difference between them and us? Is this sustainable? Can they say no?" The effectiveness of the efforts that international humanitarian agencies make depends on the relationship between their own agendas and the context in which they are working. Often they consider their values to be universal, failing to look into the historical roots of their own beliefs. This lack of self-criticism, for which guilt is not a substitute, leads to the importation of agendas that do not correspond to the reality on the ground.

In Guatemala, women are only beginning to realize that the ratification of their rights is contingent upon the existence of functioning political and social institutions, and the exercise of rights is contingent upon labor-saving devices, transportation, and help with the kids. Failure to understand this during the period under study led to the erosion of the movement for gender equality among the returnees of Guatemala.

Humanitarian agencies cannot be sued for malpractice. They cannot be made to go back and clean up their messes. There is no ethical structure, no authority structure outside the agency world from which incentives or contingencies might flow that would lead agencies to deal with their mistakes. On the contrary, there are incentives for them to keep doing what they are doing. First, there will always be another and worse emergency coming down the pipeline. There is no time and no money to backtrack. Second, agencies profit from failure. They get to do lessons-learned exercises without ever having to test the assumption that learning occurred. Emergencies will always be sufficiently different one from the other to guarantee more errors than trials.

Apart from the issues of rights and their exercise, and the transfer of donors' cultural values to recipients, there were several ways in which women benefited from these experiences in Guatemala. Foremost, a distinction can be made between organizing and the uses to which the resulting organizations were put. This chapter criticizes the latter, but it must be recognized that the women under discussion did benefit from the development of organizational skills. True, they have moved giant steps backward following the gains they experienced in the camps. But the capacity to speak on their own behalf remains strong. By comparison with women in nonreturnee communities, who did not have the opportunity to learn to stand up for themselves and articulate their views, those with the camp experience are by far the stronger. This, together with the fact that organized returnee women are, in many instances, committed to overcoming gender inequities and to encouraging the participation of nonreturnee women, indicates that this fight is far from over.

There is nothing in this experience that would indicate that in another time and place similar women's organizations should not be encouraged and facilitated. But the experience does say that there needs to be clear separation between helping to create social structures and the uses to which those structures are put. Donor organizations helped refugee women acquire the potential power that comes from collectivity and communication. Now that the need to hide old agendas has passed, these or similar organizations might be in a position to help with the acquisition of skills and planning for development. It has been shown, however, at least in the middle term, that these skills and plans do not come automatically.

Humanitarian agencies need to consider the consequences of infusing their cultural norms into recipient populations. Where that is not workable, a fallback strategy of monitoring the outcomes of strategies must be in place. In Guatemala, both the United Nations and NGOs maintained a presence long after the refugee return, beyond the need to hide loyalties to guerrilla and other factions that had largely ceased to exist. A longer-term agenda was, and remains, possible.

Notes

1. Peiro Gleijeses, *Shattered Hope* (Princeton: Princeton University Press, 1992).

2. For an earlier study by the Humanitarianism and War Project of humanitarian action in Guatemala, see Christina Eguizábal, David Lewis, Larry Minear, Peter Sollis, and Thomas G. Weiss, *Humanitarian Challenges in Central America: Learning the Lessons of Recent Armed Conflicts,* Occasional Paper no. 14 (Providence, R.I.: Watson Institute, 1993). Also available in Spanish as *Desafíos Humanitarios en Centroamérica: Lecciones de los Conflictos Armados Recientes.*

3. Alto Comisionado de Las Naciones Unidas para Los Refugiados (ACNUR), *Mamá Maquín en la lucha por el derecho de la mujer a la propiedad de la tierra y la participación en la Organización Comunitaria: Lecciones Aprendidas en el Trabajo con Mujeres Guatemaltecas Refugiadas y Retornadas* (Guatemala City: ACNUR, 1998).

4. ACNUR, *Mamá Maquín en la lucha.*

5. Itziar Lozano, *Lessons Learned in Work with Refugee Women: A Case Study of Chiapas* (Comitán, Chiapas: United Nations High Commissioner for Refugees, 1996).

6. Lozano, *Lessons Learned in Work with Refugee Women.*

7. Paula Worby, "Organizing for a Change: Guatemalan Women Assert Their Right to Be Co-owners of Land Allocated to Returnee Communities," paper prepared for the Kigali Inter-regional Consultation on Women's Land and Property Rights Conference, February 1998.

8. Interview in Guatemala City, 1999.

9. Clark Taylor, *Return of Guatemala's Refugees: Reweaving the Torn* (Philadelphia: Temple University Press, 1998).

10. Quick-impact projects are small, development-oriented projects funded by UNHCR, aimed at generating work and community services after refugees are resettled, before development agencies arrive on the scene. Typically they include the digging of wells and the construction or rehabilitation of schools and clinics.

11. Taylor, *Return of Guatemala's Refugees.*

12. Ibid.

13. Carried out for this study.

14. Personal communication.

15. Interview with a coordinator at Mamá Maquín headquarters in Guatemala City, 1999.

16. Personal communication.

Chapter 7

Sierra Leone

Peacebuilding in Purgatory

THOMAS MARK TURAY

Capacity building . . . requires outsiders who can listen to voices that have been excluded for centuries from informed participation.
—THE AUTHOR

Editor's Note: In 1996, the fifth year of the country's rebel war, I visited Sierra Leone on behalf of CARE Canada to examine relationships between international humanitarian agencies and local nongovernmental organizations. What I found was not encouraging. Most large, international, name-brand NGOs were there, delivering food, running camps for refugees, and trying to keep alive whatever development programming was possible. Local organizations played a very small part in their efforts. I was told that there was virtually no local capacity. There were tales of theft and corruption, and because the needs were great and urgent, there was no time to rectify the situation. Thus the international NGOs continued doing what they had always done—ministering directly to those in need.

Members of local organizations told a different story. Many of the organizations had been actively involved in the search for peace, and it was an undisputed fact that civil society organizations—women's groups especially—had taken to the streets at the most critical moments of 1996 to demand, successfully, that the country's military regime hold elections and hand power to a civilian government. Sierra Leonean organizations acknowledged their limited capacity for humanitarian assistance, and they acknowledged problems of probity, but they asked why, after five years of war, the international agencies had been unable to build any capacity or to find ways to ensure the honesty that seemed to be so problematic.

This chapter deviates in style from others in the book. Like other chapter authors, Thomas Turay began with a plan for the chapter, one that

157

SUM Incorporated

he took with him to Sierra Leone in November 1998. He intended to complete the chapter within a couple of months while he gathered background material for a doctoral dissertation and conducted peacebuilding workshops on behalf of a Canadian NGO. His plans were changed dramatically by the January 1999 rebel invasion of Freetown. Trapped for several weeks, Turay then stayed longer until he could make contact with his three daughters—the eldest eighteen and twins aged sixteen—trapped behind rebel lines. In order to raise the money needed to bribe rebel fighters at the many checkpoints between Freetown and Makeni, he took short-term capacity building assignments with a variety of Sierra Leonean

NGOs. *The ironies trip over each other: aiming to write about capacity building, Turay became a practitioner. Planning to study international humanitarian agencies, he represented one himself until the invasion occurred, when he suddenly became "a local." Studying war, he became its victim. Desperate to find his daughters, and a witness to murder, his belief in peace was put to tests that nobody should endure.*

Because of the way events unfolded, it was decided that he should scrap the outline he started with, and, instead, tell the story of his year in Sierra Leone in the first person. The fundamental theme of the book—building local capacities in a complex emergency—emerges in some ways much more clearly than it would have if the chapter had been written as originally intended. We believe that the convictions Turay articulates about the difficulties of capacity building amid collapsing structures and communities has special relevance and urgency.

—IAN SMILLIE

Introduction

I understand capacity building as a process through which the people of a given society are motivated to transform their physical, socioeconomic, cultural, political, and spiritual environments for their own well-being and the advancement of their society. Capacity building is about empowering people to take control of their lives. It enables people to rediscover their strengths and limitations, and the opportunities to develop their fullest potential. The process enables people to build self-confidence and self-respect, and to improve the quality of their lives, utilizing their own resources, both human and nonhuman. Capacity building provides opportunities for local organizations to establish networks at both local and international levels. Capacity building is also a process of creating opportunities for people to be creative and imaginative, to dream, and to be able to live their dreams.

Like most African countries, Sierra Leone after independence replicated the growth-oriented development paradigm it inherited from its former colonial master, Britain. This paradigm, which measured only growth, did contribute to some economic development, particularly in the first two decades after independence in 1961. The development honeymoon, however, was short-lived. The events that unfolded in the wake of the rebel war that began in 1991 made the country worse off socioeconomically, politically, culturally, and spiritually than ever before. Rampant corruption, the mismanagement of public funds, a plundering of the country's natural resources by politicians and senior civil servants, and exploitation by external agencies all contributed to this predicament. By 1999, about 90 percent of the rural areas of Sierra Leone did not have access to basic education, safe drinking water, motor roads, basic health facilities, or improved agricultural services. During the colonial and postcolonial periods, politicians and policy makers maintained an urban-centered approach to development. In addition, successive governments ignored the socioeconomic, political, cultural, and spiritual capacities of the rural people. Simply put, rural Sierra Leoneans have for decades remained the economic producers, while urban Sierra Leoneans became the consumers.

After independence in 1961, the country had only two "democratic" elections—in 1967 and 1996. Political pluralism died in 1978, when then-President Siaka Stevens declared a one-party state. In 1980, the country hosted an Organization of African Unity (OAU) summit. Millions of dollars were wasted in the process, and the country never recovered. Despite the intervention of the World Bank and the International Monetary Fund (IMF), the economy continued to fail. Today, in spite of its vast mineral resources and fertile agricultural lands, Sierra Leone is the least-developed country in the world according to the United Nations Development Program (UNDP) Human Development Index, a position it has occupied for several years.

The outbreak of the rebel war in March 1991 added insult to injury. Ostensibly fighting for a return to democracy, the Revolutionary United Front (RUF) waged war on a military government by attacking civilians. Its trademark became the brutal amputation of the hands and feet of the innocent, many of them small children. A return to democratic rule in 1996 actually worsened the war, and the only thing standing between the government and military defeat when I returned to Sierra Leone in November 1998 was a West African peacekeeping force, the Economic Community of West African States Monitoring and Observation Group (ECOMOG).

My Background

I had taught in Sierra Leone for a total of eight years between 1970 and 1985 in elementary and secondary schools. My undergraduate qualifications include a higher teacher's certificate in rural science from the Milton Margai Teachers College, Freetown (1976), and a bachelor of science degree in agricultural education from the University of Sierra Leone (1983). Between 1977 and 1986, I did a lot of work with the United States Peace Corps. During those ten years, I served as language and cross-cultural instructor and cultural coordinator, and it was through this experience that I became interested in community development work. Upon graduation from the university in 1983, I decided to go back to my village, Mapaki, to establish the Mapaki Descendants Farming Association (MADFA). Catholic Relief Services (CRS), Development and Peace (Canada), CEBEMO (Holland), and Bread for the World (Germany) eventually funded MADFA, which later became a model for the country.

By 1985, I thought this was the kind of thing I wanted to do for the rest of my life. At that time the Diocesan Catholic Development Office (also known as Caritas Makeni) needed a lay worker who would be responsible for its agricultural program. I was persuaded by the bishop to give up my role at MADFA and to serve the entire diocese; I became director in 1989. Around then I started to become critical of my own role and the role of the church in development. I felt that we were not reaching out to the people who needed us most. In fact, I kept saying that the people who needed us most didn't even know we existed. As a church, we needed long-term strategic planning, but we didn't have anything like that.

When I raised questions, they said, "Why don't you come up with something?" So I organized some conferences and seminars, involved community-based organizations to get their input, and we developed a three-year strategic plan as a pilot program. Quite a lot of it had to do with training and organizing, because one of the things I had seen was that people did not recognize their own capacities. A group, for example, would write a project proposal for a cassava farm and garri processing, then spend months or years trying to get overseas funding, when it had all the resources it needed. It is important to create awareness in order to help people examine the abilities within themselves, the capacities *they* have, the local resources, skills, and knowledge.

In 1992, I went on leave and received an award from the Points of Light Foundation, a U.S.-government program that took people from around the world to the United States for a month of reflection. While I was there I attended some seminars and conferences on change. I knew that I was trying to change myself but I didn't have the tools or the knowledge. The month in the United States helped. I had been thinking of establishing a peace institute, and when I went back to Sierra Leone, I saw my new role. I didn't call it a peace institute at the time; I called it a development-education center. The idea was to strengthen civil society groups, community groups, and the church. I invited some people I knew and trained eight of them in different aspects of development. I didn't call it peace training and conflict resolution, but I was starting to deal with those issues.

We were registered as an NGO in Makeni and called ourselves the People's Animation Center, now the Center for Development and Peace Education. Our approach from the beginning was simple: I said we are not going to ask anybody to give us money. Sierra Leonean NGOs usually begin when they hear about an NGO elsewhere. They say, "Let's form an NGO." They write a proposal, get funding, and, when the money runs out, they have a problem. I said we would start by *selling* our skills, and I resisted writing a proposal for grants. We began by getting contracts from Sierra Leonean NGOs, and then a U.S.-based foundation gave us a contract to do a needs assessment in three organizations it was funding. Based on our recommendations, the foundation asked us to do training. Then, in 1993, the International Fund for Agriculture and Development (IFAD) revived an integrated agricultural-development project. IFAD needed an NGO for parts of the program, and we won a contract to provide training to two hundred farmers' associations.

Some time later, wanting to upgrade my skills in adult education, I applied for and received a Commonwealth Fellowship that took me to Canada. Not long afterward, the IFAD project ran into trouble. The rebels invaded the north, and because our program had a $24.5 million budget over seven years, it became a target. Everything came to a standstill in 1995.

My Return to Sierra Leone

In 1998, I went back to Sierra Leone with four objectives. The first was to conduct two peacebuilding training-of-trainers workshops and to establish a microproject fund for victims of the war in Bo District. I was to do this on behalf of a Canadian NGO, Partnership Africa Canada (PAC). My second objective was to collect data for my doctoral dissertation, titled "Approaches to Conflict Resolution in Urban Secondary Schools in Sierra Leone: Implications for Building a Culture of Peace." Since I knew that the provinces I had intended to study were now dangerous rebel territories, I decided to concentrate on Freetown, where it was relatively safe at the time. The third objective was to write this chapter, although the intention was to produce something quite different from what has emerged. And my fourth objective was to visit my family. As it turned out, the events that unfolded were very different from my expectations.

The PAC Workshops

The PAC workshops were organized by a Sierra Leonean NGO, the Network Movement for Justice and Development (NMJD). NMJD was established in 1988, with headquarters in Kenema and branch offices in Bo and Freetown. It is one of the very few local organizations specialized in training community-based organizations in various aspects of development. It was also one of the few local NGOs that provided humanitarian assistance to Sierra Leonean refugees in Guinea.

At first, I was nervous about whether what we were going to do was relevant. I thought the Civil Defense Forces (CDF) would resist talking about nonviolent approaches to the conflict, about conciliation. At the time, those words were taboo. You couldn't use the word *mediation* or talk about dialogue, because the government was not prepared to accept that, and people who talked that way were seen either as rebel collaborators or even rebels. We had that kind of difficulty, but the participants were interested in learning new ways of looking at things. I remember coming out of one workshop with people saying they were for the nonviolent option in dealing with the former combatants, because they realized that war was not going to solve the problem and that violence was not helping anybody. It was clear that the participants recognized that no sustainable development process could take place without peace.

There were, of course, certain capacities that were not strengthened. The duration of the workshops was inadequate and most participants had little theoretical background in approaches to conflict resolution and peacebuilding. None had any previous training-of-trainer experience in this area. Against this background, it could be argued that a three-day workshop is too brief to develop a solid conceptual framework on approaches to conflict resolution and peacebuilding, and to transfer the skills necessary for training others. And, to be honest, a few participants attended the workshops mainly in the hope of receiving a project grant afterward.

The January 1999 Invasion of Freetown

I left Bo on December 20, when the rebels invaded Kono District, less than 100 kilometers away. The Council of Churches wanted me to stay for its Christmas party, and my idea was to go home after that to Makeni. Having been there at the beginning of the war, however, I knew how fast and how far the rebels could go, and I felt it wasn't safe to go to Makeni. So I went to Freetown. At around 2 A.M. on January 7, news came that the rebels had invaded earlier that night. I was staying in the west end of the city, and I called my brother, who lived in the east end. He said, "They are right here—they are in front of my door and we can't get out." And then the phone was cut off.

The rebels were driven out by ECOMOG forces after about three weeks, but not before burning the east end of the city, killing at least 6,000 people, and kidnapping about 2,000 children. The first time I went out was on January 28—I went as far as the stadium while the rebels were still at the east end of Freetown. At that time more than 40,000 displaced people were camped in the stadium. I was shocked by what I saw. Most of the international humanitarian agencies had evacuated to Guinea, and the only NGOs providing food—the small amounts that they had—were the Methodist Church and the Council of Churches. There were no expatriates. But the local organizations had only leftovers. There was a lot of food, but it was locked up, and the international NGOs, the

World Food Program (WFP), and others had all gone away with the keys. Eventually they came back, but the situation was far from normal. I was completely cut off from my family, which was behind rebel lines in Makeni. I had no idea how long the situation would last, and I was running out of money. I was angry, frustrated, and disillusioned, but I had to do something, so I started doing what I knew best, working with local NGOs.

I must have had a dozen or more assignments in the months that followed. For example, I cofacilitated three workshops for different local organizations on the training of trainers for disaster mitigation and preparedness. The participants included church and community leaders, leaders of community-based organizations (CBOs), teachers, women, and youth leaders from the organizations' target regions. In July 1999, the director of Caritas Makeni contracted me to conduct a participatory peacebuilding needs assessment in three Sierra Leonean refugee camps in the Forecariah region of Guinea. The contract had two main objectives. First, it aimed to assess the needs of refugees in three camps, and then to assess the capacity of the organization to promote a culture of peace among refugees. Second, I was to train the staff in conducting participatory needs assessments on their own. Third, I was to help develop a peacebuilding project proposal for refugees in the three camps.

I spent about a week in Forecariah working with the field staff. Few of them had even basic training in trauma healing and peacebuilding, although some had very good backgrounds in community animation. The organization had done a lot of sensitization among the refugees; however, it had very limited financial, material, and technical support from international NGOs. This weak institutional base created frustration among the field staff, because they could not make much difference in alleviating the refugees' appalling conditions.

Between April and September 1999, I also assisted three local Christian organizations to develop short- and long-term strategic plans. This was done through workshops and informal sessions. Participants who benefited from these workshops included church leaders, heads of government departments, and program officers. Generally speaking, I observed that most church institutions and organizations depended heavily on external support. They had a very weak financial base, and their capacity to mobilize and generate local financial and material resources had not been fully tapped. It was therefore encouraging to see these three organizations developing long-term plans with an emphasis on sustainability and self-reliance.

Between September and November 1999, I worked with three other organizations on conflict resolution and peacebuilding. All three had highly trained professional adult educators and trainers in various aspects of community development. However, they did not have trainers grounded in the theory and practice of conflict resolution and peace-building. It was against this background that they requested me to train their trainers in this critical area of their work. It was encouraging for me to see at least one of these organizations, the Centre for De-velopment and Peace Education (CD-PEACE), putting into practice the knowledge and techniques it had learned. Later in the year, this organi-zation was contracted by the Family Homes Movement (a local NGO providing humanitarian assistance and vocational training to former child-soldiers) to train its workers on approaches to peace and recon-ciliation. The organization was also invited to participate in a training and reintegration project for Paramount Chiefs, the traditional rulers of the country.

Another job involved facilitating a one-day workshop organized by the National Commission for Democracy and Human Rights (NCDHR). The purpose was to train representatives from civil society groups who were selected by NCDHR to participate as observers in the Lomé peace talks, to take place in June and July. Even though this workshop was short and poorly planned, it enabled participants to explore the mean-ing and principles of interest-based negotiations. World Vision played a very important role in this process by covering the cost of airfare and accommodation for the civil society representatives. Neither the govern-ment nor the UN Observer Mission in Sierra Leone (UNOMSIL) was enthusiastic about encouraging civil society participation at the Lomé peace talks, for fear of resistance against accommodating the rebels in a power-sharing deal.

While the peace talks were going on in Lomé, the United Nations Hu-manitarian Assistance Coordination Unit (HACU), based in Freetown, set up a committee comprised of representatives from various local and international NGOs. The main purpose of this committee was to provide feedback to UNOMSIL and government representatives on the reaction and mood of civil society toward the peace talks. HACU invited me to join this committee because of my background in negotiation and medi-ation. I felt that HACU did a good job bringing together representatives from different backgrounds to brainstorm how the government should deal with issues such as power-sharing with rebels, a cease-fire before the rebels' withdrawal from strategic mining areas, and whether to give the rebels a blanket amnesty.

HACU's initiative provided a forum for local and international NGOs and civil society groups to make informed contributions to the peace process. I saw this information-sharing as an essential ingredient of local capacity building. The unit also gave constant feedback to the com-mittee on how things were going at the Lomé peace talks. There was transparency and accountability, and discussions were held in a frank and democratic manner. There was great respect for diversity in perceptions, understandings, and interpretations of the various elements and approaches to the peace process.[1]

International Humanitarian Organizations

My initial shock when I arrived in Bo after a four-year absence had to do with the proliferation of international NGOs. When I left in 1994, Oxfam was not in Bo, nor were many of the others. Now there was Oxfam, Action International Contre la Faim (AICF), Médecins sans Frontières (MSF), and Africare, to name a few, as well as several church organizations. I saw NGO vehicles everywhere. World Vision had a fleet of vehicles and bikes. It was difficult not to notice them. If you went to the Black and White Restaurant, you could see dozens of vehicles parked outside at lunchtime. The presence of many international NGOs and few local NGOs was in my opinion a sign of weakness in the local capacity building processes that many international organizations claimed to be enhancing.

Time and circumstances do not allow me to go into a detailed and comprehensive assessment of international humanitarian approaches to local organizations. My comments are based on what I saw, heard, and observed before and after the January 6, 1999, rebel invasion of Freetown. Let me start with the local capacity building approaches of some of the organizations that impressed me the most.

The United Nations Children's Fund (UNICEF) was deeply involved in strengthening the capacities of local organizations assisting former child soldiers and other children affected by the war. UNICEF not only provided financial assistance to local NGOs, it supported the training of Sierra Leoneans in child protection, trauma healing, family tracing, and reintegration of former child combatants. The organization financed the production of posters carrying messages of peace and reconciliation, and messages decrying the use of children as soldiers and other forms of child abuse. The relationship among UNICEF and local NGOs, government ministries (especially the Ministry of Health), and other international NGOs was very cordial.

The United Nations Educational, Scientific, and Cultural Organization (UNESCO) also did a lot in local capacity building, supporting the reconstruction of educational institutions. It collaborated with the Sierra Leone chapter of the Forum for African Women Educationalists (FAWE) to develop a training module for education, culture, and peace, with a focus on trauma healing, conflict resolution, the role of women in conflict resolution, and fundamental human rights. World Vision developed a Seeds of Hope program that taught local NGOs and CBOs improved farming techniques such as pot vegetable production. This type of innovation was very timely. The Jesus Healing Ministry, the

Community Animation and Development Organization (CADO), and the International Islamic Religious Organizations (IIRO), which benefited from the Seeds of Hope project, felt that they strengthened their capacities to improve food security in their target areas.

What I also found encouraging was an increased awareness of the need for both international and local NGOs to develop short- and long-term strategic plans for the postwar period. For example, I worked as a resource person with local organizations such as the Council of Churches in Sierra Leone, NMJD, the Baptist Convention of Sierra Leone, the Methodist Church of Sierra Leone, the Young Men's Christian Association (YMCA), and the Christian Extension Services to develop long-term strategic plans for these organizations. Participants in these sessions included senior staff members, church and community leaders, and policy makers. Some international NGOs both inside and outside the country provided financial assistance for this kind of capacity building.

Some international NGOs also provided training for local organizations on various aspects of the Disarmament, Demobilization, and Rehabilitation (DDR) process that emerged from the Lomé Peace Agreement signed early in July. But this program depended heavily on donations from the international community, and the inadequacy of financial and other logistical support contributed to its slow pace. There were times when the ex-combatants would accuse both the local and international humanitarian agencies of mismanaging funds meant for them.

The DDR program however, provided unique opportunities for the local population. Many industrious Sierra Leoneans set up new businesses such as food processing, petty trading, and small construction companies. The program also created opportunities for local organizations and groups to diversify their development interests. For example, a study done by Sierra Leonean organizations revealed that half of the local conflict resolution and peacebuilding organizations had been established between 1991 and 1999. This was encouraging, because Sierra Leoneans need their own capacities to analyze, design, and implement programs to meet the challenges of the war.

While there was collaboration among some local and international NGOs and community-based organizations in capacity building, it was also obvious that there were tensions. I observed a lot of mistrust between the international "food pipeline" agencies and local organizations. The local organizations in my opinion were basically errand boys—their main role being to distribute food and take insults from hungry and angry internally displaced people who frequently accused them of misappropriation. When food supplies dried up, the local NGOs that had been engaged in such food distribution became redundant and became targets for accusations of fraud.

The only international NGO I saw seriously engaged in strengthening the capacity of local organizations in disaster mitigation and preparedness was Christian Aid (UK). But merely training local people is not enough. If, in the midst of an emergency, persons cannot apply their knowledge because they lack the logistical support and resources, the training becomes meaningless. This is what happened during the January 1999 rebel invasion of Freetown. Local NGOs were left on their own to cater for the needs of the thousands of internally displaced persons, and they lacked the capacity to do so. International NGOs with the resources fled when they had wind of the rebel invasion. Most fled to Guinea, and while some made provisions for their local staff, many others abandoned them and closed down their operations.

Between February and September 1999, several newspapers carried articles about local NGOs that had been accused of misappropriating relief food and nonfood items. For example, the *Standard Times* (September 3) carried an article alleging that rice meant for the Civil Defense Forces (CDF) did not get to them. In another article, *The Pool* (September 3) reported that some senior and junior World Food Program workers were accused of siphoning and selling relief food items to market women. In a similar story, the *New Tablet* (September 10) reported that some parliamentarians and Paramount Chiefs had been accused of stealing used clothing sent by the Kono Descendants Union in the United States.

Such reports were common, especially the first few months after the January invasion of Freetown. During this period nobody seemed to trust anybody. For example, when the Relief and Development Department of the Evangelical Fellowship of Sierra Leone (EFSL) reported that 122 million leone (about U.S.$4,700) from the income-generating credit fund had been burned during the invasion, the beneficiaries accused the ESFL of foul play (*New Sierra Leone*, February 15). To curb the incidence of such alleged corruption, some international NGOs simply decided to handle the distribution of relief supplies entirely by themselves.

Internationals were also accused of corruption. In Bo, for example, many Sierra Leoneans I met were baffled by the multitude of international NGOs operating in the Southern Province. Some were believed to be trading in diamonds, while others were accused of supporting the rebels. In the wake of the rebel invasion of Freetown, both the government and ECOMOG accused the International Committee of the Red Cross (ICRC) of providing communication equipment to the rebels. This led to a subsequent expulsion of the ICRC from the country for several months. Whether any of these accusations were true did not really matter. There was a cloud of doubt among many Sierra Leoneans about the intentions of some international NGOs, especially those operating in the diamond regions.

The influx of expatriate staff among the international NGO community was another issue. I had no problem with international NGOs employing expatriates for expertise that Sierra Leoneans could not provide. But I felt uncomfortable when I saw that many qualified Sierra Leoneans who could do some of the jobs much better were being left out. A related issue is the huge salary gap between expatriate and local staff. This issue has been present for many years. I recall my days at Caritas Makeni, when one of our overseas partners assigned a so-called agricultural technical expert to work with me to develop long-term agricultural programs with our target communities. In spite of the fact that I did most of the practical work and was in a real sense the expert, my counterpart was paid three times my salary and a lot of fringe benefits. This kind of situation was still prevalent among some international NGOs during my visit.

Another issue that created a lot of suspicion among the public, the government, and the international humanitarian agencies had to do with transparency and accountability. The government's desire to address this issue was articulated by the Minister of Development and Economic Planning, Dr. Kadie Sesay. According to the *Herald Guardian* (November 22, 1999), Dr. Sesay required all international NGOs to register their budgets and their areas of operation with government. Dr. Sesay also demanded that international NGOs report to her ministry for evaluation, and said that failure to do so would lead to expulsion. One reason for this was the failure of many international NGOs to pay customs duties on imports that were not duty-free (*Herald Guardian*, November 22, 1999).

Both the international humanitarian organizations and local NGOs were ill-prepared to cope with the immense humanitarian problems caused by the January invasion of Freetown. This led to great tensions and mistrust between local and international organizations on the one hand and between the local organizations and the direct beneficiaries on the other. The death of some personnel—both expatriates and local people—and the wanton destruction of some of the offices and property of several NGOs as a result of the rebel war caused much institutional trauma. Some NGOs would never recover from the loss.

Family Matters

I was challenged during some of the peacebuilding workshops I facilitated. Some participants questioned the relevance of the nonviolent approaches to conflict resolution and peacebuilding they had learned during the workshops. They asked me questions like, "How should we deal with these rebels who have done such barbaric things to us?" Others asked, "If it were your daughters whose hands were amputated, would you forgive and reconcile with such killers?" These were tough questions, especially for a father with three young daughters trapped in rebel-held areas.

On the first Saturday in February 1999, I decided to go into town from the west end where I had stayed during the invasion. When I got to Congo Cross there was a long queue at an ECOMOG checkpoint. We all had to pass through with our identity cards, and while I was there they spotted someone who was not well dressed. A woman pointed to this fellow and said he was a rebel, saying, "I saw him at the east end of Freetown, and he burned our house." The ECOMOG soldiers pulled him out of the queue and shot him fifteen times. Then they picked people from the queue to take the corpse to the ocean two hundred yards away. I prayed that they would not pick me. It was the most horrible experience in my life. I lost faith in many things at that moment, and I was quiet for nearly two weeks. But, in a way, it helped me. I later shared it in some of the workshops with others who had similar experiences, and talking about it became part of my own healing.

When the rebels invaded Makeni, my family managed to escape, living between villages and the bush fifteen miles northwest of town for about three weeks. They ran away with nothing but the clothes they wore when the rebels attacked. They lived on wild fruit and the support they received from people in the villages they passed through. During this period they managed to send me a letter through a relative who escaped and traveled by bush path for nearly a week before he reached Freetown. In the letter, which I received just before the invasion of Freetown, they explained where they were and what they were going through. I managed to raise some money and gave it to the same relative to take back to them. He left Freetown, and I never heard from him again. The rebels invaded Freetown the next day, and we were cut off.

I tried again in May. That was when everyone was talking about the negotiations in Lomé and there was a lull in the fighting, so I sent someone else with Le80,000 (U.S.$60). He never came back. It was a racket. If you wanted to get your relatives into Freetown, you would negotiate with someone who would promise to go and get them. It was mostly a scam, but you couldn't give up. Someone would introduce you to a man, saying, "He has just brought ten people in; he is trustworthy." But after the second attempt I was more cautious. I did not have the money, and some attempts were fatal. I knew a case in which everyone in the family was lost in the attempt.

I did not hear from my family until mid-August 1999, until my wife's younger brother was able to travel to Freetown. The family was safe, living in my late mother's village about twenty miles southeast of Makeni. But they had lost everything we had worked for over the decades. Our house was completely vandalized by the rebels and damaged by a fragment from a rocket-propelled grenade.

Now I negotiated with the fiancé of a cousin who had just brought in twenty people. This time we had to calculate everything very carefully. To escape from Makeni, you had to go to the truck park to get a rebel pass that would allow you to *recce,* a word meaning you were going to search for food. Then you would negotiate for transport and pay. And at every checkpoint you would pay more—Le4,000 per checkpoint. There were dozens and dozens of checkpoints, and we had to calculate all of them. I wanted all the small kids to come out with my three daughters— eleven people in all. The total was about Le600,000 (about U.S.$400). So I gave him the money. And he got there.

My daughters and the others left very early in the morning, and the only transport available at the time was a tractor. So they took the tractor with a small trailer and went about seven miles from Makeni, and then they got stuck because they were using palm kernel oil instead of diesel. The tractor broke down, and they were immediately abandoned. They had paid the money, but from that point they had to walk. It was life or death, and it was the last chance. They walked for two days and two nights—sixty miles—and on the journey the rebels took everything from them. By the time they got to the ECOMOG lines, they had nothing. They couldn't pay for transport, so they slept there and finally ECOMOG gave them a lift to Freetown. It was the third week of September, almost a year since I had arrived to give peace a chance.

Conclusions

Throughout my visit to Sierra Leone, I was repeatedly challenged by former colleagues who said, "Why are you coming here with this white man's stuff—nonviolence, peacebuilding, and so on?" They thought I was from a new planet; they thought I had been brainwashed by what they called the "white mentality." This sort of comment reflects a shortcoming in attitudinal capacities as much as any other. Developing human capacities must include the emotional, intellectual, psychological, cultural, spiritual, and social needs of people. Capacity building must therefore be based on the lived experiences, aspirations, resources, needs, visions, and limitations of the local people. It is about assisting the marginalized and oppressed in society to take ownership and control of their development process. Local capacity building is about empowering people to make a difference in their own communities.

Capacity building must address people's ability to ensure food security and other basic needs, to gain the knowledge and skills necessary for improving the quality of their lives, their environment, and their society. The process requires outsiders who can listen to the voices that have been excluded for centuries from informed participation. This is the challenge facing many African countries, but especially Sierra Leone today. In order to meet the challenges of the twenty-first century and to participate meaningfully in the globalization process, indigenous African capacities must be understood and developed. This will be extremely crucial for sustaining long-term peace in a postwar Sierra Leone.

A few international organizations have done a lot to strengthen the capacities of a handful of local organizations during the rebel war. However, much more needs to be done by the internationals to support long-term local capacity building. My general observation was that suspicion and mistrust between international and local organizations increased during the 1999 rebel attack on Freetown. There was more competition than cooperation regarding who was doing the most humanitarian work and who was *seen* to be doing the most. There were more short-term projects than long-term strategies. Some international NGOs behaved like tourists. They flooded the country when times were sweet and they disappeared during rough times. (In addition to January 1999, most had disappeared between May 1997 and February 1998 when the Armed Forces Revolutionary Council took power, and they disappeared again in May 2000 when there were rumors of an imminent RUF attack on Freetown.)

Local capacity building should include the creation of well-equipped, local development training and research centers. Expatriates skilled in special disciplines should be encouraged to work with local counterparts, rather than sending Sierra Leoneans away for training. This approach means fewer job opportunities for expatriates. It also means more power, control, and ownership of the development process by local organizations. But with most local organizations still largely dependent on international agencies for their daily bread and survival, I do not expect this to happen soon.

Participatory research into local capacity building issues is almost nonexistent in Sierra Leone. Virtually anybody can claim to be a trainer or adult educator in one field or the other. There are no standards for the competencies required of trainers and adult educators. Many Sierra Leoneans, having participated in short trauma-healing or peacebuilding workshops, immediately assumed they were expert trainers in a very complex field of study. In the future, much more inquiry should be encouraged into the strengths, weaknesses, and opportunities inherent in local organizations. The government, perhaps through the Ministry of Education and with collaboration from the Sierra Leone Association of NGOs (SLANGO), should work toward developing a policy and standards on the competencies required of trainers and adult educators.

Let me conclude by emphasizing that for local capacity building to be effective in the long run, there must also be peace, the rule of law, democratic governance, political pluralism, a stable economy, and transparent and accountable political leadership. The basic needs of people must be met. There must be mutual trust and respect between international and local organizations engaged in capacity building, as well as between the government and NGOs. Unfortunately this is not yet the case in Sierra Leone. The reign of terror and the jungle justice that the rebels established in Sierra Leone has made the process of building local capacities a dream that is yet to come true.

Editor's Epilogue

I had occasion to visit Sierra Leone again in October 2000, nine months after Thomas Turay's ordeal ended. The NGO world was buzzing about a new NGO policy that had been introduced by the government the previous month. The policy aimed to give clarity to the term NGO and to re-register all local and international organizations in the country. Local NGOs would be required to have at least three full-time staff members, an easily identifiable office, a postal address, and a bank account in Sierra Leone. International NGOs would be required to show proof of their legal status in their home country, to have ministerial approval of their programs, and to limit their administrative costs to 20 percent or less of their overall budget. Each international NGO would be allowed up to three expatriate staff, with special permission required for more than that number. All NGOs, local and international, would be required to submit quarterly bank statements to the government.

While some of the new regulations seemed unduly bureaucratic and even draconian, they contained elements not often found in government regulations. For example, one specification was that "programme formulation must be done with the full participation of the specific target group, and confirmation of this should be evident in the submitted programme."[2] And, "All NGOs must have commensurate numbers of national staff at senior management level with enough authority to ensure continuity of programmes, even in the absence of expatriate seniors. This will also assist in promoting the transfer of knowledge and capacity building."[3]

Among international NGOs, reaction to the policy was almost universally negative. "It came out of the blue," said one director, who believed that local NGOs had encouraged the government to crack down on the internationals. "Why didn't they discuss it with us first?" Clearly, the new policy had not come out of the blue—it represented long-held frustrations of Sierra Leoneans, now in their tenth year of a brutal war, who simply wanted to take greater ownership of the relief and reconstruction process themselves. An explanation for the nationalistic tone in the regulations could be found in the preamble: "The January 1999 crisis saw a mass exodus of expatriate staff of international NGOs. . . . [B]uilding national capacity has to be urgently undertaken."[4]

Many international aid workers make the mistake of thinking that the world they find in a country like Sierra Leone began on the day they arrived. They are not very interested in the history, past relationships, past frustrations. The new NGO policy in Sierra Leone will inevitably be amended over time, but perhaps its original shock value will have served the purpose of conveying a message about local empowerment that was long overdue.

—Ian Smillie

Notes

1. For a detailed discussion in the Humanitarianism and War Project's series on HACU and the efforts of coordination in Sierra Leone, see Marc Sommers, *The Dynamics of Coordination,* Occasional Paper no. 40 (Providence, R.I.: Watson Institute, 2000).

2. Government of Sierra Leone, *Policy Regulations on the Operations of Non-governmental Organisations* (Freetown: Government of Sierra Leone, August 2000), 5.

3. Government of Sierra Leone, *Policy Regulations,* 10.

4. Government of Sierra Leone, *Policy Regulations,* 1.

Chapter 8

From Patrons to Partners?

IAN SMILLIE

Patronage or Partnership: Local Capacity Building in Humanitarian Crises grew out of the research of the Humanitarianism and War Project, an independent policy-research initiative now based at the Feinstein International Famine Center in Tufts University's School of Nutrition Science and Policy. The book was designed to test assumptions and to investigate relationships between humanitarian agencies and local civil society in complex emergencies. The book began with a general review of the literature on capacity building and then examined experiences in six countries.

The countries were chosen for various reasons. First, we wanted geographic spread, thus one country each in Europe, Asia, Latin America, the Caribbean, and two in Africa. Second, we wanted experiences of both war and the transition out of war into reconstruction and development. Sierra Leone and Sri Lanka exemplify the former, as does the Haitian example, although Haiti's period under military rule—while certainly a complex emergency—did not entail fighting. The Mozambique, Guatemala, and Bosnia chapters describe efforts at capacity building during and/or after wars, focusing more on the reconstruction period than the conflicts themselves.

We were interested in countries in which a relatively robust and formalized civil sector predated the conflict, and we also looked for settings in which civil society was more embryonic or informal. Sri Lanka and Haiti represented the former, while Mozambique and the Guatemalan refugee story represented the other end of the spectrum. Sierra Leone was somewhere in the middle, and Bosnia represented what might be loosely termed post-Soviet space.

This rather ambitious effort to cover the entire waterfront in six chapters was complicated by another objective, which was to reverse the normal order of discourse and to solicit views, where possible, from a local perspective. Most writing on humanitarian interventions, and a great deal on the aid enterprise as a whole, is the work of Northern academics and practitioners. This is understandable in the sense that they are usually the primary readers. But they are not the primary consumer of the product that is being described. In organizing this book we were therefore looking as much as possible for views from a local perspective.

Local, of course, is a loaded word, and one writer never speaks for all. Nevertheless, Kathy Mangones says that the perspective of her chapter "is unabashedly that of Haitian civil society organizations," and she talks convincingly about the need "for new strategies and directions based on the capacity and potential of concerned populations, enabling them to move from object to subject, from victim to actor, *to the possibility of being.* Only then can we hope to see greater synergy between humanitarian assistance and development, and between humanitarian assistance and capacity building at the community level." Thomas Turay says that "local capacity building is about empowering people to make a difference in their own communities."

While we have certainly not captured all Bosnian, Sri Lanka, or Sierra Leonean viewpoints in the chapters on those countries, the views they contain are also unabashedly Bosnian, Sri Lankan, and Sierra Leonean. In the cases of Mozambique and Guatemala, the authors have solid field experience, and their work was made stronger by the background participation of Mozambicans and Guatemalans.

Much is made in general development writing about the role of civil society. In the literature on conflict—at a conceptual level, at least—civil society also finds a modest place in prescriptions for "social capital" as part of the peacebuilding process. At an operational level, however, specific policies among humanitarian agencies about working with civil society are ambiguous or unclear, and the lessons of experience often are difficult to discern. The book started, therefore, with a general review of past and current thinking about the notion of capacity building, and what application—if any—capacity building might have during and immediately after a conflict. Chapter 1 talked about definitions of *capacity building,* expanding the term beyond basic ideas of technical and managerial training to encompass the idea of strengthening whole sectors of civil society to allow their engagement—on their own terms, not those of their benefactors—at a policy level in political, social, and economic arenas.

Easier said than done, capacity building at this end of the spectrum has important implications for timing. It cannot be done quickly, and this is obviously a serious constraint for humanitarian agencies with limited time frames. A more important question has to do with the capacity to build capacity. Even in deliberate, developmental capacity building projects, there are problems in knowing how to approach the issue, how to measure, and how to evaluate it. In humanitarian emergencies, in which many aid-agency employees are young, overworked, and under great stress, the knowledge, time, and care required to build local capacities may be in short supply. Chapter 1 concluded this way:

> In order to be effective, a capacity building approach must be clear in its purpose: does it intend to create a specific capacity within a single organization, or does it aim to build the institution and its capacity to undertake independent thought and action? Second, the target must be clear—whether a single organization, a sectoral activity such as health delivery, or a societal subset such as civil society. The time required and the complexity of the exercise will increase depending on the depth of change envisaged. The simple transfer of information may not require great effort, but building knowledge, changing behavior, and altering attitudes require investments with significantly different orders of magnitude.
>
> In approaching the question of civil society, outsiders need to build their own understanding while exercising caution. Attempts to build civil society are important, but civil society may be contested space during a volatile and politicized emergency, simultaneously emerging and contracting, part solution and perhaps part problem. Training is not a panacea . . . it is not in any way synonymous with capacity building. . . . And a general lesson about capacity building, one now decades old, is that builders must have good knowledge of "buildees," their society, and the context in which the effort is expected to take place. There is no substitute for a clear understanding and analysis of the local situation, something that cannot be achieved without the intimate participation of those affected.

As it turned out, these prescriptions, while not wrong, were too general to be of much use in several of our case studies. Three of the chapters—on Haiti, Sri Lanka, and Mozambique—barely got to the question of deliberate capacity building by outsiders, because the context was fraught with more basic problems. Capacities, to be sure, were built in the food project described in the Haiti chapter, but the positive experience was soon nipped in the bud by the narrow mandate and time frames of the funding agency.

Arjuna Parakrama makes the point that opposing forces in Sri Lanka have everything to gain by weakening the capacities of local communities and displaced people, and that humanitarian agencies essentially play along. In other words, the basic concept of strengthening local organizations—not to mention more complex questions like how or why to do it—may barely be visible on the humanitarian radar. In the Mozambique case, Stephen Lubkemann argues that decades of heavy-handed government, along with nonexistent state services, caused what little organized civil society there was to opt out rather than to engage the state. The initial question for aid agencies, therefore, became one of building state capacities, albeit at a local level, before there could be any engagement with civil society.

Three chapters deal more specifically with capacity building. In Bosnia, humanitarian agencies saw capacity building in its most elementary definition: as a means of creating more effective or cheaper local delivery mechanisms. Capacity building tended to focus on training and enhancement of the most basic managerial functions. It had more to do with service delivery than with building civil society, even though the need for social capital and a stronger civil society was recognized more explicitly by international agencies in Bosnia than in any of the other countries in our selection. CARE's Project Phoenix did positively address capacity building for civil society, and its experience reinforces conclusions about the importance of ensuring that the purpose of such activities be clear, that the time frame be appropriate, and that expectations be realistic.

Humanitarian agencies working with Guatemalan refugees instilled gender awareness in native women, taking advantage of the time and the opportunity to do what often is recommended in nongovernmental organizations' manuals for women in refugee camps. There were at least two problems, however. The first was that the training turned out to be largely irrelevant for many women at the point of returning with unreconstructed men to an unreconstructed society. Or—to be more fair, perhaps—the training was not very useful in the context of the enormous developmental and economic needs for which the women had received no preparation. Second, having lived for years in a refugee-camp situation, they returned home well versed in how to ask for things, but with few of the tools required to *do* things. Here is an example of selective training— a subject close to the heart of international organizations—but without virtually any training in the subject of greatest interest to the women and their families.

Thomas Turay describes a broad set of Sierra Leonean organizations hungry—desperate almost—for the capacity to do more in situations of uncertainty and conflict. If there are surprises in his chapter, and it offers in some ways the most personal and disturbing account of any of the chapters, it is that so many international organizations were striving to understand and cope with war, and that international agencies appeared to play such a limited role in helping.

What emerges from the six chapters, therefore, is a significantly different cross section of issues from that presented in chapter 1. This revised framework can be described under four headings: conceptual issues, operational issues, political issues, and motivational issues.

Conceptual Issues

Civil Society Revisited

As a concept, civil society goes back more than three hundred years. Hegel, John Locke, Thomas Paine, de Tocqueville, and Gramsci all had important things to say on the subject. Only during the past decade or so, however, has the idea of civil society intruded on aid agencies. Much discussed but much confused, the concept has since been used to explain and justify all manner of things. In an attempt to clarify matters, Alison Van Rooy has described six different ways of looking at civil society: as a value, as a collective noun, as "space," as a historical moment, as an antihegemonic phenomenon, and as an antidote to the state.[1]

As a value, a civil society would be one that is law-abiding, tolerant, trustful, cooperative. Not surprisingly, we see little evidence of this at the national level in our six case studies, but it is there in the microcosm of the Haitian experiments with food production and distribution, and in the hopeful creation of Bosnian organizations like the VIDRA Women's Action or the Elderly Club 15–100. It is there in the efforts of Sierra Leonean organizations to help people in the face of extreme brutality. The idea of civil society as a value, therefore, even in the worst humanitarian emergencies, might well be regarded as universal.

As a collective noun, civil society describes a collection of organizations, formal and informal, working outside of government and the private sector. These include village-based organizations, advocacy groups, NGOs, human rights organizations, professional bodies, and so on. In some countries there is a long tradition of such organizations, in others there is not. In Bosnia and Mozambique, emerging from the experience of strong centralizing governments over at least two generations, the number and strength of civil society organizations was relatively small at the end of the hostilities that led to independence. The challenge of working with them, as described in the chapters on those two countries, was difficult. In Sierra Leone, civil society expanded dramatically as a direct result of the decade-long war, with many organizations emerging as a protest, some as self-help or welfare efforts, some as human rights organizations. Opportunities for collaboration with international humanitarian agencies expanded, although they were perhaps more opportunities missed than taken.

Haiti represents a mix. At the end of the Duvalier period, welfare organizations were joined by a new generation of activists. They, too, offered programming opportunities in the midst of crisis, but the opportunities described in chapter 3 were treated somewhat opportunistically, and were not institutionalized by the primary funding agency. Despite a long history of strong civil society organizations in Sri Lanka, Arjuna Parakrama argues that they have played a minor role in all but the delivery of humanitarian assistance, and even that has been compromised by the unwillingness of both the government and the Tamil Tigers to countenance anything that might give greater voice to victims of the conflict. The size and history of civil society may not, therefore, be a major factor in the ability of international humanitarians to engage it at anything more than a service delivery level.

The notion of civil society as "space" is often represented by a diagram with three overlapping circles representing government, the market, and civil society. The diagram usually shows circles of the same size, overlapping only slightly. In many countries, however—such as Bosnia before the Dayton accords and Mozambique before the end of the war—the government circle would have been large, the market small, and civil society infinitesimal. In Sri Lanka the circles might be of a similar size, but Arjuna Parakrama suggests that the overlap between civil society and government is so large that the independence of the civic voice is compromised. Working with civil society in either case presents different programming challenges from Haiti, say, where there was virtually no overlap.

Several writers describe civil society in terms of a historical moment, something that ebbs and flows according to the prevailing winds and the prevailing conditions—laws, cultural context, degree of democratic space, levels of pluralism. Bosnian's civil society before World War II was more vibrant that Hungary's, but since former Yugoslavia emerged from the Cold War later than Hungary, it was much smaller and more fragile through the 1990s. The independence or "voice" of Sri Lankan civil society would appear to have atrophied in recent years, in part because of the war and human rights violations, in part because of the increasing alignment of civil society with one side or the other in the conflict, in part because of threatening behavior—either physical or legislative—again from both sides. The space for civil society, in fact, may change much more rapidly during and after a complex emergency than at other times. Certainly the growth of civil society in Haiti, Bosnia, and Sierra Leone was a direct result of conflict, while its contraction occurred in Sri Lanka. There, as in Guatemala before the peace agreement, events bear out Paul Harvey's contention that "military strategies, extreme scarcity and displacement serve to undermine civil society."[2]

Some writers have viewed civil society, or parts of civil society, as an "antihegemonic" phenomenon. The most obvious current international examples are the NGO struggle against genetically modified food, and the battles against globalization waged in the streets of Seattle, Prague, and elsewhere. Among our cases, perhaps the most overt example can be found in Mozambique, where, during the years of Portuguese colonialism, war, and afterward, civil society became an informal coping mechanism for avoiding a heavy-handed state that offered little or nothing to the populace. This further validates Paul Harvey's contention that during an emergency, civil society may well be growing in some settings—as in the case of Haiti and Sierra Leone—but in other places it may be contracting. Mozambique exemplifies Harvey's notion of the extreme disengagement of civil society from the state and a fallback on kinship, tribal, religious, or traditional structures as a coping mechanism.[3] Stephen Lubkemann offers some important considerations for outsiders in such a situation, defining civil society as "forms of associational life involved in negotiating the political order with the state (and among actors), *premised on the degree of legitimacy granted by all of these players to that process of negotiation itself* and thus on the commitment to exercising 'voice' as opposed to 'exit' options. Perhaps the most basic prerequisite for making society 'civil' . . . is that the players grant that the presence of other players and their right to exercise voice is also legitimate."[4]

The idea of civil society as an antidote to the state is perhaps the most confused part of the package. One school of thought among aid agencies sees civil society as a cheaper, more effective alternative to the delivery of hitherto ineffective state services. Where development is concerned, this is an area of contentious debate. Where emergencies are concerned, the debate is not so contentious because time frames are limited, and where civil society organizations have been expanded, there is always the possibility of going back to the status quo once an emergency is over, no matter how much space an NGO has occupied. This is essentially what happened in the Haiti food project described in chapter 3.

Another reason for the lack of controversy is that in the worst emergencies there is often no government service to usurp, as in Sierra Leone. A more profound problem arises when the idea of civil society as antidote moves beyond simple humanitarian-service delivery into questions of human rights, democracy, pluralism, and the most basic elements of what is understood by a civil society. The tradeoffs between the need for humanitarian neutrality and the advocacy that may be required in situations of human rights abuse, for example, are serious enough for international agencies. However, they are even more problematic for organizations that do not have the luxury of plane tickets to another place if what they say displeases belligerents or if the fighting gets too hot, as it did in Freetown three times in as many years. Capacity building for service delivery, therefore, may be ideologically contentious in the longer run, but capacity building for advocacy could well put civil society organizations in harm's way. The obverse of this, however, can be found in situations like Haiti or Sierra Leone, where local groups *want* to be more than humanitarian organizations, where human rights and advocacy are high on their agendas, but where they find little in the way of concrete or moral support from outsiders nervous about "taking sides" or expressing solidarity for those who do.

Why Engage Civil Society?

This discussion, then, gets to the conceptual question about why humanitarian agencies might want to engage and strengthen civil society during an emergency. The reason is surely, in part, to help in returning a war-torn country to some sort of civility. The purpose is also to help in getting the immediate humanitarian tasks done more efficiently than might be the case if outsiders were doing it alone. With the protraction of so many emergencies, the idea of quick response and early exit has become a thing of the past, and local partnerships make eminent programming sense.

The bigger question for international humanitarian agencies is whether they are willing to go further in developing civil society for its own sake because of the more social and political roles it might play in helping to return a country to normal, or preventing a return to conflict. If the answer is yes, then the issue must be addressed explicitly. The job cannot be done carelessly, because too much is at stake. CARE's Project Phoenix in Bosnia demonstrates how much outsiders and locals have to learn in doing this work well. The answer, however, may well be no. If they are unprepared to frame their task more comprehensively, outsiders should be clear on the limitations of their intervention, and they should not cloak their desire for service delivery partners in the broader jargon of building civil society.

Operational Issues

The Capacity to Build Capacity

If anything, the six case studies in this book demonstrate the enormity of the operational challenge involved in the engagement of civil society by outsiders. One of the most basic operational issues has to do with the capacity of outsiders to augment the capacity of others. The transfer of information is a relatively simple matter, but effective skill development is something else. Providing information about how to drive a four-wheel vehicle or to operate a computer does not necessarily convey the skill to do so. The knowledge required for decisions about where to drive the vehicle, or what to use the computer for, or what to do at a military roadblock is a much higher level of capacity—one based on information, but also on experience and judgment. Changing attitudes, a critical element in building local capacities in some emergencies, may be extremely difficult, but altering behavior—at an individual and at an organizational level—is likely to be even more problematic. The greater the desired change in capacity, the greater the difficulty and the time required to accomplish it.

The Haiti chapter shows that because a Canadian organization, Centre canadien d'étude et de la coopération internationale (CECI), hired competent Haitians, and because the Haitians had not yet been completely immersed in CECI's organizational culture, they were, when left to their own devices, able to develop their own programming capacities and those of others. This may be an exception to the rule. In the case of the Guatemalan refugees, women's attitudes toward gender were changed through the provision of information, but the training did not extend to practical matters and to skill development that might have empowered the women to create real behavioral change in their families and villages when they returned home.

Some of the problem has to do with cultural understanding. Thomas Turay talks about the problem of expatriates doing work that Sierra Leoneans could do as well or better. Arjuna Parakrama argues that the use of expatriates works against capacity building at the community level in Sri Lanka because foreigners rarely (or perhaps never) speak the language, and they rarely understand the cultural context sufficiently. Their systems and hierarchies also work against capacity building, while traditional Sri Lankan deference makes groups less assertive with foreigners than they perhaps should be. Translators thus are extremely important interlocutors, becoming more than translators. In fact they become interpreters, a role for which they may be ill-equipped.

In Sierra Leone, Thomas Turay did not have a cultural or linguistic problem, and his work spanned the gamut of change from the provision of information to the desire of his clients for meaningful organizational development. Two-day workshops, however, were probably little more than a single step in the right direction. The Sierra Leone case, in fact, illustrates the problem of time—it is not just that two-day workshops have their limitations; in the midst of a crisis, even two days of training may be a real luxury.

Time and Timing

Time, in fact, is one of the most precious commodities in a humanitarian emergency. People cannot wait for food and water if they are to survive. Good timing is also crucial to any intervention—knowing when to intervene, when to modify an intervention, and when to withdraw is essential to prevention, conflict resolution, reconstruction, and development. It is also important to knowing if, when, and how to move from basic relief to activities with developmental objectives.

In Bosnia, time was a more thorny problem than money. Time was needed to rebuild institutions, the rule of law, and good governance and to break through the authoritarian nature of the regimes that followed Yugoslavia's breakup. Timing—knowing when to introduce development projects to organizations with other priorities—was also problematic, as in the case of moving too quickly with the Banja Luka student union. But time is something refugees and displaced people do not always have in abundance. With a few exceptions, such as FINNIDA in Mozambique, it seems that most aid agencies do not have or take much time either.

The source, volume, and other conditions related to money are key factors in most timing decisions—in hurrying or delaying humanitarian response or in inappropriately hastening the move from relief to development programming. Money issues can be the cause of precipitous agency withdrawal, and they are the prime motivation behind the growing demand for unrealistic exit strategies. The time-and-money nexus was at the root of CECI's problem in Haiti. Outsiders had plenty of time to work with Guatemalan refugee women while they were in the Mexican camps, but almost none after they returned home. Time and knowledge are also intimately connected: organizations in a hurry have little time to learn. Not knowing when to act, outsiders become paralyzed, as though there were no previous examples to draw on for inspiration.

Rules and Regulations, Corruption and Control

"Lack of local capacity" is often a euphemism used by international agencies to avoid the word *corruption.* This word is not used much in this book, but it lurks not far behind the scenes and is always a problem when high-value commodities are on the move. Thomas Turay writes about the mistrust between "food pipeline" humanitarian organizations and local groups that are treated essentially as "errand boys," "their main role being to distribute food aid and take insults from hungry and angry internally displaced people." Because nobody in such situations trusted anyone else, international organizations dealt with the problem by doing everything themselves.

It is perhaps unfortunate that the issue of corruption is seldom addressed openly, because although everyone knows it is a problem, the absence of discussion gives the impression that there are no ways of dealing with it, except for expatriates to retain full control. This sets up unpleasant and inaccurate images about who is honest and who is not. Rather than dealing with the issue openly, however, discussion is buried in euphemism (or jargon perhaps), and operational practice becomes mired in rules and regulations that may reduce the possibility for corruption, but that make local organizations more vulnerable to charges of incompetence. As Parakrama puts it,

> Documentation, accounting, and reporting systems, which are invariably imported from First World contexts, are seldom modified or made appropriate to the exigencies of the local situations.
>
> The failure of imported accounting and reporting systems in a given community is a failure precisely of these systems and not of

the community's ability to use them. Sri Lanka is singularly plagued by the inability of its donor community to understand this simple truth, and to work toward creating user-friendly systems, compatible with conditions and skills available within the communities themselves.

A further problem has to do with results. Many donor agencies today are, quite rightly, placing much more emphasis on results than on inputs and outputs. For example, reducing child mortality in a camp is more important than the means used to do it. Old emphases on measuring, for example, management of an inoculation program have changed in favor of a hard look at whether the inoculations accomplished their purpose. This makes sense. But where capacity building is concerned, the intended results will inevitably be long-term in nature. They will be harder to correlate with a specific intervention. Relief agencies, after all, are expected to save lives, not to build the capacity of local organizations. The first quotation in the introduction to this book was taken from the London *Sunday Times*, which accused an international organization of "squandering British aid" in Burundi because it was running conflict resolution workshops instead of saving lives.

There are, perhaps, three ways of looking at the problem. The first is that humanitarian agencies should stick to their knitting and save lives rather than building the capacity of others to do so. A good case can be made for this approach, institution by institution. But in a world beset by conflict and war, it hardly makes sense at a generic level. Humanitarian agencies represent the front line in the international response to emergencies, and they are often the only outsiders on the ground with humanitarian motives and humanitarian resources.

The second option is that someone else should build capacities. But for the reasons noted above, who that might be is hard to say. Organizations that work only in development are usually not present, and, in any case, they are unlikely to have anything to teach a Guatemalan or a Haitian NGO about humanitarian assistance.

The third option is to face the situation more forthrightly. This might include an insistence that capacity building is a legitimate and even a necessary endeavor for international humanitarian organizations, and that in an emergency that has lasted more than nine months, for example, capacity building should be a compulsory part of all humanitarian assistance.

Contracting

Unless more capacity building begins to occur, there may be little change. But there is a problem where governmental donors are concerned. A great deal of the funding for international humanitarian NGOs is derived from bilateral and multilateral agencies. As noted above, most (or even all) of this funding will be for immediate humanitarian purposes, with many of the time constraints that have been noted throughout the book. This leaves Northern organizations with two choices in building local capacity. One possibility is to use untied and untargeted donor income for this purpose. In emergencies, however, most individual donors also want to see immediate results. Given the implicit intent of donors responding to a given emergency, there may be an ethical issue in using these funds for anything not directly related to immediate humanitarian purposes. The second choice is to persuade bilateral and multilateral benefactors that change in their funding arrangements is badly needed. This may be easier said than done (a recurring phrase throughout this book, in fact), because the humanitarian-budget lines from which such funding comes are usually constrained by short time frames and narrow ground rules. This problem was mentioned in several chapters in the book.

Changing the arrangements offered by a governmental funding agency may be constrained, in fact, by something more fundamental than the rules themselves. The organization of bilateral and multilateral agencies into divisions in which there is little overlap between relief and development has created dysfunctional fiefdoms in which rules, compartmentalization, and independence have become more important than the job to be done. Specialization in humanitarian work is essential, but when it creates problems in timing, funding, and understanding that block long-term effectiveness, then the time has clearly come for an overhaul of the system.

Taking government contracts rather than grants from humanitarian agencies can present greater problems for local organizations than for NGOs. For local organizations, the rules and regulations tend to be more detailed, the framework is more narrow, and time frames may be tighter than they are for international agencies (to avoid, say, corruption). There is rarely enough money to cover administrative overheads, which are a universal problem for nonprofit organizations worldwide, both North and South. Donor agencies usually provide as little as possible, and then almost always as a blanket percentage, regardless of what work is being undertaken. This approach is justified in a variety of ways, usually with something like the 1995 explanation from the UNHCR, which "sees its relationship with its implementing partners as one of, precisely, partnership, and draws a clear distinction between such partnerships and contractual relationships.... UNHCR [expects] ... suitable agencies ... at least to cover the overhead administrative costs related to the project from their own or other non-UNHCR resources."[5]

While this statement applied mainly to Northern agencies, most donors, including Northern NGOs, apply similar conditions to Southern organizations—a case of victims passing the same problem on to their own partners. The issue was graphically illustrated in the Bosnia chapter: "Some of the NGOs created by international agencies had been 'dumped.' They had been given basic project funds for a year, a little training perhaps, and then set adrift in a sea of jargon about sustainability. Most NGOs, including several regarded by donors as the best and the strongest, faced extremely severe financial difficulties because of core funding shortfalls."

If the only other source of money is private donor funds (rarely available to Southern organizations), these must be used cautiously, because, as noted above, private donors are even more concerned than institutional donors that all of the money gets there. But when administrative overheads are not sufficiently funded, one of two things will occur. Either the organization in question will cut corners and do the job less well than might be desired, or it will—in time-honored NGO tradition—engage in rubber mathematics, hiding administration costs and inflating whatever cost the donor likes best. An apt new expression for this disappointingly common—and frequently necessary—behavior is "money morphing."[6]

Political Issues

The Concept of Neutrality

Although they may be somewhat outdated by the kinds of warfare now found in countries like Sierra Leone and Sri Lanka, the ideals of humanitarian neutrality and impartiality still occupy an important place in the thinking of most international organizations. For UNHCR and kindred agencies, *impartiality* means that "humanitarian assistance should be provided without discrimination [to] all individuals and groups who are suffering, without regard to nationality, political or ideological beliefs, race, religion, sex or ethnicity." *Neutrality* means that "relief should be provided without bias toward or against one or more of the parties to the political, military, religious, ideological or ethnic controversy."[7]

Accused of assisting bad people in Cambodian and Rwandan refugee camps as a perceived consequence of their fidelity to such principles, many humanitarian agencies have taken a more nuanced view of such terms. And even where the concepts are still diligently observed, they run the risk of clashing with the views and the work of organizations more concerned about human rights than humanitarianism. Here is the crux of the problem. At its simplest, *humanitarianism* is about providing assistance to the victims of war; *human rights* is about justice. While the two should be compatible, for practical reasons they must often be treated as separate theologies, practiced in different churches.

This may create real problems for local capacity building, because, in many cases, local organizations are highly partisan, often for good reason. Justice may be as high on their agenda as relief. This was certainly the case with Guatemalan refugees in Mexico, but it posed no serious problem there because the refugees were in a cross-border camp. The days of the cross-border camp, and of humanitarian agencies working far from the battle, however, have changed. At the aggregate level, displaced people in their own countries often outnumber refugees, and civilians—whether organized or not—are often targets. Local organizations are therefore likely to have opinions that exist in tension with basic humanitarian principles. In Sierra Leone, for example, the local chapter of the Red Cross may be able to remain neutral, but most organizations ministering to the mutilated victims of rebel atrocities in Sierra Leone, for example, were not.

Building local capacities and working through local organizations holding partisan views creates several potential risks for outsiders. The first is that the international NGO runs the danger of being charged with partiality and thus of being denied access to one side in a conflict. The second risk is the possibility of expulsion and of an inability to provide assistance to anyone. The third is the possibility that relief goods will be diverted to combatants. There is another side to the coin, however. International NGOs may not be able to go places and to do things that locals can, so it may be expeditious to work with local groups that have partisan connections. In the southern Sudan, international agencies have traditionally steered away from most local organizations because of the political implications. As one study puts it, however,

> Those local NGOs (LNGOs) which are tapped for partnerships find themselves in a difficult situation. When international NGOs (INGOs) seek out local groups they do so in order to gain access to beneficiaries they wouldn't otherwise be able to reach. This access, however, may require LNGOs to negotiate directly with armed elements, something donors wish to avoid. How then can such local partners be expected to deepen international access to needy civilians? Forced to walk a tightrope between extending the reach of international relief and remaining above the conflict, LNGOs have on occasion been forced to obscure certain aspects of their field operations from their international partners—a practice which can only weaken trust.[8]

The problem becomes even more serious when combatants actively mistrust civil society organizations, whether they are partisan or not. The Sri Lanka chapter demonstrated that the government regards all Tamil leaders as sympathizers and front men for the Liberation Tigers of Tamil Eelam (LTTE), while the insurgents have dealt ruthlessly with anyone they suspect of working with the Sri Lankan military. In such situations it would behoove any local leader or organization to behave as neutrally as possible, but neutrality—in a situation in which fealty is demanded by both sides—might well be impossible.

This leads to a situation described by Arjuna Parakrama in which international humanitarian actors avoid taking sides in a war, and, in doing so, shortchange the dispossessed victims on both sides.

> Hence, their "neutrality" is purchased at the expense of forfeiting an engagement with the broader political issues that the war engenders. This translates on the ground to a strict adherence to logistical and narrowly humanitarian issues—admittedly crucial in a time of terrible suffering—which leaves no room for the more overtly political concerns that affect the lives of the displaced communities with whom actors work.
>
> This version of humanitarian assistance does not run counter to the logic of war. On the contrary, in this case humanitarian assistance minimizes the cost of war—helps pick up the pieces or clear the battlefield—and it serves as an essential component of the grammar in which the logic of war is embedded. Humanitarian assistance can be said to help the LTTE as they help themselves to a good proportion of the supplies; it assists the government's image locally and internationally by easing civilian suffering. True, humanitarian agencies advocate against atrocities and campaign unwaveringly to ensure basic food supplies, but they do not take sides against the war itself.

Who Pays the Piper Calls the Tune

Some of the mandate problem—the tradeoff between humanitarianism and justice—derives from the ultimate source and control of funding. But the issue is even more basic than that, relating to questions of where, when, and whether a humanitarian agency will act. Interest in Somalia declined when the cameras and the various intervention forces pulled out. Sierra Leone's nine-year war made little impact on the media and therefore on the budgets of most aid agencies until May 2000, when five hundred United Nations peacekeepers were kidnapped and the CNN factor kicked in.[9]

In any emergency, the volume of money available to humanitarians will be affected by the interest of major funding bodies, but the content and quality of the money will also be affected. For many years, for example, international agencies working in Palestine, including those funded by the United States Agency for International Development, were encouraged to work closely with the Israeli-controlled civil authority. The implications for developing close and trusting partnerships with Palestinian NGOs are obvious.

This recurring dependency problem, whether political or monetary, is real. Writing about Mozambican NGOs, Stephen Lubkemann says, "Small in scale, thoroughly dependent on foreign funding, and with activities largely limited to reconstruction, many of these NGOs vanished when the reconstruction projects that gave them birth ended." Of course they were small. They were brand-new, untried, untested, unknown, and probably not very professional. And, of course, they were thoroughly dependent on foreign funding—like most NGOs everywhere in the South. (Most NGOs in the North are thoroughly dependent on government funding, and that funding, too, becomes foreign once it gets to Mozambique.) The reason these NGOs were given birth by reconstruction projects is that donors had money for reconstruction and wanted local partners (that is, contractors or "errand boys") who could do the work. The reason they vanished is that nobody was interested in supporting them, or in contracting them for anything else when the reconstruction money dried up.

This is not unlike Bosnia. But in Bosnia, civil society organizations tried to build their own longer-term capacities and sustainability. They created an NGO Council and an NGO Foundation, both of which aimed to develop better non-ethnic coordination and to provide training and support for advocacy capacities. Neither body was able to attract significant donor funding, despite the millions of dollars pumped through NGOs for reconstruction contracts, despite a variety of donor-run NGO training programs, despite almost universal declarations of support for a vibrant civil society.

Motivational Issues

This book has explored some of the reasons that international humanitarian agencies might want to build local capacities in complex emergencies. It has also demonstrated that there are more problems in doing this well than might be anticipated. Doing the job well is one thing; wanting to do it at all is another. Kathy Mangones made it clear in chapter 3 that virtually none of the humanitarian organizations in Haiti had much interest in Haitian civil society. Writing about Sierra Leone, Turay says that, if they did, it would inevitably mean fewer jobs for expatriates. "It also means more power, control, and ownership of the development process by local organizations," he writes. "But with most local organizations dependent on international agencies for their daily bread and survival, I do not expect this to happen soon."

Stephen Lubkemann describes a different way of looking at local capacity building, including the need for an overhaul of state–civil society relations. The initiative to create a Bosnian NGO Foundation was supported by CARE, World Vision, the International Rescue Committee, Catholic Relief Services, and the International Council of Voluntary

Agencies. Not generally known for coordination, much less real co-operation, these five organizations—remarkably—put time and money into getting the foundation off the ground. But it did not get far off the ground. Most of the large institutional donors approached by the foundation refused to make eye contact, and so did most other international NGOs.

As Goran Todorović puts it, "It is widely believed by Bosnian NGOs that as long as there is money for international NGOs in Bosnia, they will not leave. Further, international NGOs will rarely advise donors to work through Bosnian organizations as long as there are financial possibilities for themselves." In essence he is saying that Northern humanitarian organizations treat their counterparts in Bosnia as competition and vice versa.

This issue of competition is part of a much larger debate about the relationship between Northern and Southern NGOs, a debate that takes on one hue in development activities and another in humanitarian work. In the former, it is obvious that the heyday of the operational Northern NGO is coming to a close in the South. Southern development organizations are springing up everywhere, and many are better at what they do, cheaper, and more appropriate than outsiders. In the development field, Northern NGOs are reinventing themselves to accommodate this reality—not without angst and pain, but change is certainly occurring.

In humanitarian work, the change has been much slower. Perhaps because there are many conceptual, operational, and political hurdles, doing humanitarian work well is a greater challenge than not doing it at all. As stated at the outset of the book, it is also possible that the capacity building discourse sets the bar too high. If, after fifty years of effort, capacity building still proves to be difficult in development settings in which it is a clear priority, how much more difficult is it likely to be in emergency settings, in which the primary and most immediate goal is to save lives? This book has demonstrated that capacity building in such situations is much more difficult, and that there are, so far, perhaps more failures than success.

There *are* successes, however. Chapter 4 suggests that after generations of avoiding the state, civil society in Mozambique is reengaging through the development of government services that people value. If this is the first step in creating new space and a new role for civil society, then it is a good lesson. And if the lesson has been learned, it is a valuable one. The Guatemalan women returning from Mexico may have been less than fully equipped, but the problem was the agencies' understanding of the women's needs, not the agencies' motivations. CECI's food project in Haiti was a valuable lesson in recognizing the capacities that already existed and how they could be put to productive use if given a chance. Despite problems, the creation of the Bosnian NGO Foundation and its support by five international NGOs, along with the tentative first steps in CARE's Project Phoenix and others like it, are all steps in the right direction.

Some obvious policy-related issues arise for consideration. Those with an eye on the future would be well advised to question whether the ways of the past offer useful guidance for the future. The operational role of international agencies in complex emergencies is not likely to end soon, but it is changing, and in some places it is changing dramatically. Those that have shielded themselves behind banners marked nonpolitical, neutral, and impartial may no longer be able to do so with impunity, especially where local organizations with agendas of their own insist on being involved in the humanitarian effort in their own countries.

International humanitarian agencies concerned about local capacities may also have to grapple with the term *nongovernmental* and whether they will be able to do their job adequately in the future, when they are so closely tied to governmental apron strings. If building local capacities is an imperative, and if governmental agencies are unwilling to provide the time, funding, and the administrative overheads needed to do it well, the moment may well have come for a systemic overhaul. The compartmentalization of humanitarian relief into small boxes and short time frames is wrong for the way the world, war, and humanitarianism work in reality. Humanitarian agencies may have to choose more forthrightly between taking scraps from the official development assistance table and demanding that ODA and the menu be changed entirely.

A question has arisen throughout the book about who should build local capacities. It is clear that many international humanitarian agencies have said "not us." Then who? Sierra Leoneans have tried to do it themselves, as have Bosnians and Haitians. In most of the cases described in this book, the venturesome ones have met with a great deal of apathy and inappropriate international behavior. In the absence of an aid overhaul, the challenge for international humanitarian NGOs will be to use their privateness and their resources much more creatively in the service of longer-term ends. Despite widespread apathy on such matters, the need for change seems to be understood. This is a first step in moving away from rhetoric, no matter how resistant the reality is to meaningful change.

Maybe it has been a mistake—as most of the chapters in this book have done—to criticize humanitarian organizations for making little progress developing real partnerships with and real capacities among their Southern counterparts. Or maybe not. Maybe it would be a mistake to exonerate them, because building local capacities to deal with local problems makes increasing sense, and because—despite all the difficulties—there is evidence to demonstrate that building local capacities is possible. The challenge of the future is not to lament the disconnection between rhetoric and reality, but to find more ways to draw principles and programming closer together.

Notes

1. Alison Van Rooy, ed., *Civil Society and the Aid Industry* (London: Earthscan, 1998), 6–30.

2. Paul Harvey, "Rehabilitation in Complex Political Emergencies: Is Rebuilding Civil Society the Answer?" *Disasters* 22, no. 3 (1998): 203.

3. Harvey, "Rehabilitation in Complex Political Emergencies."

4. See Ian Smillie, *Relief and Development: The Struggle for Synergy*, Occasional Paper no. 33 (Providence, R.I.: Watson Institute, 1998).

5. UNHCR, EC/1995/SC.2/CRP.27, Geneva, September 4, 1995.

6. I am grateful to the students of Graduate Policy Workshop 591b at Princeton University's Woodrow Wilson School for this wonderful term, used in the workshop's research report, *Partnerships in Crisis: Collaboration between International and Local Organizations in Disrupted Societies*, Princeton, December 1999.

7. United Nations High Commissioner for Refugees, *A UNHCR Handbook for the Military on Humanitarian Operations* (Geneva: UNHCR, 1994), 8.

8. Graduate Policy Workshop 591b, *Partnerships in Crisis*.

9. For a discussion of the role of the media in Somalia, Sierra Leone, and elsewhere, see Larry Minear, Colin Scott, and Thomas G. Weiss, *The News Media, Civil War, and Humanitarian Action* (Boulder, Colo. and London: Lynne Rienner, 1996), 47–77.

Abbreviations

ACNUR	United Nations High Commissioner for Refugees (in Spanish)
ADRA	Adventist Development and Relief Agency
AICF	Action International Contre la Faim
ANDAH	Association Nationale des Agronomes et Agro-professionnels d'Haiti (Haiti)
CAC	Conseil d'Action Communautaire (Haiti)
CADO	Community Animation and Development Organization (Sierra Leone)
CARE	Cooperative for Assistance and Relief Everywhere
CBO	Community-based organization
CDF	Civilian Defense Forces (Sierra Leone)
CD-PEACE	Centre for Development and Peace Education (Sierra Leone)
CECI	Centre canadien d'étude et de la coopération internationale
CIDA	Canadian International Development Agency
CLC	Community Leadership Council (Conselhos de Lideres Comunitarios) (Mozambique)
CNISA	Commission Nationale Intersectorielle de Securité Alimentaire (Haiti)
CNN	Cable News Network
COHAN	Cooperation Haitiano-Neerlandaise
COMAR	Mexican Commission for Aid to the Refugees (in Spanish)
CPAU	Commission Permanente sur l'Aide d'Urgence (Haiti)
CPR	Communities of Populations in Resistance (Guatemala)
CRS	Catholic Relief Services
CSZ	Civilian Safety Zone (Sri Lanka)

CVA	Capacities and Vulnerability Analysis
Danida	Danish International Development Agency
DDR	Disarmament, Demobilization, and Rehabilitation (Sierra Leone)
DFID	Department for International Development (UK)
DGap	Development Group for Alternative Policies
EC	European Community
ECHO	European Community Humanitarian Office
ECOMOG	Economic Community of West African States Monitoring and Observation Group
EFSL	Evangelical Fellowship of Sierra Leone
EU	European Union
EVI	Extremely vulnerable individual
FAO	Food and Agriculture Organization (UN)
FAWE	Forum for African Women Educationalists (Sierra Leone)
FINNIDA	Finnish Cooperation
FRELIMO	Front for the Liberation of Mozambique
GRD	Groupe de Recherche pour le Developpement (Haiti)
GRICAR	International Group of Consultation and Aid to the Return (Guatemala)
GTIH	Groupe de Technologie Intermédiaire (Haiti)
HACU	Humanitarian Assistance Coordination Unit (United Nations/Sierra Leone)
IBHA	Independent Bureau for Humanitarian Affairs
ICRC	International Committee of the Red Cross
ICVA	International Council of Voluntary Agencies
IDP	Internally displaced person
IDRC	International Development Research Centre (Ottawa)
IFAD	International Fund for Agriculture and Development
IFOR	Implementation Force (Bosnia)
IIRO	International Islamic Religious Organizations
IM	Mediating Body (in Spanish) (Guatemala)

IMF	International Monetary Fund
INGO	International nongovernmental organization
IPKF	Indian Peace Keeping Force
IRC	International Rescue Committee
JVP	Janatha Vimukthi Peramuna (Sri Lanka)
LNGO	Local nongovernmental organization
LTTE	Liberation Tigers of Tamil Eelam (Sri Lanka)
MADFA	Mapaki Descendants Farming Association (Sierra Leone)
MHC	Maternal health care
MMOH	Mozambique Ministry of Health
MOD	Ministry of Defense (Sri Lanka)
MPF	Ministry of Planning and Finance (Mozambique)
MPIHP	Manica Province Integrated Health Project (Mozambique)
MSF	Médecins sans Frontières
NATO	North Atlantic Treaty Organization
NCDHR	National Commission for Democracy and Human Rights (Sierra Leone)
NGO	Nongovernmental organization
NHSRP	National Health Sector Recovery Program (Mozambique)
NMJD	Network Movement for Justice and Development (Sierra Leone)
NORAD	Norwegian Agency for Development Cooperation
OAS	Organization of American States
OAU	Organization of African Unity
ODA	Official development assistance
OSCE	Organization for Security and Cooperation in Europe
PA	People's Alliance (Sri Lanka)
PAC	Partnership Africa Canada
PAH	Programme d'Aide Humanitaire (Haiti)
PAPDA	Haitian Platform for Alternative Development
PDH	Provincial directorate of health (Mozambique)
PHC	Primary health care

PRA	Participatory Rural Appraisal
QIP	Quick-impact project
RENAMO	Mozambique National Resistance Movement (in Portuguese)
RUF	Revolutionary United Front (Sierra Leone)
SDC	Swiss Development Cooperation
SLANGO	Sierra Leone Association of NGOs
TA	Technical adviser
TBA	Traditional birth attendant
TMP	Traditional medical practitioner
UN	United Nations
UNDP	United Nations Development Program
UNESCO	United Nations Educational, Scientific, and Cultural Organization
UNFPA	United Nations Fund for Population Activities
UNHCR	United Nations High Commissioner for Refugees
UNICEF	United Nations Children's Fund
UNOMSIL	United Nations Observer Mission in Sierra Leone
UNP	United National Party (Sri Lanka)
UNRISD	United Nations Research Institute for Social Development
URNG	Unidad Revolucionaria Nacional Guatemalteca (Guatemala)
USAID	United States Agency for International Development
UTHR	University Teachers for Human Rights (Sri Lanka)
VIDRA	Women's Action (Bosnia)
WFP	World Food Program (UN)
WSP	War-Torn Societies Project
YMCA	Young Men's Christian Association
ZANLA	Zimbabwe African National Liberation Army

Select Bibliography

General

Anderson, Mary B., and Peter J. Woodrow. *Rising from the Ashes: Development Strategies in Times of Disaster.* Boulder, Colo.: Westview Press, 1989.

Chambers, Robert. *Whose Reality Counts? Putting the Last First.* London: Intermediate Technology, 1997.

Eade, Deborah. *Capacity Building: An Approach to People-Centred Development.* Oxford: Oxfam, 1997.

Graduate Policy Workshop 591b, Woodrow Wilson School, Princeton University. *Partnerships in Crisis: Collaboration between International and Local Organizations in Disrupted Societies.* Princeton: Princeton University, December 1999.

Harvey, Paul. "Rehabilitation in Complex Political Emergencies: Is Rebuilding Civil Society the Answer?" *Disasters* 22, no. 3 (1998).

James, Rick. *Demystifying Organization Development: Practical Capacity-Building Experiences of African NGOs.* Oxford: International Training and NGO Research Centre, 1998.

Lautze, Sue, and John Hammock. *Coping with Crisis, Coping with Aid: Capacity Building, Coping Mechanisms, and Dependency, Linking Relief and Development.* New York: United Nations Department of Humanitarian Affairs, 1996.

Morgan, Peter. "Capacity Development—An Introduction." In *Emerging Issues in Capacity Development.* Ottawa: Institute on Governance, 1994.

Pearson, Lester B. *Partners in Development.* New York: Praeger, 1969.

Smillie, Ian. *Relief and Development: The Struggle for Synergy.* Occasional Paper no. 33. Providence, R.I.: Watson Institute, 1998.

Stiefel, Matthias. *Rebuilding after War: A Summary Report of the War-Torn Societies Project.* Geneva: War-Torn Societies Project and Nations Research Institute for Social Development, 1998.

Uvin, Peter. *Aiding Violence: The Development Enterprise in Rwanda.* West Hartford, Conn.: Kumarian Press, 1998.

Van Rooy, Alison, ed. *Civil Society and the Aid Industry.* London: Earthscan, 1998.

Haiti

Americas Watch and National Coalition for Haitian Refugees. *Silencing a People: The Destruction of Civil Society in Haiti.* New York: Human Rights Watch, 1993.

Cadet, Charles. *Crise, Pauperisation et Marginalisation dans l'Haiti Contemporaine.* Port-au-Prince: United Nations Children's Fund, 1996.

Centre canadien d'étude et de la coopération internationale (CECI). *Une Aide Alimentaire Alternative (Septembre 1992–Juin 1996).* Port-au-Prince: CECI.

Maguire, Robert, et al. *Haiti Held Hostage: International Responses to the Quest for Nationhood, 1986–1996.* Occasional Paper no. 23. Providence, R.I.: Watson Institute, 1997.

Mangones, Kathy. "De la Solidaridad a la Cooperación Institucionalizada." In *La República Dominicana y Haiti frente al Futuro.* Santo Domingo, Dominican Republic: FLACSO Working Papers, 1998.

McGowan, Lisa. *Democracy Undermined and Economic Justice Denied: Structural Adjustment and the Aid Juggernaut in Haiti.* Washington, D.C.: Development Group for Alternative Policies, 1997.

Richardson, Laurie. *Feeding Dependency, Starving Democracy: USAID Policies in Haiti.* Boston: Grassroots International, 1997.

Werleigh, Georges. *Situation Alimentaire en Haiti: Une Etude sur la Production Alimentaire et la Situation Nutritionelle en Haiti.* Port-au-Prince: COHAN BRD and Caritas Nederlandica, 1987.

Guatemala

Alto Comisionado de Las Naciones Unidas para Los Refugiados (ACNUR). *Mamá Maquín en la lucha por el derecho de la mujer a la propiedad de la tierra y la participación en la Organización Comunitaria: Lecciones Aprendidas en el Trabajo con Mujeres Guatemaltecas Refugiadas y Retornadas.* Guatemala City: ACNUR, 1998.

Biekart, Kees. *The Politics of Civil Society Building: European Private Aid Agencies and Democratic Transitions in Central America.* Amsterdam: International Books and the Transnational Institute, 1999.

Fagan, Patricia Weiss. *Refugee Women in El Salvador and Guatemala: Challenges and Lessons of Reintegration.* Washington, D.C.: International Center for Research on Women (ICRW), 2000.

Gleijeses, Peiro. *Shattered Hope.* Princeton: Princeton University Press, 1992.

Lozano, Itziar. *Lessons Learned in Work with Refugee Women: A Case Study of Chiapas.* Comitán, Chiapas: United Nations High Commissioner for Refugees, 1996.

Molina, Carolina Cabarrus, Dorotea Gomez Grijalva, and Ligia Gonzalez Martinez. *Guatemalan Women Refugees and Returnees: Challenges and Lessons Learned from the Refugee Camps and during Reintegration.* Washington, D.C.: International Center for Research on Women (ICRW), n.d.

Taylor, Clark. *Return of Guatemala's Refugees: Reweaving the Torn.* Philadelphia: Temple University Press, 1998.

Worby, Paula. "Organizing for a Change: Guatemalan Women Assert Their Right to Be Co-owners of Land Allocated to Returnee Communities." Paper prepared for the Kigali Inter-regional Consultation on Women's Land and Property Rights, February 1998.

Sierra Leone

Afrique et Developpement [Africa Development], Lumpen Culture, and Political Violence: The Sierra Leone Civil War 22, nos. 3 and 4 (1997).

Lord, David, ed. *Paying the Price: The Sierra Leone Peace Process.* London: Conciliation Resources, 2000.

Reno, William. *Corruption and State Politics in Sierra Leone.* Cambridge: Cambridge University Press, 1995.

Richards, Paul. *Fighting for the Rainforest.* The International African Institute in association with James Currey. Oxford and Portsmouth, N.H.: Heinemann, 1996.

Smillie, Ian. "Sierra Leone." In *NGOs in Complex Emergencies Project.* Ottawa: CARE Canada, 1997.

www.Sierra-Leone.org

Mozambique

Alexander, Jocelyn. "Terra e Autoridade Politica no Pos-Guerra em Moçambique: O Caso da Provincia de Manica." *Arquivo* 16 (1994).

Chingono, Mark. *The State Violence and Development.* Aldershot, England: Avebury Press and Ashegate Publishing, 1996.

Hall, Margaret, and Tom Young. *Confronting Leviathan: Mozambique since Independence.* Athens: Ohio University Press, 1997.

Harbeson, John W., Donald Rothchild, and Naomi Chazan, eds. *Civil Society and the State in Africa.* London: Lynne Rienner, 1994.

Manica Province Integrated Health Project. *Manica Province Integrated Health Project Mid-term Review.* Helsinki: Finnish Cooperation (FINNIDA), April 1997.

Mozambican Ministry of Health. *African Health Care Systems and the War in Mozambique, a Six-Part Study.* Maputo: Mozambican Ministry of Health, 1990–91.

Mullin, Guy. *National NGOs in Zambezia Province, Mozambique—Inventory of NGOs and an Analysis of Their Work and the Potential for Investment in NGO Coordination and Capacity Building.* Maputo: LINK Forum Report, 1996.

Pavignani, Enrico, and Joaquim Ramalho Durao. *National Coordination of External Resources in the Health Sector: The Mozambican Case Study.* Maputo: Swiss Cooperation, September 1997.

Sogge, David. "The Civil Sector." In *Mozambique: Perspectives on Aid and the Civil Sector,* edited by David Sogge. Amsterdam: Gemeenschappelijk Overleg Medefinacierig, 1997.

Bosnia

Dialogue Development. *European Union Civil Society Development Project in Bosnia and Herzegovina.* Copenhagen: November 1997.

Ignatieff, Michael. "Nationalism and the Narcissism of Minor Differences." *Queen's Quarterly* 102, no. 1 (spring 1995).

———. *The Warrior's Honour: Ethnic War and the Modern Conscience.* New York: Viking, 1998.

Rieff, David. *Slaughterhouse: Bosnia and the Failure of the West.* New York: Touchstone, 1976.

Stubbs, Paul. *Social Reconstruction and Social Development in Croatia and Slovenia: The Role of the NGO Sector.* Research Report R6274. Zagreb: Overseas Development Authority, 1996.

Woodward, Susan L. *Balkan Tragedy: Chaos and Dissolution after the Cold War.* Washington, D.C.: Brookings Institution, 1995.

World Bank, *Bosnia and Herzegovina: From Recovery to Sustainable Growth.* Washington, D.C.: World Bank, 1997.

Sri Lanka

Bastian, Sunil. "Development NGOs and Ethnic Conflicts." In *Culture and Politics of Identity in Sri Lanka.* Colombo: ICES, 1998.

Goodhand, Jonathan, and Nick Lewer. "Sri Lanka: NGOs and Peace-Building in Complex Political Emergencies." *Third World Quarterly* 20, no. 1 (1999).

Rotberg, Robert I., ed. *Creating Peace in Sri Lanka: Civil War and Reconciliation.* Washington, D.C.: Brookings Institution Press, 1999.

Saravanamuttu, Paikiasothy. "Sri Lanka: Civil Society, the Nation, and the State-Building Challenge." In *Civil Society and the Aid Industry,* edited by Alison van Rooy. London: Earthscan, 1998.

Somasunderam, Daya. *Scarred Minds: The Psychological Impact of War on Sri Lankan Tamils.* New Delhi: Sage, 1998.

United Nations High Commissioner for Refugees. *A Primer on Micro-projects in Sri Lanka: A Formula for Consolidating Durable Solutions.* Colombo: UNHCR, 1993.

Van Brabant, Koenraad. *The Coordination of Humanitarian Action: The Case of Sri Lanka.* Network Paper 23, Relief and Rehabilitation Network.

About the Contributors

Ian Smillie, an Ottawa-based Canadian, has worked for more than thirty years in international development as a practitioner and writer. Recent publications include *The Alms Bazaar: Altruism under Fire—Non-profit Organizations and International Development,* and *Relief and Development: The Struggle for Synergy,* a monograph in the Humanitarianism and War Project series.

Mike Leffert has reported on Central America for ten years as an independent journalist. He lived and worked in Guatemala for six years, writing for a number of international publications and wire services, including *Time* and the Associated Press.

Stephen C. Lubkemann is a postdoctoral fellow at the Thomas J. Watson Jr. Institute for International Studies and the Population Studies and Training Center at Brown University. He has lived and worked in Mozambique, and his doctoral dissertation was on Mozambican refugee migration.

Kathy Mangones served for ten years as executive director of the Association Haïtienne des Agences Bénévoles, an NGO umbrella group. Since then she has worked as an independent development consultant in Haiti.

Arjuna Parakrama is a former senior fellow at the United States Institute for Peace and a former dean of arts at Colombo University. He is director of the Centre for Policy Alternatives in Sri Lanka and has been instrumental in the design and implementation of innovative community-activist training programs throughout the country.

Goran Todorović began the 1990s as a Yugoslavian journalist and finished the decade having run CARE's emergency relief program in Sarajevo throughout the war. He subsequently founded and managed the Bosnian NGO Foundation, which aims to foster the development of Bosnian civil society. He currently works for CARE in East Timor.

Thomas Turay, a longtime Sierra Leonean NGO worker, is currently a lecturer at the Coady International Institute in Nova Scotia.

Index

The Humanitarianism and War Project

THE HUMANITARIANISM AND WAR PROJECT is an independent policy research initiative underwritten since its inception in 1991 by some fifty UN agencies, governments, NGOs, and foundations. To date it has conducted thousands of interviews on complex emergencies around the world, producing an array of case studies, training materials, books, articles, and opinion pieces for a diverse audience.

During the years 1997–2000, the Project examined the process of institutional learning and change among humanitarian organizations in the post–Cold War period. In 2001, the Project is working to synthesize and disseminate its findings and recommendations in order to assist practitioner organizations in improving their effectiveness.

Following earlier residences at the Refugee Policy Group in Washington, D.C., and the Thomas J. Watson Jr. Institute for International Studies, the Project is now located at the Feinstein International Famine Center in Tufts University's School of Nutrition Science and Policy. A detailed list of its contributors and publications is available at the web site below.

THE HUMANITARIANISM AND WAR PROJECT
Feinstein International Famine Center
Tufts University
11 Curtis Avenue
Somerville, MA 02144
(617) 627-5949
e-mail: h&w@tufts.edu
web site: hwproject.tufts.edu

Suivez-nous

Achevé d'imprimer en avril 2017
sur les presses de Marquis-Gagné
Louiseville, Québec